# SILENT STUDIO DIRECTORY

By
Ed and Susan Poole

2015 Edition

Thousands of silent film producers and distributors, including names, addresses, principals, logos, etc.

A Publication by
LearnAboutMoviePosters.com
of the
Learn About Network, L.L.C.

**Silent Studio Directory**
2015 Edition

Published by:
Ed and Susan Poole
P. O. Box 3181
Harvey, LA 70059
edp@LearnAboutMoviePosters.com

ISBN: 978-0-9815695-9-8

© 2015 by Ed and Susan Poole
All Rights Reserved.

No part of this publication may be reproduced, stored in a database, or transmitted in any form, or by any means, electronic, mechanical, photocopying, recording, or otherwise, without prior written permission of the Authors/Publishers.

**LIMIT OF LIABILITY/DISCLAIMER OF WARRANTY**

The Authors/Publishers have used their best efforts in preparing this publication. Authors/Publishers make no representation or warranties with respect to the accuracy or completeness of the contents of this publication and specifically disclaim any implied warranties of merchantability or fitness for any particular purpose and shall in no event be liable for any loss of profit or any other commercial damage, including but not limited to special, incidental, consequential, or other damages.

**ADDITIONAL COPIES**:

Additional copies of this publication are available through the authors.

Ed Poole
P. O. Box 3181
Harvey, LA 70059
(504) 298-LAMP
Email: edp@LearnAboutMoviePosters.com

or online at www.LearnAboutMoviePosters.com

# HERITAGE®
## VINTAGE MOVIE POSTER AUCTIONS

### Seeking Quality Consignments

How can you be sure the offer to purchase your poster or poster collection is the absolute maximum? At Heritage, our goal is to present each and every one of your items to the largest number of qualified buyers in the world. Why sell outright to a single buyer when our auction platform will bring multiple buyers to compete against each other? When the time comes to sell your treasures, call us; we'll be happy to give you a free appraisal.

*Dracula* (Universal, 1931)
One Sheet (27" X 41") Style F
Sold For: $310,700 | March 2009

 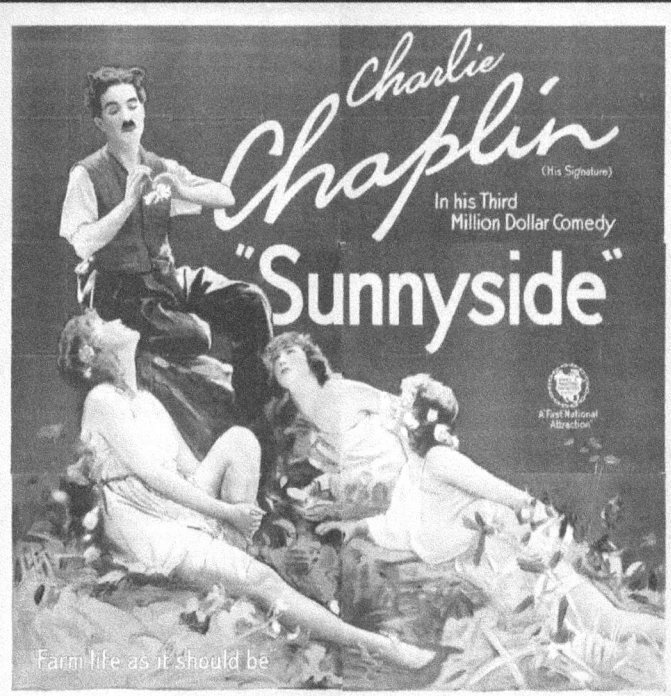 

*Frankenstein* (Universal, 1931)
Insert (14" X 36")
Sold For: $262,900 | July 2013

*Sunnyside* (First National, 1919). Six Sheet (81" X 81")
Sold For: $71,700 | July 2014

*Casablanca* (Warner Brothers, 1942). Insert (14" X 36")
Sold For: $191,200
November 2012

**CONSIGN YOUR VALUABLE POSTER COLLECTION NOW**
Additionally, be sure to check out our weekly Sunday Internet Movie Poster Auctions all year long.
To view lots and bid online visit **HA.com/MoviePosters**

Inquiries:
877-HERITAGE (437-4824)
GREY SMITH
Director, Movie Poster Auctions
Ext. 1367 | GreySm@HA.com

ALWAYS ACCEPTING QUALITY CONSIGNMENTS IN 39 CATEGORIES | IMMEDIATE CASH ADVANCES AVAILABLE

Annual Sales Exceed $900 Million | 850,000+ Online Bidder-Members
3500 Maple Avenue | Dallas, TX 75219 | 877-HERITAGE (437-4824)

DALLAS | NEW YORK | BEVERLY HILLS | SAN FRANCISCO | HOUSTON | PARIS | GENEVA

Paul R. Minshull #16591. BP 19.5%; see HA.com. 34461

THE WORLD'S LARGEST COLLECTIBLES AUCTIONEER

# From the Authors

The silent era was one of the most fascinating times in human history. The introduction of the film industry had an unbelievable impact on society. To quote the *Guinness Book of World Records*:

> *Few inventions have spread more rapidly than cinematography. By the end of 1896, a mere twelve months after the real start of commercial cinema in France, nearly all the major countries of the western world had witnessed their first demonstration of the new art.*

For the first time, silent films presented to the public a VISUAL version of news, travel, comedy, drama, and entertainment that had never been experienced before. And, since they were silent, it was presented as an international point of view with no language barriers. Cue cards could present any explanations needed.

Immediately, movement, travelogues and factuals were the craze. But by 1902, people grew tired of this type of entertainment, so much so that films began to be used to clear the vaudeville halls at the end of the performances.

Between the years 1902-1907, there was turmoil in the industry. As stories were beginning to be told and Georges Melies ignited the public imagination with his special effects and science fiction, the public clamored for more.

## Demand

Everyone was trying to get into some form of this new exciting industry. Feeding this frenzy was the ability to quickly, easily and cheaply get into EXHIBITING films. Theaters were opening rapidly.

This wasn't just in the U. S., it was worldwide. For example, to supply the demand, there was an estimated 500 production companies formed in Italy between 1905 and 1910 alone.

In 1908, Sears Roebuck and Co. released a catalogue selling moving picture equipment through Sears (see ads on next page). In every community, corner theaters were becoming common place.

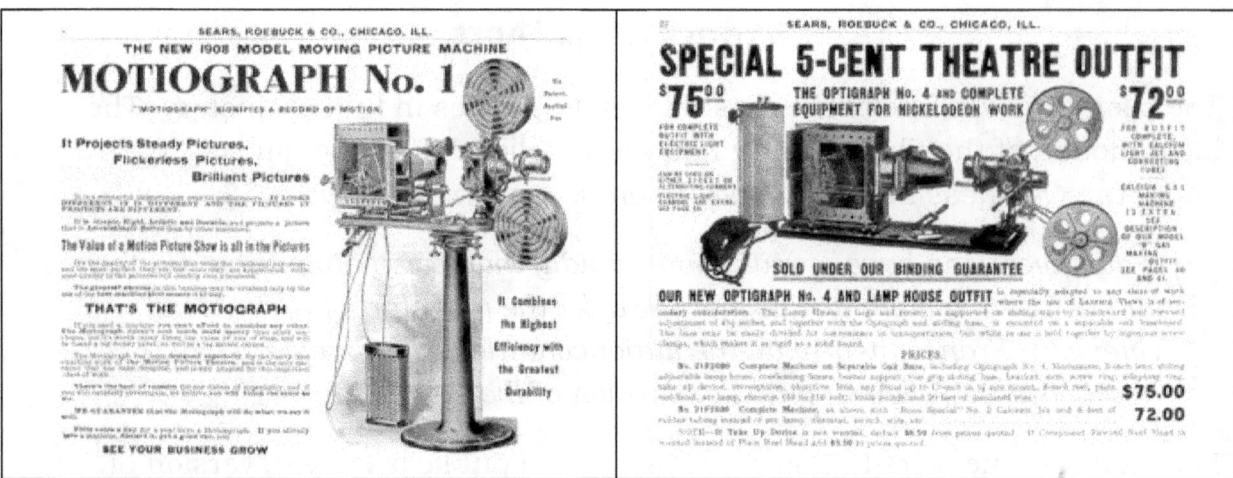

In 1909, *Moving Picture World* printed some stats on the U. S. film industry under the title, "Do You Know..."

Here are a couple of excerpts from that page:

- That 250,000 people visit motion picture theaters in New York City every weekday?
- That 500,000 people visit motion picture theaters every Sunday?
- That there are 6000 licensed motion picture theaters in the U. S.?
- That there are now almost a 1000 more licensed theaters in the U. S. then there was 3 months ago?

**Now, this was in 1909.**

Before 1910, France had dominated the worldwide industry. However, World War I turned the film industry upside down by eliminating most of the European film industry, leaving the public screaming for more entertainment. The film industry's shift to the United States caused a massive void, and the rapid growth made it very hard to control.

But while the public was screaming for more films and all of the new theaters were looking everywhere to try to satisfy their consumers, Edison was trying to allow only those people who would pay him royalties through his Motion Picture Patents Co. to exhibit films.

Here is a quote from the March 12, 1910 issue of *Moving Picture World* by Edwin Thanhouser who started Thanhouser Films:

*I saw its possibilities. I became filled with the idea that I could produce better pictures than a majority of those I had seen. The idea became a determination. I studied the situation on the market. To be frank with you, I applied for a license as a manufacturer, but was, of course, refused, as I then had no plant and may be said to have known nothing of the business. I have great respect for the Motion Picture Patents Company and appreciate what their protection means to the licensed manufacturer and to the moving picture business, but this was not helping me to realize my ambitions. So I set about seeing how I could make pictures without infringing upon patent rights... EDWIN THANHOUSER, The Moving Picture World, MARCH 12, 1910*

There was no complicated sound equipment or microphones, no scripts, no unions, no stages and many times, no experience. The demand was so great with the rise of the independents trying to fill the void that it made it definitely worth the risk of avoiding legal problems. Films could be shot in a few days and it was like panning for gold. If you were good at it, you could strike it rich almost instantly.

## Documentation

Documentation during the silent era is a historian's nightmare. From an international view point, documentation of the silent era was almost completely reliant upon the company's registration within the country archives (which was usually voluntary), historians (which primarily looked at the major companies or titles), preservation societies or film institutions (which were limited or non-existent) or the films themselves. So, massive amounts of production and distribution information have gone undocumented.

Plagiarism was such a problem that European companies established offices in the U. S. primarily to try to stop or at least try to slow it down. Logos became one of the major tools used for both the production and distribution side to try to establish and protect territory and identity.

Even though we are covering the world studios, let's focus for a few minutes on the U. S., mainly because we have more statistics and documentation and can more easily present the situation. Unfortunately, most countries, from a research and documentation view point, are in **WORSE** shape than what we are presenting here.

To get a better feel for how bad the situation really is in the U. S., the U. S. Congress commissioned David Pierce, a noted historian and archivist, to do a report. He did a phenomenal job and his report has been widely used. But, while it brought a lot of needed attention to the situation and a few stats have been quoted, from our point of view, it only scratched the surface.

When thinking about the silent era, most people, whether in the business or not, automatically think of Keystone Kops, Chaplin, Laurel and Hardy, Harold Lloyd, Our Gang, Will Rogers, Charley Chase, Ben Turpin, Mabel Normand, Fatty Arbuckle, etc.

But is that what Congress was thinking of? You see, Congress commissioned the report to cover U. S. feature films from 1912-1929. **NOTE:** A feature film is considered a film over one hour in length (normally 5+ reels). That brings the question: Why would they start the report in 1912? Take a glance back at the stats *Moving Picture World* reported in 1909 and all the activity!

Here's the answer. There are two reasons for this time period. The year 1912 was the first year the U. S. produced what was classified as a feature film AND they are more easily documented. *Guinness Record Book of Movie Facts and Feats* states that in 1912, the U. S. produced their **FIRST TWO** feature length films: *Oliver Twist* produced by H. A. Spanuth with five reels and *Beloved Vagabond,* a six reeler produced by Gold Rooster.

What about all the hundreds of others like Mack Sennett (who produced over 1000 films such as Keystone Kops, cross-eyed Ben Turpin, Fatty Arbuckle, Andy Clyde and Hank Mann) and Hal Roach, who produced Our Gang, Laurel and Hardy, Harold Lloyd and Charley Chase?

Consider this. In that same time period between 1912 and 1929, Hal Roach produced 853 films. Of those, **THIRTEEN WERE FEATURE FILMS!** The OTHER 840 **are NOT included in the stats or the report!** Thanhouser (quoted above) produced 1086 films between 1910 and 1917. When he retired, 51 of those were feature films, **leaving 1,035 NOT included**.

Thousands upon thousands of newsreels, shorts, documentaries, travelogues and regionals are not covered in the statistics to Congress of what has been lost.

**From Bad to Worse**

If so much has been lost, what has been done to try to save it?

Film preservation has been going on for a LONG time. Will Hayes, of the Hayes Commission, actually started film preservation in the U. S. in 1926. Since that time, MILLIONS of dollars have been spent in the U. S. on film preservation.

But STILL, with all that money spent, the American Film Institute declared that 90% of all silent films made in the U. S. are lost forever AND 50% of all U. S. films made before 1951 (when they invented safety film) are already LOST FOREVER.

Even if we accept those statistics, when you don't have the film anymore, what do you do to get information? You could go to the copyright offices, or in our case in the U.S., the Library of Congress. You could go to a film institution or try to find books that could at least give a few basics.

Well, what about the posters, stills, pressbooks and trade ads? – you know, the documents issued WITH the film, what we call, the film accessories. But there is a problem.

With all the millions spent in the U.S. on film preservation, we have not been able to find a single organization dedicated to film accessories preservation. No poster preservation societies, no groups to preserve film accessories. In fact, most institutions don't want to handle film accessories because film accessories were considered an "unimportant necessity of the business."

Film accessories were normally produced on cheap acidic paper that is costly to maintain. They are also a pain to store, a pain to handle and a pain to present. Because they are such a problem, and cost so much of their maintenance budget to preserve, many institutions quietly just allow them to decay and disintegrate so they can be removed from their inventory.

This has been unfortunate, because when you don't have the actual film, the film accessories are the primary source of information. They are actually the historical documents issued WITH the film and are invaluable when you want to reconstruct more than just the basic information about a film title.

Over the last 10 years of advance research of film accessories, we have been completely SHOCKED that a complete industry is being allowed to gradually disappear mainly because it doesn't fit into the current archival structure.

Here is a small example of what we're talking about.

In 2010, there was a HUGE find in the film community. A film was found that had Charlie Chaplin in it! The film community in California didn't realize Charlie Chaplin was even in the film!

It became the headliner for the 2010 Cinecon Convention. The following is an announcement that they issued:

# Lost Chaplin Film

A Thief Catcher (Keystone, 1914), featuring a previously unknown performance by silent comedy star Charlie Chaplin, will have its West Coast re-premiere during the 46th annual Cinecon Classic Film Festival at the Egyptian Theater in Hollywood California over Labor Day Weekend, September 2-6, 2010

Chaplin is officially credited with appearing in thirty-five films during his year at Keystone in 1914, but he claimed in various interviews that he had also played bit roles as a cop and a barber while at the studio--but he did not name the films, and although there has been some speculation about the possibility of additional Chaplin-Keystone appearances, none has turned up until now. Film collector Paul Gierucki found a 16mm film print in a trunk at a Taylor, Michigan, antique store last year. "I could tell it was a Keystone comedy, so I haggled and got it for $100," says Gierucki, but he didn't get around to looking at the print for several months. When he did put it on a projector this past March, he was astonished when Chaplin appeared as a cop about six minutes into the film for an extended two-minute cameo. "My heart stopped," Gierucki recalls. "I recognized him immediately."

Starring Keystone's famed comic villains Ford Sterling and Mack Swain, with support from Edgar Kennedy, A Thief Catcher was in production between January 5-26, 1914, soon after Chaplin arrived at the Keystone studio, and it represents the second or third screen role for the soon-to-be world famous comedy star.

A Thief Catcher is one of nearly forty rare and unusual films to be screened during the five-day Cinecon film festival, and will be shown on Saturday afternoon during a themed film preservation segment of the program.

You can see from the article that the film community was ecstatic to find this unknown Charlie Chaplin film (and it wasn't his second or third film – it was his fourth). While we have not found material from the original release, it was rereleased numerous times during the teens and twenties.

**If they had just taken the time to look at the poster that was issued WITH the film, this would not have been such a surprise. Several re-releases in the teens and twenties used this image on the posters for *The Thief Catcher* with varying backgrounds. But where do you find a reliable database that records them.**

# Reconstructing Lost History

Then your next question should be: WHY aren't museums and institutions compiling and reconstructing the lost film history using film accessories?

Simply put, they can't.

Museums, institutions and universities are not set up to reconstruct the film accessories because of their structure. All regular museums, institutions and universities are set up on the same principle.

> They acquire a collection (preferably donated).

> They have a curator and archivists to take care of that collection.

> Then people have to come to that facility to SEE the collection. This brings in revenue, interest and stability for that facility.

The archivist job is to take care of that collection. If it is NOT in that collection, it is NOT part of their job – **AND THEREFORE DOES NOT EXIST** to that archivist and facility.

In most cases, this system works GREAT! (and has for many decades). If it is documenting the life of a famous person or an important event, **GREAT!!**

You see, normally a collection will come from a director, or an actor, or sometimes even a studio. For a specific film, they might get the script, production notes, a costume or two and a couple of stills or posters. **That would be a pretty good acquisition!!!**

If you have a couple of posters for each film, isn't that enough?

When it comes to film accessories, suddenly you're in a different and still largely undocumented world. **Very few realize the magnitude of FILM ACCESSORIES!!!**

For a medium size film, you have HUNDREDS of different film accessories created.

It all starts with the keybook. During production hundreds and hundreds of production stills are taken by the unit photographer. A keybook is created containing the best production stills taken for the advertising department to use to promote the film. The rest of the stills are put in storage in case they are needed later. The stills pulled for the keybook are numbered with production codes. These are used for promotions, AND used in the making of the promotional material. These are also sent with a synopsis to the other countries where the film is being distributed for them to prepare their posters and promotional material.

On the right is an example of the 1934 medium size film *Zoo in Budapest* featuring Loretta Young. It had 99 stills pulled, numbered and used for promotions. From this would start the trade ads and fan magazine articles.

It also started the process of making all the advance advertising material. Then came premier material and then the massive amount of promotional material to be used to market the film throughout the country: pressbooks, insert cards, promos, portraits, heralds, lobby cards in sets, mini lobby cards, jumbo lobby cards, half sheets, window cards, mini window cards, jumbo window cards, 30x40s, 40x60s, one sheets, 2 sheets, 3 sheets, 6 sheets, 12 sheets, 24 sheets, door panels, banners, standees, and sometimes varying sets and several styles.

That did not include any oddities such as trolley cards, secondary printers, and local or regional production. Here are just a few of the larger posters from *King Kong* shown in the pressbook to order.

Rereleases were a MAJOR source of income for the studios because there were no production costs involved, only new promotional material. But, when you rereleased OR renamed the film, you had to do MANY OF THOSE SIZES OVER AGAIN. So, most films were re-released numerous times.

Many releases would also have to deal with varying sizes of: awards issues (for local, regional, national, international or festival awards), anniversary issues, combo issues, duotone, limited editions, military issues, strikes, review issues, roadshow, serials, shorts, stock and semi-stock issues, etc.

THEN for the films exported to other countries, you had to do a completely different set FOR EACH COUNTRY!!! And any rereleases for that country.

## An exhaustive amount of material for documentation!

The current academic and archival systems are not able to record or research these massive and specialized areas of documentation. We have spent the past 20 years developing methods and systems that can. We truly believe that film accessories are the key to reconstructing a lot of the lost film history.

We have taken a reverse approach of documentation and reconstruction to try to preserve these areas that are so important to international film heritage. We began researching in 1995 and released the first reference book on the industry in 1997. Everything began to come together when we created the only research database dedicated to film accessories in 2006. Our Movie Poster Data Base has over 100,000 posters shown and is continuously generating tremendous amounts of compiled information that has never been available before. We have documented previously unknown areas such as our research on production codes with over 50,000 codes to help identify unknown movie stills; reconstruction of National Screen Service history with over 25,000 poster accounting codes and over 18,000 trailer codes; reconstruction of film industry lithographers with over 10,000 litho plate numbers used for dating purposes, reconstruction of movie poster artists filmographies with thousands of poster artists around the world including their signatures and lists of works; etc.

As we continue to bridge the gap between the academic, commercial and collecting communities, we hope this edition is a starting point for another major area to help establish a base to cross reference, expand the scope and continue to make our dating process more accurate.

*ed and Susan Poole*
**Film Accessory Researchers**

# CHRISTIE'S

## The Art People

## www.Christies.com

# Acknowledgements

We consider this book as "the next step". It's the first-of-its-kind, none-other-like-it, etc. It has been the hardest and one of the most enjoyable books we've ever written. It has been on our minds for many years, but was always a future thought. We never believed we would be able to put it together. It is our 19th reference book and honestly could not have been feasible without the research and books before it. It has been like a series of standing dominoes, each one triggering and making the next possible.

So, when it comes to acknowledgements, it is really not appropriate to just say that all information and images were either in our files or provided by our sponsors and members. Only through the time spent in telephone interviews, the patience of those who taught us specific areas, the dedication of members who constantly send us material, and the sponsors who loan us rarities that we could never afford , and give us support to keep the wolves from our door, could this book have been possible.

This book is "the next step" across the line. The first step across the line of just documenting posters, was our *Movie Still Identification Book* to reconstruct production codes to help identify unknown movie stills. That made Production Code Basics possible, reconstructing how they came about and how each studio utilized them.

This book goes a step further by expanding to the trade ads and using all types of film accessories to reconstruct silent film history to help with identification and dating of obscure silent material. It crosses from being a reference book about movie posters to a book to help anyone involved with the silent film industry.

We have to acknowledge Grey Smith from Heritage Auction, whose constant support and encouragement keeps us pushing to fill in the next blank space, and Bruce Hershenson, whose team is constantly searching for more information and accuracy.

We really have to acknowledge our sponsors and members whose financial support allows us the privilege of doing what we enjoy, researching, untangling and documenting film accessories to help make this a better and more stable hobby and industry. Please see the list on the last page of this book which shows where their ads are. Please take time to notice the ads throughout this book and support these wonderful people as they have invested financially in YOUR education by sponsoring this book.

# DO YOU HAVE POSTERS YOU WANT TO SELL?

There is NO auctioneer of vintage movie paper who has lower fees or who delivers consistently higher prices than eMoviePoster.com, and we are the only auctioneers who can take ALL of your movie paper!

eMoviePoster.com
P.O. Box 874
306 Washington Ave.
West Plains, MO 65775
www.emovieposter.com
417-256-9616 · mail@emovieposter.com

---

## Movie Poster Frames
*Direct from Studio Supplier*

*Specializing in framing your collectibles since 1984*

*Made to order custom frames*
*At Wholesale Prices*
*~ Delivered to your door ~*

www.hollywoodposterframes.com
(800) 463-2994

**9260 Deering Ave**
**Chatsworth, CA 91311**

**Open to public:**
**Thur-Fri: 10-5 p.m.**
**Sat: 9-2 p.m.**

# About This Book

This book is the first of its kind, but NOT because of the topic. There have been other books published that have documented some of the better known and larger companies from the silent era. This book is the first of its kind because of the approach.

In 2006, we created the first and only research database. Each poster entered into the database has all the information on it fed into the computer. There are currently over 100,000 poster images in the database. With this volume, we are able to resort the information from a wide variety of directions.

To create this book, we started with studio and distributor information and logos that we had compiled from our database. We then factored in trade ads and other information that we had gathered from our research.

This has created some very positive results and a unique foundation that has not been available before. One perk is that it is not confined to particular country borders. Another, that you should notice immediately, is that it presents many companies that you have never heard of before, including their names, the principals, addresses and, in some cases, the logo they used in their business endeavors.

However, there are some considerations that must be addressed when using this book. Since film accessories were used to document these companies, there are potentially some gaps in the operational time periods referenced. Dates were gathered based on documentation found; however, companies may have existed for a longer period than shown. Also, some companies released ads and film accessories for an extended period of time but went out of business before completing their plans.

This will be continually refined and expanded as we continue documenting the film accessories. For this reason, this book is not intended to be an all-inclusive reference work on silent production and distribution companies. Quite the contrary, literally thousands of listings were cut because of lack of enough additional information for them to be included. We look at it as a starting point to BEGIN the expansion and reconstruction of this important time period in our cultural heritage.

# A

**A & H Andrews - UK - 1902-1910 -** production and distribution company formed by Arthur Henry Andrews and Horace Edward Andrews; merged to become Andrews Pictures Ltd in 1910.

**A & W Film Corp - US - 1916 -** distribution company formed by Abraham Press, Ernest V. Reiss and William G. Keir and managed by A. and H. M. Warner (who later formed Warner Bros.); offices located at 523-525 Longacre Bldg. 42st St. Cor. Broadway, New York.

**A. B. Biografernas Filmdepot - SWEDEN - 1922-1934 -** [see Biografernas Filmdepot]

**A. B. Fribergs Filmbyra - SWEDEN - 1920 -** distributor for Pathe films located in Stockholm.

**A. B. Maescher Productions - US - 1922-1923 -** production company formed by Mrs. A. B. Maescher of Los Angeles, California; distribution through Arrow Film Corporation.

**A. C. L. Feature Films - UK - 1913-1915 -** distributor of Ambrosio Films, Herkomer and Henderson's Exclusives with offices at 94 Wardour Street, Westminster.

**A. Drankov & Co. - RUSSIA - 1907-1917** (also known as Drankov Studio) production company formed in Saint Petersburg by Aleksandr O. Drankov, the first Russian production studio; released the first Russian newsreels in 1908 and then moved to feature films introducing crime films and serials to Russia; studio closed in 1917.

**A. E. Abrahams Ltd. - UK - 1913-1914 -** distributor of Ambrosio Films with offices located at 73 Romford Rd. E. Stratford.

**A. E. Hubsch and Co. Ltd. - UK - 1913-1914 -** distributor of Deutsche Bioscop, Mutoscope, Express, Hepworth, Ludwig Freund, Messter, Vesuvio, Vitascope and Biograph Films; offices at 29a Charing Cross Rd. Winchester.

**A. G. Steen Corp. of New York - US - 1925-1926 -** production company located in New York. [see Miller and Steen]

**A. G. Whyte - US - 1909-1910 -** distribution, import and export company with offices located at 1 Madison Avenue, New York and 91 Dearborn Street, Chicago, Illinois.

**A. H. Features, Inc. - US - 1919 -** production company with filming at Thanhouser studios in New Rochelle, New York and distribution through Rolfe Productions.

**A. H. Fischer Features, Inc. - US - 1919-1921 -** production company located at 18 E. 41st St., New York and owned by S. Schwartzberg, I. Schmal and B. A. Braham; in 1919 production moved to the Thanhouser Studio at 322 Main Street in New Rochelle featuring Robert W. Chambers stories.

**A. H. Jacobs Photoplays, Inc. - US - 1917-1919 -** production company located in New York featuring Jane Grey and Thomas Holding.

**A. H. Sawyer Film Features, Inc. - US - 1914-1915 -** production and distribution company founded in May 1914 by Arthur. H. Sawyer with William H. Rudolph as the general manager to produce comedy shorts; offices were located at 1600 Broadway, New York; utilized studios in Asbury Park, New Jersey and Saratoga Springs, New York; distribution released under the trade name Sawyer Film Mart and distributed for Bosburn Photoplay, Canadian Bioscope, Esanja Film Co. of Detroit, Japanese-American Film, Liberty Motion Picture, Santa Barbara Motion Picture, and Trans-Oceanic Films; reorganized as Sawyer Film Corp. in December 1914.

**A. Khanzhonkov and Co. - RUSSIA - 1905-1919 -** first Russian production company formed by Aleksandr Khanzhonkov with over 100 films produced during this time.

**A. Lincoln Miller Production, Inc. - US - 1921 -** production company located at 1139 Coronado Terrace, Los Angeles, California with A. Lincoln Miller as president and general manager.

**A-B Company - CZECHOSLOVAKIA - 1921 -** production company with studio in Vinohrady.

**A1 Features and Exclusives Ltd - UK - 1914-1916 -** formed from A1 Film Service with John Arthur Ward as president and general manager; offices located at 11 Denman Street, Westminster from October 1914 until December 1914 and then to 31 Wardour Street, Westminster.

**A1 Film Service - UK - 1913-1914 -** distribution company with John Arthur Ward as president and general manager; offices located at 48 Rupert Street, Westminster; in October 1914, company moved and changed their name to A1 Features and Exclusives Ltd.

**Aafa-Althoff-Anvil Film AG (Aafa) - GERMANY - 1920-1934 -** production company formed through merger of Radio Film AG, Gustav Althoff, Ambos Film Export, and Anvil-Film; located in Berlin; closed due to Nazi takeover.

**Aafa Film - NETHERLANDS - 1927 -** distribution company located in Amsterdam.

**ABC Films - US - 1917 -** [see American Bioscope Corporation]

**Abbey Pictures, Inc. - US - 1922-1923 -** production company located at 1674 Broadway, Earle Bldg, New York with John A. Murphy as president and Maurice Kriger as production manager.

**Abo Feature Film - US - 1914 -** distribution company with offices located at 229-231 West Erie Street, Chicago, Illinois with W. S. Bastar as general manager.

**Academy Pictures - US - 1925 -** distribution company.

**Ace Comedies - US - 1914- 1915 -** trademark name for a series of one reel comedies produced by Centaur Film Co.

**Ace-High Productions - US - 1924-1925 -** distribution company.

**Achievement Film, Inc. - US - 1921-1923 -** production company.

**Acme Pictures Corporation - US - 1919 -** production company with distribution through Pathe Exchange.

**Action Pictures, Inc. - US - 1924-1928 -** production company specializing in westerns; distribution through Associated Exhibitors but changed to Pathe Exchange in 1927.

**Active Film Co. - US - 1922 -** located at 729 7th Ave., New York.

**Actophone Company - US - 1909-1910 -** production company founded by Mark M. Dintenfass to produce one reel comedies and dramas; offices located at 573 11th Ave. New York and studio in

Philadelphia; sued by the MPPC and ceased production in May 1910 but immediately formed Champion Film Company to continue production. [see Champion Film Co.]

**Adamson Productions - US - 1927-1928 -** [see Victor Adamson Productions]

**Adanac Producing Company - US - 1920 -** production company.

**Advance Film Service Ltd - UK - 1913-1914 -** distribution company with offices at 13 Gt. Ducie St. Manchester.

**Advance Pictures - US - 1923-1937 -** distribution company through states rights.

**Advanced Motion Picture Corp. - US - 1917-1922 -** production company formed by Arthur Hammerstein, Ralph W. Ince, and Lee Shubert with offices at 1493 Broadway, New York.

**Adventure Films, Inc. - US - 1921-1923 -** production company with Amadee J. Van Beuren as president and general manager, Clayton J. Heermance as secretary and A. E. Siegel as treasurer with offices located at 1562 Broadway, New York and distribution through Pathe. [see AyVeeBee Corp.; V. B. K. Film Corp; Timely Topics Inc.; Fables Pictures Inc.; Timely Films Inc.]

**Aetna Film Company - US - 1914 -** distribution company located at the Longacre Building, Broadway and 42nd Street, New York.

**Aetna Pictures Corporation - US - 1924 -** production company in New York with distribution through Selznick Distributing Corporation.

**Affiliated Distributors Corp. - US - 1918-1922 -** distribution company located at 1476 Broadway, New York; formed May, 1918 and headed by Frank Rembusch and Sydney Cohen; merged with Allied Producers Corp and acquired 51% of Mutual Film Corp.; changed their name to Exhibitors' Mutual Distributing Corp.

**Affiliated Distributors, Inc. - US - 1921 -** distribution company located at 135 W. 44th St. New York and studio at 54th St.; Charles C. Burr was president and W. T. Lackey was secretary and treasurer.

**Affiliated Enterprises - US - 1921 -** production company for states rights located at 301-302 Merchants National Bank Bldg. Broadway, Los Angeles, California.

**African Expedition Corp. - US - 1922 -** production company.

**African Films Trust Ltd - UK - 1913-1915 -** distribution company for Ambrosio Films with offices at 2 Gerrard Street, Westminster; general manager was Robert Dalglish Graham who was later replaced by Leo Weinthal.

**African Jungle Films - US - 1922 -** production company.

**Agence Generale Cinematographique - FRANCE - 1915 -** distribution company located in Paris.

**Agfar Corp. - US - 1923 -** production company.

**Aggressive Pictures - US - 1925 -** production company.

**Ajuria Productions - ARGENTINA - 1928 -** production company located in Argentina.

**Al Dia Feature Co. - US - 1914 -** distribution company located at 220 W. 42d Street, New York.

**Al Gilbert Film Productions - US - 1921-1922 -** production company with offices located at the Chandler Bldg. 220 W. 42nd St. New York Al Gilbert was president; distribution by states rights.

**Al Jennings Feature Films, Inc. - US - 1920-1921 -** production company located at 6049 Hollywood Blvd., Hollywood, California formed by Selma Green, Tillman Eggleston, M. E. Jennings, V. Williams and Young Rogers.

**Al Jennings Productions Co. - US - 1918-1919 -** production company formed in July 1918 by Al Jennings and his brother Frank to make films about their exploits as outlaws and bank robbers; offices located at 70 Fleet St., London, 17 W. 44th St., New York, and 430 S. Broadway, Los Angeles; studios located in Tucson and Los Angeles. W. S. Van Dyke was the director of production and distribution was through Ernest Shipman.

**Al Lichtman Corp. - US - 1922-1924 -** distribution company formed by Al Lichtman; offices at 576 5th Ave. New York; company was acquired by Preferred Pictures in 1923. [see Alco Film Corp., Metro Pictures, Preferred Pictures]

**Al Rockett Productions - US - 1926-1927 -** production company.

**Al St. John Comedies - US -** production company producing comedy shorts; Jack Warner was president and Al St. John was V. P.; offices were located at 220 W. 42nd St. New York and studio at 6050 Sunset Blvd. Hollywood, California.

**Al Wilson Productions - US - 1925-1926 -** production company.

**Aladdin Comedies - US - 1921 -** trade name for comedy shorts distributed by Realcraft Pictures Corp.

**Alamo Film Exchange - US - 1910 -** distribution company located at 722 Maison Blanche Building, New Orleans, Louisiana.

**Alaska Film Corp. - US - 1915 -** distribution company formed with Dr. Leonard S. Sugden as president and A.B. Ferguson.

**Alaska Moving Picture Corp. - US - 1924 -** production company with Austin E. Lathrop as president.

**Alaskan-Siberian Motion Pictures - US - 1912** - production company.

**Alba-Film - AUSTRIA - 1923** - production company.

**Albatros Produktions - GERMANY - 1924** - production company.

**Alberini and Santoni Co. - ITALY - 1905-1906** - first production company to open in Italy; owned by Filoteo Alberini and Dante Santoni and located in Rome; Alberini patented the first Italian projector in 1895 called the Kinetografo Alberini, a combined camera, projector and printer; the company name was changed to Cines Co., Inc. in 1906.

**Albert Capellani Productions, Inc. - US - 1919-1920** - production company.

**Albertini-Film GmbH - GERMANY-ITALY - 1920** - production company with Luciano Albertini as president.

**Albion Cinema Supplies Co - UK - 1915** - distribution company with offices at 121 Wardour Street, Westminster.

**Albion Exclusives Ltd - UK - 1914** - distribution company founded by Archibald Robert Boult and Gilbert Louis Wild for Eclair Films; offices located at 13 Old Compton Street, Westminster; offices closed later that year when manager and staff were called back to France due to WWI.

**Albion Productions - US - 1922** - production company with Charles Giblyn as president.

**Albuquerque Film Co. - US - 1913-1918** - production company located at 1745 Allesandro St., Los Angeles, California formed from Albuquerque Film Manufacturing Co. and owned by Gilbert P. Hamilton; produced one reel comedies and comedy/dramas under the trademark name of Luna Films featuring Dot Farley and Augustus Carney (Alkali Ike); distributed through Warner's Features. In 1918, Hamilton declared bankruptcy.

**Albuquerque Film Manufacturing Co. - US - 1913** - production company formed by Gilbert P. Hamilton and located at 406 Court St., Los Angeles, California to produce 3 reel westerns featuring Dot Farley; reincorporated in October 1913 as Albuquerque Film Co of Los Angeles with distribution through United Film Service.

**Alco Film Corp. - US - 1914-1915** - distribution company formed by Al Lichtman (former GM of Famous Players) and Walter Seeley (newspaper exec) in August 1914; offices located at Alco Building, 218 West 42nd Street, New York; distributed for All Star Feature Co., California Motion Picture Corp., Popular Plays and Players, Favorite Players Film Co., Excelsior Feature Film Co., Tiffany Film Corp., B.A.

Rolfe, and Life Photo through Universal Film; Lichtman left company in November due to internal dissension; company filed for bankruptcy in early 1915; reorganized in 1915 to become Metro Pictures with Al Lichtman, William Sievers, Richard Rowland and James B. Clark.

**Alerta Exclusive Film Co Ltd - UK - 1913-1915** - distribution company formed by Francis Parkes, Francis Robinson, and George Rowen with William Horan as general manager; offices located at 167-169 Wardour Street, Westminster.

**Alexander Film Corp. - US - 1920-1922** - production company with offices located at 130 W. 46th St., New York; William Alexander was president, Jack Levy was secretary and Harry H. Thomas was treasurer.

**Alexandra Palace - UK - 1912-1916** - distribution company (and theater) located at Muswell Hill; released films under the trade name Big Ben; owned by Union Film Publishing with Al Pickering as general manager.

**Alhambra Film - FRANCE - 1921** - production company located in France.

**Alhambra Motion Picture Co. - US - 1914-1915** - production company formed to produce films written and featuring Betty Harte; distribution through Kriterion; merged to form Associated Film Sales in 1915.

**Alice Howell Comedies - US - 1921** - trade name used for comedies featuring Alice Howell and distributed by Reelcraft Pictures Corp.

**Alkire Productions - US - 1919-1920** - production company.

**All American Film Co. - US - 1921** - production company.

**All American Photo Plays, Inc. - 1921** - distribution company located at 20 West 45 Street, New York.

**All Celtic Film Co. - US - 1915** - production company located in New York formed by Charles J. O'Hara; used the Physioc Studios at 624 West 24th St. New York.

**All Feature Booking Agency - US - 1915** - distribution company.

**All Star Comedies - US - 1922** - production company specializing in comedy shorts; shorts distributed by Mastodon Films, Inc. in New York.

**All Star Feature Corp. - US - 1913-1915** - production company located at 220 West 42nd Street, New York; founded in Albany, N.Y. with Harry Raver as president, Archibald Selwyn as V. P. and Augustus Thomas as head of production; studio located on Staten Island; distribution by Exclusive Supply Corp, with Raver as president of that as well; Alco Film Corp. became the distributor in August 1914; soon afterward, Raver and Thomas left the company and John Dunlap became president and George Platt became head of production; All Star went bankrupt in early 1915 as did Alco.

**All Star Feature Distributors - US - 1915-1917** - distribution company located at 191 Golden Gate Ave. San Francisco, California and 514 W. 8th St. Los Angeles; Sol Lesser was president and general manager.

**All Star Negro Motion Pictures - US - 1927** - [see Famous Artists Corp. of America]

**All Star Productions - US - 1929** - production company.

**All-Story Films Corp. - US - 1921** - located at 45 Pinehurst Ave. New York with Rev. Clawrence J. Harris as president; specialized in historical and educational shorts.

**Allan Dwan Productions - US - 1919-1921** - production company located at 6642 Santa Monica Blvd. Hollywood, California with W. W. Kerrigan as general manager; distribution through Associated Producers, Inc.

**Allen Feature Film Corp - US - 1914** - distribution company with home office located at the Union Theatre, Providence, Rhode Island, and branch offices located throughout New England.

**Allen Holubar Productions - US - 1922-1923** - production company with Allen Holubar as president, Jimmy O'Shea as business manager and Harry Bucquet as production manager; offices located at Union League Building, Third and Hill Streets, Los Angeles, California.

**Allgood Picture Corp. - US - 1920** - production company located in New York.

**Alliance Film Co. - US - 1916-** - distribution company for states rights; offices located at 1905 ½ Commerce St. Dallas, Texas; distributor of Christie's Comedies et al for Texas, Arkansas and Oklahoma.

**Alliance Film Corp. - UK - 1919-1922** - production company formed October 1919; located at 74 Old Compton St. London with Harley Knolls as head of production; acquired British Actors Film Co. and studio at Twickenham in 1920; distribution in the U. S. by First National Exhibitors Circuit of America.

**Alliance Films Corp. - US - 1914-1915** - formed as an organization of exchanges in an attempt to eliminate states rights; located at 11 Floor, Leavitt Building, 126 West 46th Street, New York; officers of the Corporation were Andrew J. Cobe, Hector J. Streyckmans and P. P. Craft.

**Allied Artists - US - 1920-1923** - production company.

**Allied Artists Ltd. - UK - 1926** - distribution company.

**Allied Distributing Corp. - US - 1921** - distribution company for states rights located at 117 W. 46th St. New York; Charles H. Rosenfeld was president and general manager, Frank D. Reitman was V. P., Murray F. Beier was secretary and Samuel D. Scherlin was treasurer.

**Allied Independent Attractions, Inc. - US - 1920** - distribution company.

**Allied Producers and Distributors Corp. - US - 1918-1924** - production and distribution company located in Grand Rapids, Michigan; took over Mutual Films in 1918 and changed the company name to Exhibitor's Mutual Distributors Corp.

**Allied Productions - US - 1920** - production company located at 533 Security building, New York with H. M. Owens as general manager.

**Alpha Pictures, Inc. - US - 1919-1921** - distribution company by states rights located at 126 W. 46th Street, New York; H. M. Rothfleish was president and Bernard H. Mills was general manager.

**Alpha Trading Co. - UK - 1907-1908 -** production company with offices and studio located at St. Albans, Hertfordshire, England; Arthur Melbourne-Cooper was president.

**Alpine Film Corp - US - 1926 -** production company located at 291 Broadway, New York; formed by G. Gatalano, S. Noto, and J. Spano.

**Alpine Production, Inc. US - 1926 -** production company located at Corporate Service Association, Alexander Building, San Francisco, California; formed by Edward C. Boyle, Mary E. Boyle, William M. Klink, A. L. Hanscome, and Emmett O'Brien.

**Alt and Howell Comedies - US - 1921** - trade name for comedies released by Union Film Co.

**Amalgamated Pictures - AUSTRALIA - 1911-1912 -** production company formed in 1911 by John and Nevin Tait, Millard Johnson, and William A. Gibson; produced feature films and newsreels; studio located in St. Kilda; merged with West's Pictures and Spencer's Pictures in 1912 to form General Film Company of Australasia.

**Amalgamated Producing Company, Inc. - US - 1922-1923 -** production company formed by Gilbert M. Anderson (and Jess Robbins?); distribution through Metro Pictures Corp.

**Ambassador Pictures - US - 1924-1937 -** distribution company

**Ambassador Pictures, Inc. - US - 1921 -** production company located at 906 Girard St. Los Angeles, California; produced films featuring Katherine MacDonald; formed from Katherine MacDonald Pictures Corp.; B. P. Schulberg was president, B. P. Fineman was V. P. and general manager; films released under trade name of Preferred Pictures and distributed by First National.

**Amber Star Comedies - US - 1917-1918 -** trade name for comedy shorts produced by Amber Star Film Co.

**Amber Star Film Co. - US - 1917-1922** - production company that acquired the old Lubin studios in Jacksonville, Florida from VIM Comedy Co. when they closed in 1917; went out of business in 1922.

**Ambrosio Film Co. - ITALY - 1906-1914** - production company founded by Arturo Ambrosio and located in Turin, Italy; distribution in the US by Ambrosio American, and in the UK by New Agency Film Co., American and Continental, American Co., American Film Releases and American Quo Vadis Films.

**Ambrosio American Co. - US - 1912-1914** -American distribution offices of Ambrosio with offices located at 15 E. 26th St. New York

**AmerAnglo Corp. - US - 1925-1929** - distribution company formed from Lee-Bradford Corp (after Bradford died in 1925) and Arthur A. Lee to import and distribute British films by states rights; distributed for British Instructional Films, Gainsborough Pictures, Gaumont Co., Piccadilly Pictures, and Welch Pearson Elder Films; AmerAnglo was closed with the coming of sound.

**America-Japan Picture Co. - US - 1917** - distribution company located at 15 William Street, New York.

**American and Continental Film Co - UK - 1911-1915** - distributor for Ambrosio Films, Film D'Art, Pharos, Mono, Triton, Solax, Melies, Captain Kettle, Minerva and Vaude; offices located at 5A New Compton Street, Holborn and 7 Rupert Court, Westminster.

**American Bioscope Corp. - US - 1917** - distribution company located at 6242 Broadway Chicago, Illinois with J. E. Willis as president and general manager.

**American Cinema Association - US - 1926-1927** - distribution company for films by David M. Hartford productions.

**American Cinema Corp. - US - 1918-1921** - production company with offices located at 220 West 42nd Street, New York; formed by Frederick W. Ritter, S. P. Blackman and Thomas F. Dwyer.

**American Cinema Corporation - US - 1919-1921** - production company located at 411 Fifth Avenue, New York with Walter Niebuhr as president.

**American Cinematograph Co. - US - 1904** - distribution company located at Room 205, 5 Beekman Street, New York; formed by Eberhard Schneider.

**American Colored Film Exchange - US - 1923** - distribution company specializing in black race films.

**American Commercial Film Co. - US - 1915-1917** - production company located at 148-152 W. Austin Ave. Chicago, Illinois.

**American Co (London) Ltd. - UK - 1911-1915** - distributor for Ambrosio Films, Flying A and Beauty Films; located at 193 Wardour Street, Kinematograph House, Westminster; expanded to film production in 1914-1915.

**American Correspondent Film Co., Inc. - US - 1915-1918** - production company located in Bridgeport, Connecticut with offices at 30 East 42nd Street, New York; formed by M. B. Clausson (Felix Malitz?; Gustave Engler?) to produce films of the war in Europe, with cameramen along the fighting fronts; company admitted to having made an arrangement to propagandize for Germany; after the U.S. entered the war, some executives of the company went to prison for violations of war laws.

**American Eclair Feature Films - US - 1913** - distribution company located at 225 W. 42nd Street, New York as branch of Éclair Films.

**American Feature Film Company - US - 1914** - distribution company located at 162 Tremont, Boston, Massachusetts, with Louis B. Mayer as president; New England distributor for Jesse L. Lasky Feature Play Company.

**American Feature Film Corp. - US - 1918-1919** - distribution company located in Greensville, South Carolina with offices at Suite 616, Candler Building, 220 West 42nd Street, New York; H. A. Tansil was president.

**American Feature Film Co. - US - 1924** - distribution company for New England territory; offices located at 37 Piedmont Street, Boston, Massachusetts; Harry Asher was president.

**American Film Co., Inc. - US - 1915-1922** - production company with Samuel S. Hutchinson as president and P. G. Lynch as general manager; previously American Film Manufacturing Co.; offices located at 222 S. State St. in Chicago, Illinois; studios located at Santa Barbara, California; expanded production under the trademark names of American Star Films, Beauty Films, Clipper Star Films, Flying A Films, Mustang Films, Signal Films and Vogue Films; distribution through Mutual until 1918, when they changed to Pathe; went out of business in 1922.

**American Film Manufacturing Co., Inc. - US - 1910-1915 -** production company formed by Samuel S. Hutchinson, Harry E. Aitken, Charles J. Hite and John R. Freuler; offices located at 6227-6235 Broadway St., Chicago, Illinois; studio located in Santa Barbara, California; initially staffed by executives from the Essanay Film Manufacturing Co.; produced one reel comedies, dramas and westerns; American Film became a subsidiary studio in the creation of Mutual Film Corp. in 1912; in 1914 began releasing a weekly comedy under the trademark of Beauty Films; released their first feature film and their first serial the following year; in 1915, several studios left to form Triangle and they changed their name to American Film Co., Inc.

**American Film Releases - UK - 1911-1915 -** distribution company for Ambrosio, Atlas, Comet, Rep, Dansk, Kinograph, Royal, Volsca, St. Louis, K. W. (Colonia Berlin), Helios, Life Photo Film Co., and Players Film Corp.; offices located at 19 Cecil Court, Westminster.

**American Film Trading Co - UK - 1910-1912 -** distribution company located at 81-83 Shaftsbury Ave. Westminster; owned by Harry Aitken, Arthur Cohen, Arthur Crook, and Frederick Wilkins; management was C. P. Crawford and Jack Reece; distributed for Kalem, Gaumont, Pathe, Urban, Eclipse, Essanay, Vitagraph, Lubin, Selig and Edison; moved to 166 London Road, Liverpool in June, 1911.

**American Gaumont - US - 1912-1915 -** American branch office of Gaumont Film in France.

**American Kinema - FRANCE - 1910 -** trade name for a series released by Pathe Freres

**American Kineto Corp. - US - 1913-1914** - distribution company located at 1018 Long Acre Bldg, Broadway at 42nd Street, New York; offices moved to the World's Tower Bldg, 110 West Fortieth Street, New York in 1914.

**American Kinograph Company - US - 1909-1910** - production and distribution company located at 124 E. 25th Street, New York.

**American Legion Film Service - US - 1926** - distribution company specializing in war films.

**American Lifeograph Co. - US - 1915-1920** - production company located in Portland, Oregon and headed by Lewis H. Moomaw; specialized in westerns and distributed through states rights, i.e. Globe Feature Picture Booking Co. and United Booking Office Feature Co.

**American Movies, Inc. - US - 1922** - located at 238 E. 3rd St. New York.

**American Mutoscope & Biograph Co. - US - 1902-1909** - production company formed from the American Mutoscope Co.; moved in 1906 to offices and studio located at 11 East 14th Street in New York; opened a studio in Los Angeles at Pico and Georgia Sts; in 1908, D. W. Griffith joined as writer and actor and became their lead director; company name changed again in May 1909 to the Biograph Company.

**American Mutoscope Co. - US - 1895-1902** - production and distribution company formed by George Blanchard, Herman Kasler, J. J. Kennedy, Elias B. Koopman, and Henry N. Marvin to market the Mutoscope (a flip card machine created by Casler); William Dickson (inventor of the original Edison Kinetoscope camera) joined to help create a the Biograph project which would not infringe on Edison's patent; production studio was created on the roof at 841 Broadway in Manhattan, then known as the Hackett Carhart Bldg.; name was changed to American Mutoscope & Biograph Company in 1902.

**American Pathe - US - 1923-1931 -** production and distribution company formed by the acquisition of Pathe Exchange by Merrill Lynch; changed name to American Pathe; acquired by Orpheum Circuit in 1927; American Pathe was divided off of the RKO merger and given to Joe Kennedy who moved it to California and merged it with DeMille's Culver City studio in 1928; Kennedy sold to RKO in 1931.

**American Pictures Associates - US - 1922 -** located at 209 E. 124th St. New York.

**American Quo Vadis Film Co. - UK - 1914 -** distribution company for Ambrosio Films and Quo Vadis Films; offices at 12 Cecil Court, Westminster.

**American Releasing Corp. - US - 1922-1923 -** distribution company located at 15 W. 44th St. New York; Walter E. Green was president and F. B. Warren was V. P.

**American Rotograph Co. - US - 1914 -** production company.

**American Sportagraph Co. - US - 1899 -** production company.

**American Standard Motion Picture Corp. - US - 1917-1918 -** production and distribution company located on the 9th Floor of the Consumers Bldg in Chicago, Illinois; Samuel Quinn was president and M. G. Watkins was head of production; New York offices were located at 130 West 46th Street with Samuel D. Pelzman as general manager.

**American Star Films - US - 1915 -** trademark name used by American Film Manufacturing Co.

**American Vitagraph Co. - US - 1897-1900 -** production company formed by J. Stuart Blackton and Albert E. Smith; company name changed to Vitagraph Company of America in 1900.

**American Woman Film Co. - US - 1916-** production company located in Los Angeles, California with Mary Whitney Emerson as president and J. Farrell MacDonald as head of production.

**America's Feature Film Co. - US - 1911-1913 -** production company located in Room 403, Schiller Building, Chicago, Illinois and headed by E. J. Eichenlaub.

**Amkino Pictures - US - 1927-1940 -** distributor of Russian films located at 723 7th Ave. New York; distributed 15-20 feature films a year plus shorts; changed name to Artkino Pictures after WWII and continued until 1980.

**Ammex Motion Picture Mfg. Company - US - 1912-1914 -** production company of mostly western films; general offices in American National Bank Bldg, San

Diego, California and studio in San Diego, California; Charles Oesting was president; New York office listed as **Ammex Film Co** at 145 W. 45th Street, New York; distribution through Film Supply Co.

**Amsterdam Studios Inc. - US - 1922 -** located at 344 W. 44th St. New York.

**Anchor Films Corp. - US - 1917-1922** - production company located in Freeport, New York.

**Anchor Film Distributors - UK - 1914-1918 -** distribution company for Paramount Pictures, et al; formed by Harold Heath, Arthur William Gosse, and James Julian McEnnery; offices located at 2 Gloucester Street, Freshford House, Holborn and Gerrard St. London.

**Anchor Film Distributors, Inc. - US - 1922-1928 -** distribution company.

**Anderson Vay Hubert & Blumberg Ltd - UK - 1914 -** formed from EGM Co. as production company for Anderson Films; distribution company for Anderson and Treumann Larsen Series; name changed to Anderson's Film Agency Ltd. later 1914.

**Anderson's Film Agency Ltd - UK - 1914-1915 -** production company for Anderson Films; distribution company for Anderson, Centauro, Colonia, Dart, D.K.G., Dragon, Uranus, N & H, Roma, Phoebus, and Pasquali Films; formed from Anderson Vay Hubert & Blumberg Ltd.; owned by Gustav Auerbach, Harris Blumberg, and Philip Blumberg; offices located at 52 Rupert Street, Westminster; merged into Argus Film Service in 1915.

**Anderson Pictures Corporation - US - 1923 -** production company located at 723 Seventh Avenue, New York with distribution through F.B.O.

**Anderson-Brunton Co. - US - 1918-1919 -** production company with Robert Brunton as president; distribution through Pathe Exchange.

**Andlauer Productions - US - 1921 -** production company formed by W.A. Andlauer.

**Andrew J. Callaghan Productions, Inc. - US - 1920-1921 -** production company formed by Andrew J. Callaghan to produce Bessie Love feature films; offices located at 25 West 43rd Street, New York and 6642 Santa Monica Blvd. Hollywood, California; distribution through Arrow Film Corp.

**Andrews Pictures Ltd. - UK - 1910-1914 -** distribution company formed from acquisition of A & H Andrews by Arthur Henry Andrews, Horace Edward Andrews, and Harold Booth; located at 5 New Compton Street, Holborn and 49 Greek Street, Cine House, Westminster.

**Andrews' Pictures Ltd - UK - 1913-1914 -** distributor with offices at 26 Cannon St. Manchester.

**Angelus Studios - US - 1917 -** production company located at 2221 E. Washington St., Los Angeles, California.

**Anglia Films - UK - 1923-1930 -** production company formed by Archibald Nettlefold.

**Anglo-American Film Co. - UK - 1910-1914 -** production and distribution company located at 13 Gerrard Street, Film House, Westminster; studio located at Wanstead in Essex; distribution offices at 5-11 W. Register St. Edinburgh.

**Anglo-American Film Corp. - UK - 1913-1914 -** distribution company with offices in London and New York; London office managed by Edward Laurillard and located at 14 Hanover Sq. London; New York office managed by George W. Lederer and located at 1423 Broadway, New York.

**Anglo-French Film Exchange - UK - 1911 -** distribution company formed by Joseph Jay Bamberger, C. Hobson, M. Hobson, and E. W. Schiff.

**Anglo-Hollandia Film Co. - NETHERLANDS - 1919-1923 -** production company formed from existing company Filmfabriek Hollandia by owner Maurits Binger after getting production contracts from the UK; production continued until Binger died April 9, 1923; bank foreclosed after his death.

**Anima Film Co. - UK - 1915-1916 -** distribution company with office at

99a Charing Cross Road, Westminster.

**Animated Photograph Co. Ltd - UK - 1906 -** production company with offices in London.

**Animatophone Syndicate - UK - 1909 -** production company.

**Anita Stewart Productions, Inc. - US - 1918-1922 -** production company formed to produce films featuring Anita Stewart with Louis B. Mayer as president, Colman Levin as V. P. and P. C. Mooney as general manager; Distribution was through First National Exhibitors Circuit.

**Anti-Trust Film Co. - US - 1908-1909 -** distribution company located at 77-79 So. Clark Street, Chicago, Illinois.

**Anti-Vice Motion Picture Co. - US - 1916 -** production company located in New York.

**Apex Film Co. - UK - 1913-1920 -** distributor of Anderson Films and formed by Edward Ellis Lyons, Louis Zimmerman, Jocelyn Brandon, Ludwig Gungel, and Ludwig Gungel; Company sold in 1918 to Morris Dollar, Sarah Dollar, Sigmund Brandon and Bernard Dollar with offices at 36 Little Newport Street, Westminster.

**Apex Film Co. - US - 1913-1921 -** production company with P. P. Craft as general manager and located at 145 W. 45th St. New York; Later moved to 140 W. 42nd St. New York

**Apex Motion Picture Film Corp. - US - 1921 -** formed Jan. 28, 1921 and located in San Francisco, California.

**Apfel Productions - US - 1922 -** production company.

**Apollo Films, Ltd. - UK - 1922 -** distribution company located at 5 Denmark Street, Charing Crosshead, London; U. S. office under the name of Apollo Trading Corporation.

**Apollo Pictures Co. - US - 1913-1916 -** production company in New Rochelle, New York; incorporated in 1916 as Apollo Pictures, Inc.

**Apollo Pictures, Inc. - US - 1916-1922 -** production company formed by Harry R. Raver with studio in New Rochelle, New York; products released under the trade name of Apollo Films; initial distribution was through Art Dramas, Inc.; leased the Solax studios in 1917 with offices located at 1402 Broadway St. New York.

**Apollo Trading Corp. - US - 1922 -** distribution company located at 220

West 48th Street, New York with Lawrence Weber as president and Bobby North as secretary, treasurer and general manager; London office under the name of Apollo Films, Ltd.

**Approved Pictures - US - 1924-1925 -** production company located in New York and formed by C. Lowenthal, E. Boudin and I. Lazarus.

**Aquila Film - ITALY - 1907- -** production company formed by Camillo Ottohenghi in Turin, Italy.

**Archibald Nettleford Productions - UK - 1926-1960 -** production company formed by Archibald Nettleford; located on Walton-on-Thames, England with production released as Anglia Films; purchased Hepworth Studios and changed name to Nettlefold Studios.

**Arctic Film Co. - US - 1914 -** production company founded by "Caribou Bill" Cooper in Saranac Lake, New York; offices located at 220 West 42nd Street, New York.

**Ardath XLNT Comedies - US - 1921 -** trade name for comedy shorts released by Arrow Film Corp.

**Arden Photoplays, Inc. - US - 1918 -** production company.

**Ardsley Art Film Corp. - US - 1917 -** production company owned by Marion Davies' brother-in-law.

**Argosy - UK - 1928 -** distribution company.

**Argosy Film Co. - US - 1918 -** (possibly same as Argosy Film Corp.)

**Argosy Film Corp. - US - 1916 -** production company located in New York.

**Argus Enterprises - US - 1914-1920 -** production company; later became Argus Motion Picture Co.

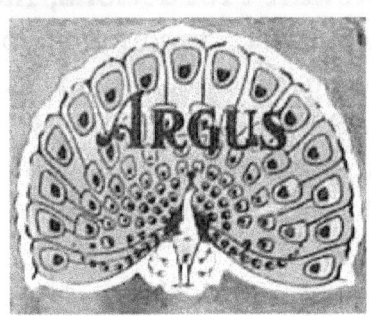

**Argus Enterprises, Inc. - US - 1921 -** production company located at 815-823 Prospect Ave., Cleveland, Ohio with H. H. Cudmore as president, George W. Armstrong as V. P., C. E. Roeshe as secretary and H. A. Brereton as treasurer.

**Argus Film Service - UK - 1915-1919** - distribution company formed with merger of Anderson's Film Agency and Clarion Film Agency; owned by Harris Blumberg, Philip Blumberg, Horace Dickerson, and Joseph Fuller; offices located at 99a Charing Cross Road, Westminster; later moved to 30 Gerrard Street, Wesminster.

**Argus Motion Picture Co. - US - 1920** - production company formed from Argus Enterprises.

**Arista Film Corp. - US - 1922-1930 -** production company located in New York.

**Aristo Productions - US - 1919 -** production company located at 310 Hollingsworth Building, Los Angeles, California.

**Arizona Film Co. - US - 1917 -** production company located in Chicago, Illinois; produced under the direction of George Siegmann; distributed through the state rights market.

**Arizona Motion Pictures, Inc. - US - 1921 -** production company located at 205 International Bldg. Los Angeles, California; studio located in Phoenix, Arizona; Dr. Norman H. Morrison was president, J. B. Bayless was V. P. and Elton E. Kunselman was secretary, treasurer and general manager.

**Armenkino - RUSSIA - 1926-1935 -** production company with studio in Armenia, Russia.

**Arnold Film Co. - US - 1920 -** production company formed by Harold L. Arnold; located in Los Angeles, California.

**Arrow Film Corp. - US - 1915-1925 -** production company formed with Wilbert Edgar Shallenberger as president and W. Ray Johnston as V.P.; studio located in Mirthquake, California; offices located at 220 W. 42nd St. New York; released feature films and serials with distribution through Pathe Exchange; also produced Bobby Dunn comedies released under Mirthquake Comedies trade name; by the late teens, distributed for Blazed Trail Productions and Atlantic Features, Inc. but primarily a distributor for states rights; distribution in the UK was through Inter-Ocean Photoplays; Johnston left in 1924; reorganized as Arrow Pictures Corp.

**Arrow Films - US - 1912 -** trade name used by Crystal Film Co. with offices at Wendover & Park Ave., New York.

**Arrow Pictures - UK - 1920 -** UK distribution branch of US company distributing under the name Mercury Film Service and Dispatch Film Service.

**Arrow Pictures Corp. - US - 1925-1926 -** re-organization of Arrow Film Corporation after Johnston left; undoubtedly an administrative change because Arrow continued for 2 more years with the same logo.

**Art & Science Photo Plays, Inc. - US - 1922 -** production company that distributed by states rights; offices located at 160 W. 45th St. New York.

**Art Cinema Corp. - US - 1926-1933 -** production company formed July 1926 by Joseph M. Schenck; absorbed Art Finance Corp. and distributed through United Artists.

**Art Dramas, Inc. - US - 1916-1917 -** distribution company located at 116 West 39th Street, New York with William Sherrill as president and Hebert Blache as treasurer; Harry Raver became president in 1917, but resigned a few months after; distributed for Apollo Films, Erbograph Films, Van Dyke Film and William L. Sherrill Feature Corp.

**Art Film Co. - US - 1915 -** production company located at 25th Street and Lehigh Avenue, Philadelphia, with Gaston Mervale as general manager; distributed through states rights.

**Art Finance Corp. - US - 1925-1926 -** production company formed April 25, 1925 by Joseph M. Schenck, Mary Pickford, Charlie Chaplin, Douglas Fairbanks and the banking firm of Lehman, Lasker and Paul Block to produce films featuring Rudolph Valentino; absorbed by Art Cinema Corp in 1926.

**Art Mix Productions - US - 1924-1934 -** production company formed by western star Victor Adamson (a/k/a Denver Dixon, Art Mix, Al Mix, and Al James). [see Victor Adamson Productions]

**Art-Film AG (Aktiengesellschaft) - GERMANY - 1920-1922 -** production company.

**Art-O-Graf Film Co. - US - 1919-1923** - production company formed by Otis B. Thayer; studio located in Englewood, Colorado; offices at Guardian Trust Bldg. Denver, Colorado; distribution through Arrow Film Corp.

**Artclass Pictures Corp. - US - 1919-1926** - production company headed by Lewis Weiss with George M. Merrick as production manager; produced Snub Pollard comedies after Pollard left Hal Roach; offices were at the Longacre Bldg at 42nd and Broadway, New York; studio was located in Yonkers.

**Artco Productions, Inc. - US - 1919-1920** - production company formed in 1919 by Harry R. Raver; used the trademark name of Four Star Productions; Raver left the company in August 1919 and Artco continued by leasing Kalem Studios.

**Artcolor Pictures Co., Inc. - US - 1920-1921** - production company located at 126 W. 46th St. New York with Louis J. Dittmar as president.

**Artcraft Pictures Corp. - US - 1916-1921** - distribution company formed as a subsidiary of Paramount; located at 720 Seventh Avenue, New York with Walter E. Greene as president; distributed films produced by Mary Pickford Film Corp; in 1921, Paramount was part of a Federal monopoly investigation which caused Artcraft to be closed.

**Arthur C. Bromberg Attractions US - 1926-1929** - distribution company through states rights with several branches. [see Progressive Pictures]

**Arthur Henry Gooden Productions - US - 1921** - production company and studio (old D. W. Griffith studio) located at 4534 Sunset Blvd. Hollywood, California with Charles Roberts as general manager; specialized in westerns with distribution through Continental Film Co.

**Arthur F. Beck Serial Productions - US - 1920-1923** - production company located at 135 W. 44th St. New York.

**Arthur S. Kane Pictures Corp. - US - 1921-1923** - distribution company located at 25 W. 43rd St. New York with Arthur Kane as president (who was also president of Associated Exhibitors, Inc.) and John C. Ragland as general manager.

**Artig Animated Cartoons - US - 1921** - located at Lissner Bldg. Los Angeles, California.

**Artistica Gloria - FRANCE - 1912** - production company.

**Artistic Cinema Negatives - ITALY - 1913** - production company located in San Remo, Italy.

**Artistic Pictures - UK - 1916-1928** - production and distribution company located in UK.

**Artlee Pictures, Corp. - US - 1926-1927** - distribution company with Arthur A. Lee as president.

**Artograph Co. - UK - 1913-1914** - distribution company located at 8 New Compton St. Winchester.

**Artograph Co. - US - 1921** - located at Merchant's National Bank Bldg. Los Angeles, California.

**Arton's Film Service - UK - 1913-1915** - distribution company formed by F. R. Arton; located at 156 Charing Cross Road, Westminster.

**Ascher Productions, Inc. - US - 1921-1922** - production company located at 117 W. 46th St., New York, with Sidney Ascher as president.

**Asher's Enterprise - US - 1920** - distribution company.

**Ashley Exclusive Films Ltd - UK - 1913-1920** - distribution company formed by Braham Julian Friend, George Poole, W. A. Underwood, and Emmanuel Woolf; located at 5 Great Newport Street, Westminster; absorbed by British Famous Films Ltd. in June, 1920.

**Ashton Dearholt Productions - US - 1923-1924** - production company.

**Asia Film Co. - HONG KONG - 1909** - formed by US businessman Benjamin Brodsky who helped established the Chinese film industry.

**Associated Arts Corp. - US - 1924-1925** - production company.

**Associated Authors - US - 1923-1924** - production company.

**Associated Exhibitors, Inc. - US - 1921-1926** - production company with Samuel Harding as president; offices located at 25 W. 45th St., New York; moved in 1923 to 35 West 45th Street, 7th Floor, New York with Arthur S. Kane as president; in 1925, John S. Woody became president and distribution moved to Pathe Exchange.

**Associated Film Sales Corp. - US - 1915-1916** - distribution company located at 110-112 West 40th Street, New York with Arthur Bard as general manager. Distributed for Alhambra Motion Picture Co., Burke Film Manufacturing Co., Empire Film Manufacturing Co., Federal Film Co., Ideal Film Co., Liberty Film Co., Navajo Film Manufacturing Co. and Santa Barbara Motion Picture Co

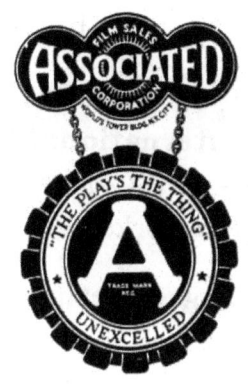

**Associated First National Pictures, Inc. - US - 1919-1924** - distribution company formed by a change of name from First National Exhibitors Circuit and located at 6 West 48th St., New York with Robert Lieberas president and J. D. Williams as general manager; Distributed films for 26 independent theater chains. They started producing films in 1924 and changed company name to First National Pictures, Inc.

**Associated Independent Film Manufacturers - US - 1910-1928** - production company formed by A.G. Whyte.

**Associated Independent Producers (AIP) - US - 1910s** - distribution company for Capital, Great

Northern, Nestor, Thanhouser, Eclair, and Lux films.

**Associated International Pictures, Inc. - US - 1922 -** located at 6 E. 39th St. New York.

**Associated Negro Pictures Distributors - US - 1926-1927 -** distribution company located at 152 W. 45th St. New York.

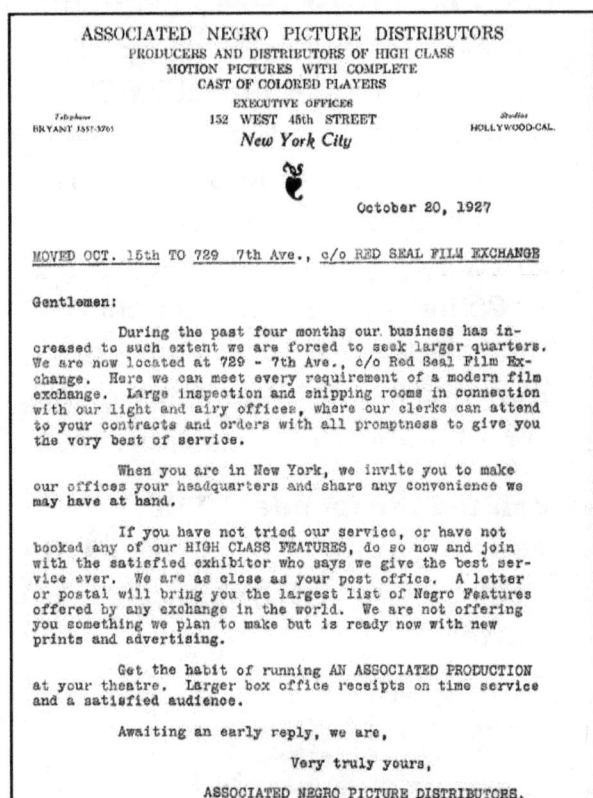

**Associated Photoplays Corp. - US - 1920-1923 -** distribution company located at 25 W. 45th St. New York and the Baker-Detwiler Bldg., Los Angeles.

**Associated Pictures Corp. - US - 1924-1925 -** production company formed by Lewis H. Moomaw in Portland, Oregon.

**Associated Pictures Inc - US - 1918 -** distribution company formed by Arthur H. Sawyer, Herbert Lubin and Louis Joseph Vance to distribute Ralph Ince films.

**Associated Producers, Inc. - US - 1920-1922 -** distribution company formed to distribute films by Maurice Tourneur, Allan Dwan, Thomas H. Ince, J. Parker Read, Mack Sennett, Marshall Neilan and George Loane Tucker; Thomas Ince was president; turned it over to Oscar Price in 1921; Mack Sennett was treasurer; offices located at 729 7th Ave. New York; merged with First National Pictures, Inc. to become Associated First National Pictures, Inc. in 1922.

**Associated Screen News Inc. - US - 1921-1922** - distributed newsreels with offices located at 120 W. 41st St. New York; G. Baynes was president and general manager.

**Astor Pictures Corp - US - 1925-1963** started as a distributor of reissued classic films, but expanded to film production; operated three subsidiary companies in 1930s: Vigilant Pictures Corp., B 'n' B Film Corp. and Promotional Films, Inc.; in the 1950s, formed Atlantic Television Corp. to release inventory to TV; Astor purchased by Franklin F. Bruder in 1959; filed for bankrupcy in 1963.

**Astoria Studios - US - 1920-current** - located at 34-31 35th St. Astoria, N.Y.; studio opened as the production center for Famous Players-Lasky; produced more than 100 silent features; became a production studio for Paramount; from 1940-1946, taken over by the War Department to create propaganda films; rental studio after the war.

**Astra Film Co. - US - 1915-1916** - production company with Louis Gasnier as president; distributed through Pathe Exchange; became Astra Film Corporation.

**Astra Film Corp. - US - 1916-1921** - production company formed from Astra Film Company; located at 1 Congress St. Jersey City, New Jersey; Louis J. Gasnier was president, George Baker was V. P., George B. Seitz was secretary and A. T. Dobson was general manager; George Fitzmaurice and Edward Jose also involved; distribution through Pathe Exchange; leased the Pathe Studios in New Jersey until 1919 when they purchased the Diando Film Company studio at Verdugo Road in Glendale, California.

**Astra Films - UK - 1920-1923 -** production company formed by Herbert Wilsox; offices at Walthamstow, England.

**Astra-Film - GERMANY - 1917-1918 -** production company.

**Astra-National - UK - 1922-1923 -** distribution company.

**Asty Film Co. - GREECE - 1916-1925** - production company established in Athens, Greece by Demos Vratsanos and Josef Hepp; produced newsreels, advertisements, and feature films.

**Atelier Apollo - FINLAND** (before independence) **- 1906-1913 -** production company formed by K. E. Stahlberg in Helsinki; primarily produced short documentaries; produced Finland's first feature length film, which was filmed in 1907 but not shown until 1913.

**Athene Films - GREECE - 1910 -** production company formed by Josef Hepp.

**Athini Film - GREECE - 1910 -** production company formed by comedian Spyros Dimitrakopoulous; located in Athens; Filippo Martelli was director and Erich Buhbach was cameraman.

**Athletic Feature Films - US - 1917 -** production company.

**Atlantic & Pacific Film Co. - US - 1922 -** offices located at 47 W. 34th St. New York; went out of business in 1922.

**Atlantic Distributing Company - US - 1918-1919 -** distribution company located in the Times Building, New York.

**Atlantic Features, Inc. - US - 1923 -** production company with offices located at 110 W. 40th St. New York; distribution through Arrow Film.

**Atlantic Films - DENMARK - 1922 -** distribution company for Svenska Biografteatern.

**Atlantic Films - UK - 1919 -** production company.

**Atlantic Union Films, Ltd. - UK - 1924 -** production company formed by Henry Edwards and Hugh MacLean; they moved to 19 London Wall, London in 1925.

**Atlas - UK - 1924 -** production and distribution company.

**Atlas Biocraft - UK - 1922-1924 -** production company formed by Miles Mander and Adrian Brunel.

**Atlas Bioscope Co. - UK - 1911 -** distribution company with offices at 52 Wardour Street, Westminster.

**Atlas Educational Film Co. - US - 1913-1942 -** production company located at 29 E. Madison St. Chicago, Illinois; studio located at 1111 S. Blvd. Oak Park; I. R. Rehm was president and J. M. Boggs was V. P.

**Atlas Feature Film Co. - UK - 1913-1914 -** distribution company with offices located at 7 Gerrard St. Winchester.

**Atlas Film Co. - US - 1910-1913 -** production company with distribution through Motion Picture Distributing and Sales Company.

**Atlas Film Company of America, Inc. - US - 1921 -** production company located 705 W. 8th St. Los Angeles, California; H. A. Crempw as president and general manager; released Charlie Conklin films; distribution through Mt. Olympus Distributing Co.

**Atlas-Biocraft - UK - 1924 -** production and distribution company.

**Athletic Feature Films - US - 1917 -** distribution company located at 218 West 42nd Street, New York with Marty McHale as president, Tris Speaker as V. P. and Tom McEvoy general manager.

**Atroy Film Service - UK - 1913-1914** - distribution company with offices located at Cromwell Hall, Lancaster.

**Attractions Distributing Corp. - US - 1920 -** distribution company located at 1476 Broadway, New York with B. P. Schulberg as president; distributed Katherine MacDonald productions through First National Exhibitors Circuit.

**Augustus Film - ITALY - 1928 -** production company.

**Aurora Film Plays Corporation - US - 1915 -** production company located at 1476 Broadway, New York.

**Australasian Cinematograph Company Pty, Ltd - AUSTRALIA - 1907-1929 -** production company.

**Australasian Film Co. - AUSTRALIA - 1913- -** production company formed in January 1913 from the merger of newly formed General Film Co. of Australasia and Greater J. D.

Williams Amusement Co; newly formed merger was called "the Combine" and dominated the film industry in Australia; during the war, all production was under government control until after the war; in the 1920s, after a series of changes, became Greater Union.

**Australasian Films Ltd - UK - 1915 -** distribution company located at Regent Street, Carlton House, Westminster.

**Australasian Films Ltd. - US - 1922 -** distribution company located at 729 7th Ave. New York.

**Australasian Kinematographic Co. - AUSTRALIA - 1901-1909 -** production company formed from the Salvation Army Limelight Department; produced the first feature length documentary and many other firsts for the country.

**Australian Film Co. - 1911-12 -** [see Australian Film Syndicate]

**Australian Film Syndicate - AUSTRALIA - 1911-12 -** production company located in North Sidney, Australia; a/k/a Australian Film Co.

**Australian Life Biograph Co. - AUSTRALIA - 1911 -** production company located in Sidney, Australia; produced films featuring Gaston Mervale and Louise Lovely.

**Australian Photo-Play Co. - AUSTRALIA - 1911-1912 -** production and distribution company formed by Stanley Crick and Herbert Finlay with distribution outlets in Australia and New Zealand.

**Austral Super Films - AUSTRALIA - 1922 -** production company formed by Lawson Harris and Yvonne Pavis; located in Sydney, Australia.

**Austring Film - AUSTRIA - 1928 -** distribution company.

**Austro-Servian Film Co. - US - 1914 -** production company located at 220 W. 42nd St., New York.

**Authors & Photo Players Co. Inc. - US - 1922 -** located at 512 5th Ave. New York.

**Authors Film Co., Inc - US - 1915 -** distribution company located at 1432 Broadway, New York; distributor for Topnotch Motion Pictures, Inc.

**Autoscope Co. - UK - 1901-1906 -** production company established by William George Barker; open-air studio located at Stamford Hill, London; sold to Warwick Trading in 1906.

**Avenue Film Co. - UK - 1915 -** distribution company located at 97 Shaftsbury Avenue, Westminster.

**Award Film Service - UK - 1913-1915** - distribution company located at 5 Edward Street, Westminster.

**Aycie Film Corp. - US - 1921-1922 -** located at 117 W. 46th St. New York.

**Ayers Motion Picture Co. - US - 1910** - formed by Milton Ayers in San Francisco, California.

**Aylesworth's Big Game Pictures - US - 1915** - production company formed by Arthur J. Aylesworth; taken over by the Paramount Pictures Corporation.

**AyVeeBee Film Corp. - US - 1920-1922 -** production company with Amadee J. Van Beuren as president and general manager; offices located at 1562 Broadway New York; distribution through Pathe. [see Adventure Films, Inc.; V. B. K Film Corp; Timely Topics Inc.; Fables Pictures Inc.; Timely Films Inc.]

**Aywon Film Corp. - US - 1919-1929 -** founded in New York by Nathan Hirsch, who had been president and general manager of Pioneer Film Co.; Hirsch purchased 16 5 reel features which he re-edited, changed the titles and distributed through states rights. He re-edited and released other material such as D. W. Griffith shorts. Offices were located at 729 7th Ave. New York. Also distributed Joy Comedies produced by Gold Seal Film Corp.

**Azerbaidjani - RUSSIA - 1924-1935 -** production studio was also named at various times, AFKU, Azerfil'm, Azgoskinprom, Azgoskino, and Azerkino.

**Azteca Studios - MEXICO - 1917 -** production company formed by Herminia Perez de Leon (known as Mimi Derba) and Enrique Rosas in Mexico City. They made 5 films and went bankrupt. This was the first feature film studio in Mexico and Mimi Derba was the first female to direct a feature film in Mexico.

# B

**B & C Kine. Co. - UK - 1913-1914** - distribution company for Brightonia Films; located at 33 Endell St. Winchester.

**B & H Film Co. - US - 1910** - distribution company located at 61 West 14th Street, New York.

**B & W. Exclusive Films - UK - 1913-1914** - distribution company located at 120 Wardour St., Winchester.

**B. A. Goodman - US - 1926** - production company.

**B. A. Rolfe Photoplays, Inc. - US - 1914** - production company formed by Benjamin A. Rolfe, Charles B. Maddox and Maxwell Karger; located at 1493 Broadway, New York; distribution through Alco Film Corp; changed name to Rolfe Photoplays, Inc. in December, 1914.

**B. A. Rolfe Productions - 1918-1920** - [see Rolfe Productions, Inc.]

**B. B. Features - US - 1919** - production company for films featuring Bessie Barriscale; distribution through Exhibitors Mutual and internationally through Robertson-Cole.

**B. B. Pictures - UK - 1913-1914** - distribution company located at Dunlop St., Glascow, Scotland.

**B. B. Productions - US - 1922** - production and distribution company for films featuring Betty Blythe; located at 15 West 44th Street, New York; used the Whitman Bennett studios on Riversdale Ave. in Yonkers, New York.

**B. F. Zeidman Productions - US - 1922-1939** - production company formed by Benjamin F. Zeidman (Bennie of Lubinville).

**B. P. Schulberg Productions - US - 1921-1942** - production company. [see Preferred Pictures.]

**B. S. Moss Motion Picture Corp. - US - 1915-1918** - production company located in Times Square, New York; formed by Benjamin S. Moss after leaving Reliance Feature Film Co., to provide films to Moss theater chain, and distributed by states rights to other theaters; ceased production in 1918.

**B. Y. S. Films, Inc. - US - 1920** - distribution company located at 130 West 46th Street, New York with Herbert H. Yudkin as general manager.

**Bacon Backer Film Corp. - US - 1918-1919** - production company located at 230 West 38th St. New York; owned by George Backer and Gerald F. Bacon.

**Balboa Amusement Producing Co. - US - 1913-1918** - production company located at Sixth and Alamitos in Long Beach, California with H. M. Horkheimer as president and general manager and Elwood Horkheimer as secretary and treasurer; formed from purchase of California Motion Picture Manufacturing Co in April 1913 by the Horkheimer brothers; initial financing and distribution through Pathe; also distributed through Alliance, B. S. Moss, Eclectic, Mutual, Paramount, Triangle, Universal and Warner Features; released films under several trade names such as Falcon Features and Fortune Photoplay which were distributed through General Film; in 1917, contracted with General Film Co. to produce a series called Knickerbocker Star Features; rented out production space to such companies as Arbuckle's Comique Film, Equitable Motion Picture, Golden Rooster, Joy, Kalem, Nemo, Oakdale, Panama, Plaza, Selig, VIM, and White Star; turned over to creditors in March 1918 and liquidated in 1919.

**Balshofer Productions Inc. - US - 1920-1928 -** production company and studio with Fred Balshofer as president and director; located at 1329 Gordon St. Hollywood, California.

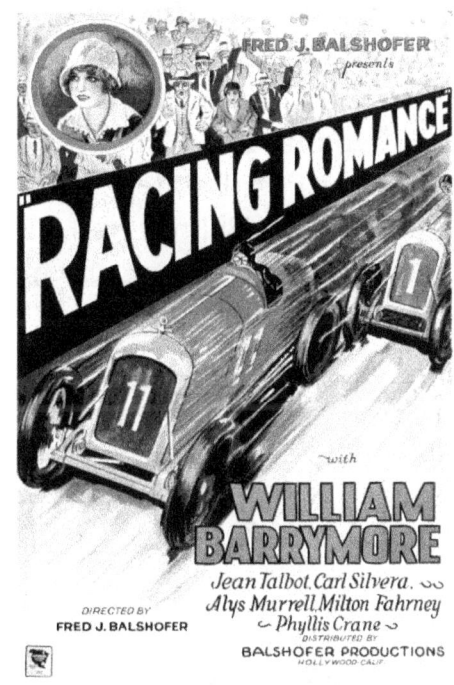

**Bamforth and Co. - UK - 1898-1915 -** production company located at Holmfirth in Yorkshire, England; produced comedies and marionette cartoons under the trade name Mario-Cartoons; distribution through Yorkshire Cine Co.; absorbed by Holmfirth Producing Co. in October 1915.

**Banba Co. - IRELAND - 1915 -** production company formed by C. A. McEvoy; located in Dublin.

**Banner Productions - US - 1924-1925 -** production company distributed through Henry Ginsberg Distributing Corp.

**Barker Films - UK - 1913-1914 -** trade name for films released by Barker Motion Photography Ltd.

**Barker Motion Photography Ltd. - UK - 1913-1914 -** production company located at 1 Soho Square, Winchester; released under the trade name of Barker Films.

**Barrett's Australian Productions - AUSTRALIA - 1922 -** production company formed by Franklyn Barrett.

**Barsky - US - 1925 -** production company owned by Irving J. Barsky.

**Bayoumi Photo Film - EGYPT - 1926-1927 -** production company located at 16 Saad Zaghloul St. at Ramleh Station in Alexandria; formed by Mohamed Bayoumi to produce documentary shorts.

**Beacon Film Co., Inc. - US - 1914 -** distribution company located at 110 West 40th Street, 3rd Floor, New York using the trade name Beacon Productions.

**Bear State Film Co. - US - 1918-1921** - production company and studio located in Hollywood, California with C. Hanford Harrison as president and general manager.

**Beating Back Film Corp. - US - 1915** - distribution company located at 71 West 23rd Street, Suite 1417, New York.

**Beauty Films - US - 1914-1916** - trade name used by American Film Manufacturing Co. in 1914; changed to American Film Co. in 1915.

**Bech, Van Siclen & Co., Inc. - US - 1919** - distribution company located at 45B East 17th Street, New York.

**Bee Hive Film Exchange - US - 1920** - distribution company merged into Reelcraft Pictures.

**Bejac Film Co. - US - 1925** - distribution company founded by Andrew F. Jackson specializing in black films; located at 240 W. 134th St. New York.

**Belge Cinema Film - BELGIUM - 1912-1919** - production company formed as a Belgian subsidiary to Pathe Freres with Alfred Machin as head of production; during the war, primarily produced war documentaries; after the war produced animal documentaries; closed in 1919.

**Bell Pictures - US - 1922-1929** - production company specializing in westerns.

**Belmar Historical Film Features, Inc. - US - 1912-1914** - production company with offices in Rosebank, New York; studio located at Post Estate, South Beach; Henry Belmar was president and Walter L. Evans was secretary/treasurer.

**Belmont Film Company - US - 1912-1917** - production and distribution company with offices located at 145 West 45th Street, Suite 710, New York; specialized in westerns; absorbed roster from Unicorn Film Services when they closed in 1916.

**Bendon Trading Co. - UK - 1913-1914** - distribution company located at 26-28 Wilson St. Glasgow, Scotland.

**Benjamin B. Hampton Productions - US - 1919-1922** - production company with distribution through W. W. Hodkinson.

**Ben Miller Productions - US - 1922** - production company specializing in westerns.

**Ben Roy Productions - US - 1921** - production company specializing in westerns.

**Ben Wilson Productions - US - 1921** - production company located at 5821 Santa Monica Blvd. Hollywood, California; produced 5 reel features and serials; distributed through Arrow Film Corp.

**Benned Film Co. - US - 1914** - production company located in the World's Tower Building, 110 W. 40th Street, New York.

**Berg-und Sportfilm - GERMANY - 1920-1927** - production company; translates as Mountain and Sports film.

**Bernstein Film Productions - US - 1917-1922** - production company located at Boyle & Stevenson Aves, Los Angeles, California; went out of business in 1922.

**Berolina Film GmbH - GERMANY - 1924** - production company located at Kochstr.12, Berlin.

**Bert Lubin Pictures - US - 1920** - distribution company located at 1476 Broadway, New York; formed by Bert Lubin to distribute 5 reel westerns.

**Berwilla Film Corp. - US - 1920-1924** - production company located at 5821 Santa Monica Blvd. Hollywood, California with Ben Wilson as president and William La Plant as V. P. and general manager; distribution through Arrow Film Corp.

**Best and Baker - AUSTRALIA - 1906** - production company located in Melbourne.

**Better Day Pictures, Inc. - US - 1923-1924** - production company formed with Bruce Barton as president, Elmore Leffingwell as V. P., and James S. Brown as head of production; produced films featuring Bruce Barton stories.

**Betzwood Film Co. - US - 1918-1922** - production company formed by the acquisition of the

500 acre Lubin studios outside of Philadelphia, Pennsylvania; Clarence Wolf was president and Ira M. Lowry (Lubin's son-in-law) was general manager; offices located at Empire Bldg. 13th and Walnut St., Philadelphia.

**Big A Features Ltd. - UK - 1913-1914** - distribution company located at 24 Gerrard St. Winchester.

**Big A Film Corporation - US - 1916** - distribution company located at 145 West 45th Street, New York.

**Big Ben Films - UK - 1913-1915** - trade name for one and three reel comedies produced by Union Film Publishing Co.

**Big Otto Brand - US - 1914** - trade name for films produced by Nash Motion Picture Co.

**Big V Comedy - US - 1918-1920** - trade name used for a series of comedy shorts produced by Vitagraph featuring Vitagraph's Big V Riot Squad including Larry Semon and Joe Rock.

**Bijou Film Service - UK - 1913-1914** - distribution company located at 160 Cheetham Hill Rd., Manchester, England.

**Bijou Films, Inc. - US - 1926-1927** - production company for Pat Sullivan Comics distributed through Educational Film Exchanges.

**Billy Franey Comedies - US - 1921** - trade name for comedy shorts released through Reelcraft Pictures Corp.

**Billy Ruge Comedies - US - 1921** - trade name for one reel comedies featuring Billy Ruge; released by Film Sales Co.

**Billy West Comedies - US - 1921-1924** - trade name for comedies produced by Bull's Eye Film Corp. and later moved to Cumberland Productions, Inc.; distributed through Arrow Pictures Corp.

**Biltmore Productions - US - 1919-1920** - production company specializing in westerns.

**Bio-Tableau - AUSTRALIA - 1901-1909** - trade name for factuals and newsreels produced by J. C. Williamson.

**Biograph Co. - US - 1909-1917** - production company formed from American Mutoscope and Biograph Co.; located at 796 East 176th Street, New York; D. W. Griffith became principle director and Mary Pickford became "the Biograph Girl"; many of film industry's foundation began here including Lionel Barrymore, Lillian Gish, Dorothy Gish, Florence Auer, Robert Vignola, Alan Hale, Blanche Sweet, Harry Carey, Mabel Normand, Henry B. Walthall, Dorothy Davenport and Mack Sennett; Griffith started filming in California but left in 1913 to move to feature films; Biograph produced last film in 1916 and moved to studio rental and rereleasing old films.

**Biografernas Filmdepot - SWEDEN - 1922-1934** - production company; the translation is AB Cinema Movie Depot.

**Biorama - DENMARK - 1909-1912** - production and distribution company formed by Soren Neilsen in Copenhagen; in 1912, the company name changed to Filmfabrikken Skandinavien (Film Factory Scandinavia).

**Bioscop Konzern - GERMANY - 1920** - production company subsidiary of Bioscop acquired by Decla.

**Bioscope Film Co. - US - 1920-1921** - production company located in Goldstein's Springs, Florida with A. B. McMullen as president to produce comedies.

**Birth of a Race Photoplay Corp. - US - 1917-1918** - production company formed to produce race films.

**Bischoff Productions - US - 1922-1928** - [see Samuel Bischoff Productions]

**Bison Life Motion Pictures** - trade name used by New York Motion Pictures Co. shortened to Bison.

**Bison Motion Pictures - US - 1909-1912** - trade name used by New York Motion Pictures; became Bison 101 from use of the Miller 101 Ranch winter camp in California; merged to become part of Universal in 1912.

**Blache Features, Inc. - US - 1913-1914** - production company owned by Herbert and Alice Guy Blache; located in Fort Lee, New Jersey; filming done at Solax, which was their studio.

**Black Diamond Productions - US - 1916-1918** - production company with studios at Talleyrand Ave. Jacksonville, Florida and Wilkes-Barre, Pennsylvania; distribution through U. S. Moving Pictures Co.

**Black Diamond Comedies - US - 1916-1918** - trade name for single reel comedies produced by Black Diamond Productions.

**Blair Coan Productions, Inc. - US - 1923** - production company located at Room 713, 108 S. La Salle Street, Chicago, Illinois.

**Blanchfield - US - 1921** - production company specializing in westerns.

**Blaney Spooner Feature Film Corp. - US - 1913** - production company located near Clason's Point, New York; produced films featuring Charles Spooner; later that year, changed company name to Charles E. Blaney Feature Play Co.

**Blazed Trail Productions - US - 1919-1923** - production company and studio located in 19 Elm St. Gloversville, N.Y. with J. L. Russell as president and Royal W. France as V. P. and general manager; produced a series set in the Canadian north woods; distribution by Arrow Film Corp.

**Blinkhorn Photoplays Corporation - US - 1913-1914** - production and distribution company formed by Albert Blinkhorn; located in the World's Tower Building, 110-112 West 40th Street, New York.

**Bluebird Photoplays, Inc. - US - 1915-1919** - production subsidiary of Universal for slightly bigger budget films.

**Border Feature Film Corp. - US - 1920-1921** - production company with studios at Bisbee and Tombstone, Arizona; offices at Wesley Roberts Bldg., Los Angeles, California with Miles M. Merrill as president and Rex Thorpe as secretary/treasurer and general manager; produced two reel westerns featuring Grant Merrill and Peggy Parkan.

**Boris Thomashefsky Film Co. - US - 1915 -** production company formed to produce Yiddish classics featuring Boris Thomashefsky.

**Bostock Jungle and Film Co. - US - 1915 -** production company founded in July 1915 by David Horsley after purchasing the Bostock collection of animals; studios situation on 5 acres with 6 stages located at Main and Washington Sts. Los Angeles, California; produced animal films; distribution through Mutual Film Corp.

**Bosworth, Inc. - US - 1913-1917 -** production company formed by Frank A. Garbutt, Joseph Garbutt, H.T. Rudisill and Hobart Bosworth and featuring Jack London stories; located at 110 West 40th Street, New York; later moved to 201 N. Occidental Blvd. Los Angeles with filming at the J.A.C. Studios; distribution was moved to Paramount in 1914; Bosworth left the company in March 1915 and production was taken over by Morosco and Pallas Pictures; merged into Famous Players-Lasky Corp on June 20, 1916.

**Bosworth-Paramount - US - 1914 -** trade name for Bosworth films distributed through Paramount.

**Box Office Attractions Co. - US - 1914-1915 -** distribution company formed from Box Office Attractions Film Rental Co. in May 1914 as Fox gained exclusive contracts from Solax, Blache, American Film, Film Releases of America, Ramo, and Great Northern for distribution in the New England area; offices located at 130 West 46th Street, New York with William Fox as president; absorbed into Fox Film Corp in February 1915.

**Box Office Attractions Film Rental Co. - US - 1913-1914 -** created in 1913 from the Greater New York Film Rental Co., a distributor of states rights material in New York and the New England area when William Fox decided to go into film production; offices were located at 130 West 46th St. New York with Fox as president and Winfield R. Sheehan as general manager; originally distributed films by Balboa Amusement Producing Co. but by 1914 began their first feature production (*Life's Shop Window*); name of the company was shortened in May 1914.

**Boy City Film Corp. - US - 1918 -** production company formed by Judge Willis Brown who created a boy's town to show a series of ½ hour films; about a dozen films were made at Culver City by King Vidor and distributed through General Film Co.

**Brabo Films - FRANCE - 1921 -** production company.

**Bradley Feature Film Co. - US - 1920-1921 -** production company located at 2147 Prospect Ave. Cleveland, Ohio; studios located at 3001 Euclid Ave. with S. R. Bradley as president and B. W. Rueben as V. P. and general manager; distribution through Federated Exchanges and by states rights.

**Bray Pictures Corp. - US - 1919-1926 -** Bray changed name to Bray Pictures Corp. when the International Film Services closed and Hearst moved IFS series to Bray; Bray moved distribution to Goldwyn who bought controlling interest but Bray bought back control in 1921; Bray divided off the military and training films and reopened Bray Studios while continuing the movie animation through Bray Pictures Corp.; Bray closed Bray Pictures Corp. in 1926 and focused on training films at Bray Studios. [see Bray Studios]

**Bray Studios, Inc. - US -1912-1919, 1921-2003 -** production company for animation formed by John Randolph Bray who created the first animated film series, Heeza Liar, distributed through Pathe Exchange; offices located at 23 E. 26th St. New York; in 1914, Bray developed and patented a process to streamline film animation and started charging license fees to other studios; Bray trained and started many major animators' careers, such as Max Fleischer, Paul Terry and Walter Lantz; in 1916, Bray supplied Paramount a one reel weekly cartoon and formed the Paramount Bray Pictograph Screen Magazine to incorporate live action with animation; Bray also started drawing training films for the military; in1919, he changed the name to Bray Pictures Corp; in 1921, he reformed Bray Studios, Inc, to handle military animation and training films that continued to operate until 2003 under Bray's grandson.

**Brentwood Film Corp. - US - 1918-1921 -** production company formed by nine doctors in the Los Angeles area to produce Christian Science oriented films directed by King Vidor; filmed at 4811 Fountain St. which was the old Mena Film Corp. studio; Lloyd C. Haynes was president and W. H. Rimmer was V. P.; signed with Robertson Cole Co. for national distribution; in September, 1919, after four films, Vidor left to go to First National Exhibitors; Brentwood closed in 1921.

**Brewster Kemble Production, Inc. - US - 1921 -** production company with studios located at 7100 Santa Monica Blvd. Hollywood, California; George H. Brewster was president and John Kemble was V. P. and general manager.

**British Actors Film Co. - UK - 1915-1921 -** production company headed by Charles Macdona, with Gerald Malvern as general manager and A. E. Matthews as head of production; utilized studio facilities at Bushey; acquired by Alliance Film Corp. in 1920 and closed in 1921 due to financial problems.

**British and Colonial Kinematograph Company Ltd. - UK - 1908-1924** - production company located at 33-35 Endell St. London; studio located at Hoe St. Walthamstow and headed by J. B. McDowell with Edward Godal as general manager.

**British Empire Films - UK - 1915-1917** - production company formed from Zenith Film Co.; studio at Whetstone; liquidated May 1917 and studio bought the following year by Famous Pictures.

**British Exhibitors' Films - UK - 1915-1922** - distribution company; in 1922, released series of one and two reel dramas produced by Master Films using the trade name Master-British Exhibitors.

**British Famous Films - UK - 1917** - production company formed to produce two reel historical films.

**British Filmcraft - UK - 1928-1929** - production company.

**British Instructional Films, Ltd - UK - 1921-1933** - production company.

**British International Pictures, Ltd - UK - 1927-1937** - production company formed by John Maxwell through purchase of Elstree Studios and British National Studios and merger with his ABC cinema circuit; in 1937, Maxwell purchased and merged in British Pathe and changed the name to Associated British Picture Corp.

**British Isle Exclusives Ltd. - UK - 1913-1914** - distribution company with offices at 1 Victoria Square, Leeds.

**British Lion Film Corp. - UK - 1927-current** - production and distribution company formed by Sam W. Smith in November 1927.

**British Mutoscope & Biograph Co. - UK - 1910s** - distribution arm for the American Mutoscope & Biograph Co. in the UK.

**British National Pictures, Ltd - UK - 1926-1927** - production company located at Heddon House, 149-151 Regent Street, London; headed by George T. Eaton; New York offices located at Suite 815, 565 Fifth Avenue with J. D. Williams as general manager.

**British Oak Film Co. - UK - 1912-1915** - production company; taken over in 1915 by New Agency Films Co. Ltd to make newreels and war films for WWI.

**British Screen Productions, Ltd - UK - 1928-1930** - production company.

**British Super Films - UK - 1922-1923 -** distribution company formed from acquisition of British Film Renters to release films featuring Fred Paul through Jury.

**Brittania Films - UK - 1911-1915 -** production company formed to supply Pathe.

**Broadway Comedies -** US - 1923-1926 - trade name for comedies produced by Cumberland Productions, Inc. and distributed through Arrow Pictures, Corp.

**Broadway Distributing Corp. - US - 1925 -** distribution company.

**Broadway Features - US - 1915 -** trade name for series released by Universal Film Manufacturing Co.

**Broadway Film Co. - US - 1915 -** distribution company located at 110 W. 40th Street, New York.

**Broadway Picture Producing Co. - US - 1914 -** production company with offices located at 1400 Broadway, New York; David Young, Jr. was president; closed same year due to financial problems.

**Broadway Star Features - US - 1914-1917 -** production company; product directed by Vitagraph.

**Broadwest Film Company, Ltd - UK - 1917 -** production company located at 175 Waldour St. London.

**Brockliss-Motiograph - UK - 1912** - distribution company located at 4 New Compton Street, London.

**Broncho Films - US - 1912-1915 -** trade name for westerns produced by Broncho Motion Picture Co.

**Broncho Motion Picture Co. - 1912-1915 -** production company located at 150 E. 14th St., New York; formed by Adam Kessel and Charles Bauman (after they left Universal) to produce westerns; distribution under the trade name of Broncho Films through Mutual Film Corp.

**Brownie Comedies - US - 1921-1922** - production company located 54 W. 40th St., New York headed by A. J. McAllister.

**Bryant Washburn Productions, Inc. - US - 1923** - production company formed by Bryant Washburn.

**Buckeye Film and Projecting Co. - US - 1910** - distribution company located at 309 Arcade Bldg, Dayton, Ohio; merged with Cincinnati Film Exchange to form Cincinnati-Buckeye Film Co.

**Bud Barsky Corp. - US - 1924-1927** - production company founded by Bud Barsky to produce films featuring Al Hoxie and Frank Merrill.

**Bud Fisher Film Corporation - US - 1913-1926** - production company located at 49th Street at 7th Avenue, New York. [see Mutt and Jeff, Inc.]

**Buffalo Bill and Pawnee Bill Film Co. - US - 1910** - production company located in New York; distribution through Motion Picture Distributing and Sales Co.

**Buffalo Films - US - 1912-1916** - trade name promoted as a Buffalo Drama and distributed by Unicorn.

**Buffalo Motion Picture Co. - 1919-1921 -** production company located at 844 6th Ave., New York with Frank W. Caldwell as president and J. W. Prouse as general manager.

**Bulldog-film GmbH - GERMANY - 1921 -** production company.

**Bull's Eye Film Corp. - US - 1918-1921 -** production company formed to produce short comedies featuring Billy West for state rights distribution located in New York, but their production was filmed at the King Bee Studio, 1329 Gordon St. Hollywood, California; Milton L. Cohen was president and Charles Parrott was production manager. Merged into Reelcraft Corp. in 1920.

**Burlingham Adventure Scenics - US - 1921 -** production company featuring one reel scenics; released by Inter-Ocean Film Corp.

**Burlingham Films - US - 1919 -** trade name for travel films released by Burlingham Travel Pictures.

**Burlingham Travel Pictures - US - 1919 -** production company formed by Frederick Burlingham; released as Burlingham Films.

**Burr Nickle Productions - US - 1922 -** production company located at 1017-1018 Story Building, Los Angeles, California.

**Burr Scenics - US - 1922-1923 -** trade name used by Mastodon Films, Inc.

**Burrud (Sunset) Scenics - US - 1921 -** production company for one reel scenics distributed by Reelcraft Pictures Corp.

**Burston Films, Inc. - US - 1921 -** production company located at Longacre Bldg., New York and 6050 Sunset Blvd. Los Angeles, California; Louis Burston was president.

**Burton Holmes Corp. - US - 1898-1946** - production company formed by Burt Holmes who started presenting travel shows in 1891 using slides; Holmes created his first film in 1897 and travelled presenting films and slides; in the 1920s, Holmes produced travelogue shorts for Paramount called Burton Holmes Travel Pictures; offices located at Aeolian Bldg. 33 W. 42nd St. New York; in 1931, produced a series for MGM and continued with personal travel shows until just after WWII, when Holmes retired.

**Buster Keaton Productions, Inc. - US - 1922-1928** - production company formed by Joseph M. Schenck, Marcus Lowe and A. H. Giannini as a successor company to Comique; specialized in Buster Keaton features and shorts; filming done at 1205 Lillian Way, Hollywood, California; dissolved in 1928.

**Butcher & Sons, Ltd - UK - 1913-1914** - distributor for Broncho Films with offices at Farringdon Ave. E. C.

**Butcher's Film Service - UK - 1903-1940s** - production and distribution company formed from W. Butcher's and Son, a photographic supply seller since 1896; F. W. Baker took control in 1903 when William Butcher committed suicide and turned it into a distribution company and expanded in production in 1917.

**Butterfly Pictures - US - 1917** - production company with distribution through Universal.

# C

**C. A. Film - DENMARK - 1922-1923** - [see Carl Alstrup Film]

**C. B. C. Film Sales Corp. - US - 1919-1924** - distribution company located at 1600 Broadway, New York with Joseph Brandt as president, Harry Cohn as treasurer and Jack Cohn as general manager; company name stands for Cohn-Brandt-Cohn; originally distributed westerns but soon moved to production of Hall Room Boys comedies, Screen Snapshots and other low budget comedy shorts; in 1922, switched to feature films and in 1924, changed their name to Columbia Pictures Corp.

**C. B. Price Co., Inc. - US - 1919 -** distribution company located in the Times Building, New York.

**C. C. Burr Pictures - US - 1921 -** [see Master Pictures, Inc. and Mastodon Pictures]

**C. E. Shurtleff, Inc. - US - 1920-1921 -** production company located at 729 7th Ave., New York; distribution through Metro Pictures Corp.

**C. Gardner Sullivan Productions - US - 1924-1925 -** production company; closed to do production work for Cecil B. DeMille.

**C. K. Y. Film Corp. - US - 1917 -** production company formed in August 1917 to produce films featuring Clara Kimball Young.

**C. L. Chester Productions - US - 1918-1922 -** production company with offices at 1438 Gower St. Hollywood, California and 130 W. 41st St. New York; C. L. Chester was president and treasurer, Albert Britt was V. P., and William S. Campbell was production manager; produced a variety of series which included Chester Comedies and Chester Junior Comedies that were distributed through Federated Exchanges, and Chester Outings, Chester Screenics, and travelogues which were distributed through Educational Film Corp; a major fire in 1921 destroyed the studio; a few chimp based comedies were produced after the fire.

**C. R. Macauley Photoplays, Inc. - US - 1919-1921 -** [see Macauley Photoplays, Inc.]

**C. S. Clancy Productions - UK - 1922-1930s -** production company formed by Carl Stearns Clancy; became C. S. Clancy Production Syndicate, Inc. with change to sound.

**Cactus Features - US - 1921-1922** - trade name for a series of features starring Maryon Aye and "Bob" Reeves released by Rogell-Brown Productions and distributed by Western Pictures Exploitation Company of Los Angeles and Hollywood.

**Caesar Film - ITALY - 1914-1935 -** production and distribution company.

**Caesar-Film - GERMANY - 1920-1924 -** production and distribution company.

**California Film Exchange - US - 1912-1917 -** distribution company of serials, comedies and features with M. L. Markowitz as general manager; offices located at 54 7th St., San Francisco, 110 E. 4th St., Los Angeles and Lewis Bldg. Phoenix, Arizona; distributed for Universal, 101 Bison and leading brands.

**California Motion Picture Corp. - US - 1914-1916 -** production company founded in San Francisco, California with studios in San Raphael; Herbert Payne was president and Alexander E. Beyfuss was V. P. and general manager; company featured opera singer Beatriz Michelena with her husband George Middleton as production manager and director; distribution was through Alco Film Corp. until Dec. 1914 when they changed distribution to World Film Corp.; in 1916, changed again to states rights but soon ran out of money and closed down the same year.

**California Motion Picture Manufacturing Co. - US - 1910-1913** - production company founded in Long Beach, California by a group of entrepreneurs with T. L. Howland as president and V. L. Duhem as general manager; in April 1913, sold to the Horkheimer brothers who changed the name to Balboa Amusement Producing Co.

**California Producers Corp. - US - 1921** - production company located at 7100 Santa Monica Blvd. Hollywood, California with George Newberger as president, S. L. Warner as V. P. and J. L. Warner as general manager; produced two reel comedies for Educational Film Corp.

**Callahan Film Co. - US - 1921** - production company located at the Curtiss Airport Grounds in Atlantic City, New Jersey; produced two reel comedies released under the trade name of Jimmy Callahan Comedies and distributed through Film Market, Inc.

**Campbell Comedies - US - 1921-1922** - trade name used by Campbell Comedy Corp.

**Campbell Comedy Corp. - US - 1921-1922** - production company formed by William S. Campbell, who was production manager for C. L. Chester Productions when the fire burned down his studio; offices were located at 4534 Sunset Blvd., Hollywood, California; used Fine Arts studio to produce two reel animal comedies for Educational Film Corp.

**Cameo Comedies - US - 1915** - trade name used by Colonial Motion Picture Corp.

**Cameo Film Co., Inc. - US - 1915** - production company located at 1400 Broadway, New York.

**Camus Productions - US - 1922** - production company.

**Canadian Bioscope Co, Ltd. - CANADA - 1912-1915** - production company formed December 1912 at 108 Pleasant St. Halifax, Nova Scotia by Capt. H. H. B. Holland; offices located at 1209 Candler Building, 220 West 42nd Street, New York; company closed February 1915 due to WWI.

**Canadian Photoplays, Ltd - CANADA - 1919-1921** - production company formed by Ernest Shipman with offices in Calgary and Alberta. [see Ernest Shipman and Associates]

**Canadian Releasing Corporation Ltd. - CANADA - 1922** - distribution company located at 12 Mayor Street in Montreal with J. P. O'Loghlin as general manager, and 1 Alice Street, St. John, New Brunswick with Phil Hazza as manager.

**Canyon Picture Corp. - US - 1919-1922** - production company with offices located at 126-130 W. 46th Street, New York; Jack Weinberg was president and Joseph M. Goldstein was treasurer; produced westerns featuring Franklyn Farnum.

**Capital Film Co. - US - 1918-1924** - production company formed February 1918 in Indianapolis, Indiana with William H. Miller as president; Miller was replaced by Ike Schlank; June 1918, began distributing Selig films; closed in 1924.

**Capital Film Co. - US - 1920-1921** - distribution company located at the Consumers Bldg, Chicago, Illinois with B. Herbert Milligan as general manager; records conflict listing Hugh Wood and S. L. Barnhard as president.

**Capitol Comedies - US - 1915-1923** - trade name for two reel comedies featuring "Smilin" Bill Parsons produced by National Film Corp. of America and distributed through Goldwyn.

**Capitol Film Co. - UK - 1913-1914** - distribution company located at 7 Rupert Ct., Wardour St. Winchester.

**Capitol Film Co. - US - 1910** - production company located at 405 11th Street, N. W. Washington, D.C.

**Captain Kettle Films - UK - 1914-1915** - production and distribution company with studios at Towers Hall, Bradford; formed to produce one reel comedies; bought out in 1915 by Pyramid Films.

**Caravel Comedies - US - 1920-1921** - trade name for Marx Bros. comedies with offices located at 130 W. 46th St., New York.

**Cardinal Pictures Corp. - US - 1916-1917** - production company located at 485 Fifth Avenue, New York.

**Carl Alstrup Film - DENMARK - 1922-1923** - production

company with distribution by Fotorama.

**Carlo Rossi & Co. - ITALY - 1906-1908 -** production company founded in Turin by Carlo Rossi; in 1908, the company name was changed to Itala Film.

**Carlos Productions - US - 1921-1928 -** production company formed by A. Carlos with W. G. Smith as president to create a series featuring Richard Talmadge; offices located at 117 W. 46th St., New York; distribution through Fidelity Pictures Corp.

**Carlton Motion Picture Laboratories - US - 1910 -** distribution company located a 1 Union Square, New York.

**Carric Film Co. - US - 1921 -** distribution company located at 104 W. 49th St., New York with H. A. Ricciardy as general manager.

**Carson Company - US - 1909 -** production company with distribution through Phoenix Film Co.

**Carter Cinema Distributing Co - US - 1920-1921 -** distribution company specializing in educational documentaries;

offices located at 220 W. 42nd St. New York.

**Carter de Haven Productions - US - 1920-1921** - production company located at 3800 Mission Road, Hollywood, California; produced two reel and five reel comedies distributed through First National.

**Cartoon Film Co. Ltd. - UK - 1918** - production company located at 76 & 78 Wardour St., London.

**Casino Star Comedies - US - 1915** - trade name for a series of comedies produced by the Gaumont Company.

**Castle Films - US - 1926-1929** - production and distribution company located at 729 Seventh Avenue, 10th Floor, New York with exchanges around the country.

**Catherine Curtis Corp. - US - 1920-1921** - production company located in Los Angeles, California to produce Catherine Curtis material with Ernest Shipman and Associates; distributed through First National Exhibitors Circuit, Inc.

**Caulfield Photoplay Co. - US - 1917-1918** - production company for one reel comedy shorts released under the trade name Strand Comedies; distributed by Mutual Film.

**Caws Comedy Corp. - US - 1917-1918** - production company for comedy shorts formed by Charles Abrams, Samuel Cummins, Nathaniel Spitzer and Arthur C. Werner.

**Cecil B. DeMille Pictures Corp. - US - 1925-1928** - production company for DeMille films with F. C. Munro as president and John C. Flinn as V. P. and general manager; product distributed through Producers Distributing Corp.; company was absorbed in re-organization with W. W. Hodkinson as part of an acquisition of Pathe.

**Celebrated Comedies - US - 1920-1921** - trade name for one and two reel comedies released by Celebrated Players Film Corp.

**Celebrated Players Film Company - US - 1914** - production company located at 64 West Randolph Street, Schiller Building, Chicago, Illinois.

**Celebrated Players Film Corp. - US - 1920-1921** - production company located at 207 S. Wabash Ave. and 810 S. Wabash Ave., Chicago, Illinois with J. L. Freidman as president, treasurer and general manager.

**Celio Film - ITALY - 1912-1921** - production and distribution company.

**Celtic Film Co. - FRANCE - 1917** - production company.

**Celtic Photo Plays, Inc - US - 1920-1921** - production company.

**Centaur Film Co. - US - 1913-1914** - production company founded by David Horsley in Bayonne, New Jersey when he left Nestor Film Co after a dispute with Universal; Horsley reformed his older production company in same location but changed the name and produced one reel comedies under three different trade names, MinA Films (the winning name in a contest that Horsley held short for "Made in America"), Ace Comedies and Cub Films.

**Centaur Film Manufacturing Co. - US - 1908-1910** - production company founded by David Horsley and located at 900 Broadway in Bayonne, New Jersey; Centaur considered the first independent company after Edison's Trust was formed; ceased production until he took on a partner, Ludwig G. B. Erg, but they didn't get along so Horsley bought him out and Erb formed Crystal Film Co.; Horsley stopped production and moved his operation to California and opened as Nestor Films.

**Centauro Films - UK - 1913 -** distributed in the U.K. by Anderson's Film Agency.

**Certified Pictures - US - 1922 -** distribution company.

**Central Film Company - US - 1915** - distribution company located at 110 S. State Street, Chicago, Illinois.

**Central Feature Film Co. - UK - 1913-1914 -** distributor with offices at 72 Shaftesbury Ave. Winchester.

**Century Comedies - US - 1917-1929 -** trade name used by Century Film Corp.

**Century Film Corp. - US - 1917-1929 -** production company with Julius Stern as president, Abe Stern as V. P. and Louis Jacobs as general manager; produced two reel comedies under the trade name of Century Comedies; studio located at 6100 Sunset Blvd, Los Angeles and offices located at 1600 Broadway, New York; distribution by states rights through Longacre Distributing Co. but changed to Universal in 1918.

**Century Films, Inc. - US - 1919-1920** - distribution company located at 207 So. Wabash Avenue, Chicago, Illinois with Maurice A. Salkin as president.

**Chadwick Pictures Corp. - US - 1924-1928 -** production company formed by I. E. Chadwick to produce feature films.

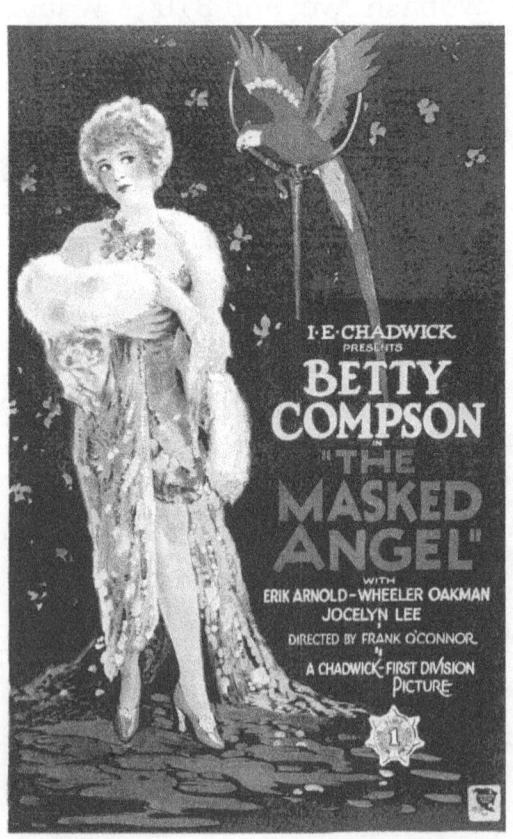

**Champion Film Co. - US - 1910-1912** - production company formed by Mark Dintenfass after the close of Actophone Co. in Philadelphia; offices located at 12 East 15th Street, New York; studio located at Coytesville, just outside of Fort Lee, New Jersey; Champion was part of the merger to form Universal.

**Chaplin-Mayer Pictures Co., Inc. - US - 1921** - production company located at 2 W. 45th St. New York and 3800 Mission Road, Los Angeles, California with Louis B. Mayer as president.

**Chaplin Classics, Inc. - US - 1922** - formed to distribute rereleases of the 12 Chaplin shorts produced by Mutual Film; offices located at 147 W. 46th St. New York.

**Character Pictures Corp - US - 1920** - production company located at 17 West 42nd Street, New York.

**Chariot Film Co. - US - 1914** - formed by Alex Yokel who was president and general manager; located at 110 West 40th St. New York.

**Charles E. Bartlett Productions - US - 1922** - production company.

**Charles E. Blaney Feature Play Co. - US - 1914** - production company formed from the Blaney Spooner Feature Film Co. and purchased a short time after the name change by Lewis J. Selznick for the World Film Corp.

**Charles Chaplin Film Corp. - US - 1921-1923** - production company and studio with Charles Chaplin as president, Sydney Chaplin as V.P. and Alfred Reeves as general manager.

**Charles Frohman, Inc. - US - 1922** - production company formed to convert some of Charles Frohman's theater productions to film (since Frohman had died in the sinking of the Lusitania in 1915); Alolph Zukor was president and David Frohman was V. P.

**Charles Gramlich Feature Plays, Inc. - US - 1920-1921 -** production company and studio located at Miami and Brickel Ave. 25th St. Miami, Florida with Charles Gramlich as president and general manager and William Cromer as V. P.

**Charles K. Harris Feature Film Co. - US - 1915 -** production company located in New York and formed to produce films based on Charles Harris; distributed through World Film Co.

**Charles Miller Productions, Inc. - US - 1919-1922 -** production company; part of formation of Hallmark Pictures Corp.

**Charles Ray Productions - US - 1920-1923 -** production company located at 1428 Fleming Street, Los Angeles, California with Charles T. Ray as president and Richard Willis as V. P. and general manager; distribution through First National.

**Charles R. Macauley Photoplays, Inc. - US - 1919-1921 -** production company. [see Macauley Photoplays, Inc.]

**Charles Urban Trading Co. - UK - 1904-1914 -** production company founded by Charles Urban with offices located at 89-91 Wardour St. Winchester London; released films under the trade names of Urbanora Films and Urban Eclipse, Uranus and Screen Chat Films; distributed Radios Films.

**Charter Features Corporation - US - 1915 -** production and distribution company located at 110 West 40th Street, New York.

(Charter Features)

**Chautauqua Film Exchange - US - 1911 -** distribution company located at 538 S. Dearborn Street, Chicago, Illinois.

**Cherry Kearton Co. - UK - 1913-1914** - distribution company for Champion Films with offices at 11 Haymarket St. London.

**Chester Conklin Comedies - US** - trade name for two reel comedies featuring Chester Conklin and released by Special Pictures Corp.

**Chester Bennett Productions - US - 1922-1923** - production company.

**Chester Photoplay - US - 1917** - production company located at 502 W. 38th St. New York.

**Chesterfield Pictures Corp. - US - 1925-1932** - production company with George R. Batcheller as president and Joseph Klein as V. P. and general manager; located at 1540 Broadway, New York; production done on the Universal lot until they merged with Invincible Pictures to become Chesterfield-Invincible.

**Cheyenne Feature Film Co. - US - 1912-1913** - production company formed by Charles Burton Irwin; offices located at 1482 Broadway, Room 1214, New York with F. J. Carroll as general manager; Irwin was a promoter of the Union Pacific Railroad, helped make rodeos popular and owned the Y-6 Ranch.

**Chicago Feature Film Co. - US - 1914-** production and distribution company located at 214 N. State Street, Chicago, Illinois.

**Chicago Film Co. - US - 1909** - production and distribution company.

**Chicago Film Exchange - US - 1908-1910** - distribution company located at 120 East Randolph Street, Chicago, Illinois with branches throughout the U.S.

**Child Players Co. of America, Inc. - US - 1914** - production company located at 45 West 34th Street, New York with Martin P. Korn as president.

**Christie Comedies - US - 1920-1924** - trade name for comedy shorts produced by Christie Film and distributed through Educational Film Corp.

**Christie Film Co. Inc. - US - 1916-1920s** - production company; Al Christie had been director of comedies at Nestor Films until David Horsley left; January 1, 1916, Al and his brother, Charles formed Christie Film Co. to produce two reel comedies for Universal under the Nestor brand; Al was president and director of production and Charles was general manager; offices and studio located at 6101 Sunset Blvd. Los Angeles, California; Al stopped producing for Universal and began supplying independent exchanges in July 1916; in April 1918, Christie began releasing through First National and in 1920 used Educational Film Corp.; comedies were also released under the trade names of Vanity Comedies and Gayety Comedies.

**Chronicles of America Picture Corp. - US - 1923-1924** - production company formed by Yale University to reconstruct American History on film. 15 episodes were filmed.

**Chrono Biorama Co. - AUSTRALIA - 1900-1901** - distribution company for factuals.

**Cinart, Inc. - US - 1921 -** distribution company with R. A. Nickell as president, N. J. Burnside as V. P., and L. C. Troupe as secretary/treasurer; offices located at 614-623 Hollingsworth Bldg., Los Angeles, California and Longacre Bldg., New York; purchased independent films and distributed primarily through states rights.

**Cincinnati-Buckeye Film Co. - US - 1910** - distribution company formed from Cincinnati Film Exchange and Buckeye Film and Projecting Company; offices located at 315-317 W. Fourth Street, Cincinnati, Ohio and 309-321 Arcade Building, Dayton, Ohio.

**Cincinnati Film Exchange - US - 1910** - distribution company located at 315-317 W. Fourth Street, Cincinnati, Ohio; merged with Buckeye Film and Projecting Company to become Cincinnati-Buckeye Film Company.

**Cine-Art Motion Picture Productions - 1920-1921 -** production company located in the Shalet Bldg., Bridgeport, Connecticut with C. Miller Fraser as president, treasurer and general manager; produced shorts and newsreels for Fox News

**Cine-Documentaire - FRANCE - 1928 -** production company.

**Cinema & General Supply Co. - UK - 1913-1914 -** distributor with offices at 49 Whyteville Rd. Forest Gate, London.

**Cinema Feature Film Co. - UK - 1913-1914 -** distribution company with offices at 21 Mount Pleasant, Liverpool.

**Cinema Film Agency - UK - 1913-1914 -** distribution company with offices at 165 Shaftesbury Ave., Winchester.

**Cinema Halles Film Co. - UK - 1913 -** distribution company located at 29a, Charing Cross Road, Winchester.

**Cinema News Service - US - 1925 -** founded by Andrew F. Jackson with A. Johnson as secretary; produced and distributed Negro News Reels; offices in the Presidential Bank Bldg in Washington, D. C.

**Cinema Studio de Joinville - FRANCE - 1919 -** production company formed July 23, 1919 as a subsidiary of Pathe.

**Cinema-Halles Film Co. - UK - 1913-1914 -** distribution company with offices at Charing Cross House, Charing Cross Rd. Winchester.

**Cinemacraft, Inc - US - 1921 -** production company located at 735 Van Nuys Bldg., Los Angeles, California with Charles H. Hickman as general manager.

**Cinematographes Kuhnen Reysbosch - BELGIUM - 1923 -** production and distribution company located in Bruxelles.

**Cinematographie G. Gilbert - BELGIUM - 1910 -** distribution company.

**Cineromans Filmes de France Cines -** [see Italiana Cines]

**Cines Co. - ITALY - 1905-1926 -** production company formed from the Alberini and Santoni Co., and owned by Filoteo Alberini and Dante Santoni; in 1907, opened a distribution office in New York and in the UK in 1913(?); after World War I, Cines fell under control of the Giuseppe Barattolo holding company which was part of the Italian Cinematographic Union (UCI); in 1929, Cines was acquired by Stefano Pittaluga of SASP; films were exported under several trade names including Cines Films and Verafilm. [see Societa Anonima Stefano Pittaluga (SASP)]

**Cines Co. - UK - 1913-1914 -** British distributor for the Italian Cines Co. films with offices at 22 Denman St. London.

**Circle Film Attractions - US - 1920-1921 -** distribution company located at 130 W. 46th St. New York with Reuben Nadler as president and Joseph Sultan as V. P.; distributed states rights films.

**Circle Ranch Film Co. - US - 1905** - production company specializing in documentaries of ranch life.

**Cite Elge Studios - FRANCE - 1905-1953 -** studio complex built for film production for

Gaumont Film Co. and used over the decades until destroyed by fire in 1953; Elge was named for Leon Gaumont's initials (LG).

**Civilization feature Co. - US - 1916 -** distribution company located at 130 West 46th Street, New York, with Nathan Hirsh, General Manager.

**Civilization Film Corp. - US - 1917** - production company with Frank Hall as president and John McNally as treasurer.

**Clara Kimball Young Film Corp. - US - 1916-1919** - production company formed by Lewis Selznick in 1916, after leaving World Film Corp., to produce films featuring Clara Kimball Young; offices located at 126 West 46th Street, New York with Lewis J. Selznick as president and general manager; filming done at Solax studios and distribution through Lewis J. Selznick Productions, Inc.

**Clara Kimball Young Productions - US - 1921 -** production company located at 1854 Glendale Blvd. Los Angeles, California; formed to produce films featuring Clara Kimball Young with distribution through Equity Pictures Corp.

**Clarendon Film Co. - UK - 1913-1914 -** production and distribution company with offices located at 167-169 Wardour Ave. Winchester and Limes Rd. Croydon

**Claridge Films, Inc. - US - 1916 -** distribution company.

**Clarion Photoplays - US - 1915-1924 -** production company formed by the Weiss Bros.; soon after they formed Artclass Productions to be the parent company.

**Clark-Cornelius Corp. - US - 1919-1922 -** distribution company formed by the board of Exhibitors Mutual Distributing Corp. to acquire and redistribute Charlie Chaplin Mutual comedies; William J. Clark was president and H. C. Cornelius was V. P.; offices located at 117 W. 46th St. New York; distribution through Republic Pictures.

**Clayplay Comedies - US - 1921 -** trade name for comedies released by Special Pictures Corp.

**Cleopatra Film Co. - US - 1918 -** distribution company formed to redistribute films.

**Clermont Photoplays Corp. - US - 1920-1921 -** production company formed by Hannibal Clermont; offices located at 6070 Sunset Blvd., Los Angeles, California; reorganized in January, 1921 with W. D. Ball as president, Fred Le Blond as V. P., and F. W. Heidel as secretary/treasurer.

**Clever Comedies, Inc. - US - 1921 -** production company located at 6040 Sunset Blvd. Los Angeles, California; produced two reel comedies.

**Cliff Smith Productions - US - 1921 -** production company located at 1511 Cahuenga Ave., Hollywood, California; produced five reel westerns featuring Pete Morris; distributed through Associated Photoplays.

**Clifford S. Elfelt Productions - US - 1923-1926 -** production and distribution company formed by Clifford S. Elfelt and located in the Chandler Building, New York.

**Climax Film Corp. - US - 1921 -** located at 729 7th Ave., New York with J. H. Friedenwald as president and F. Goldfarb as secretary and general manager.

**Clipper Star Features - US - 1915-1916 -** trade name used by American Film Co.

**Clover Comedies - US - 1918 -** trade name used by National Film Corporation of America.

**Cloverio Film Corp. - US - 1921 -** production company located at the Lents, Portland, Oregon with

Hector Cloverio as president and P. J. Strand as general manager.

**Clune Film Exchange - US - 1913-1924** - distribution company located at 611 Marsh Strong Exchange, Los Angeles, California; distributor for Clune Film Production Co.

**Clune Film Production Co. - US - 1913-1924** - production company and studio located at 5320 Melrose Ave., Hollywood, California with William H. Clune as president, O. K. Evans as secretary/treasurer and O. L. Little as general manager; studio acquired by Tec Art in 1924.

**Clyde Cook Comedies - US - 1921** - trade name for two reel comedies featuring Clyde Cook; produced and distributed by Fox Film Corp.

**Co-Operative Cine Co. Ltd. - UK - 1913-1914** - distributor for Comet Films with offices at 31 Litchfield St. Winchester.

**Cohn-Brandt-Cohn Studio - US - 1919-1924** - [see C. B. C. Films Sales Corp]

**Col. W. F. Cody Buffalo Bill Historical Film Co. - US - 1914** - production company located at 521 First National Bank Building, Chicago, Illinois.

**Colonia Films - UK - 1913** - production company distributed in the U.K. by Anderson's Film Agency

**Colonial Film Producting Co., Inc. - US - 1921** - production company and studio located at 100 Boylston St. Boston, Massachusetts with Enid Mayo as president and general manager.

**Colonial Motion Picture Corp. - US - 1913-1916** - production company located at 18 East 41st Street, New York with James D. Law as president and Frederick S. Dudley as V. P. and general manager; in 1915, began producing Cameo comedies featuring Harry Kelley.

**Colored Pictures Distributing Co. - US - 1929 -** distribution company located at 317 Herndon Bldg., Atlanta, Georgia with P. L. Taylor as general manager; specialized in black films.

**Colored Players Film Corp. - US - 1927 -** production company with offices located at 1322 Vine St., Philadelphia, Pennsylvania with David Starkman as general manager; studios located at 1135-1137 S. 58th St., Philadelphia, Pennsylvania; specialized in black race films with.

**Columbia Film Company - US - 1909-1910 -** production company located at 301 West 37th Street, New York, with distribution through Associated Independent Film Manufacturers. (Not related to Columbia Pictures)

**Columbia Pictures Corp. - US - 1915-1917 -** production company with distribution through Metro Pictures. (Not related to larger Columbia Pictures).

**Columbia Pictures Corp. - US - 1924-current -** formed from C.B.C. Film Sales Corp. with offices at 1600 Broadway in New York; studio is still in existence today and owned by Sony Pictures.

**Columbus Film - US - 1914 -** production company located at 110 West 40th Street, New York.

**Comedyart Comedies - US - 1921 -** trade name used for two reel comedies released by Special Picture Corp.

**Comenius-Film GmbH - GERMANY - 1921-1931 -** production company.

**Comerio Production Co. - ITALY - 1907 -** production company formed by Luca Comerio in Milan; later that year merged with SAFFI-Comerio.

**Comet Film - US - 1917 -** production company located at Hanan Mills Bldg., Detroit, Michigan.

**Comet Film Co. - US - 1911-1913 -** production company located at 344 E. 32nd St. New York with William B. Gray as president.

**Comiclasses - US - 1921 -** trade name used for two reel comedies released by Special Picture Corp.

**Comique Film Corp. - US - 1916-1921 -** production company located at 1493 Broadway, New York with Joseph M. Schenck as president and Lou Anger as general manager; formed to produce 'Fatty' Arbuckle comedies; filming done at the Norma Talmadge Film Studios at 318 East 48th St. New York; Buster Keaton joined Arbuckle's film company and later that year, the company moved to the Balboa Studios in Long Beach, California; last move was to the Diando Studios in Glendale, California and distribution moved to Metro Pictures Corp.

**Commercial Feature Film Co. - UK - 1913-1914 -** distribution company with offices at 97 Shaftesbury Ave., Winchester.

**Commercial Motion Picture Co. - US - 1914-1916.** - located at 102 W. 101st St. New York with Edward M. Roskam as president and Jesse J. Goldburg as secretary and general manager; distributed through states rights; briefly signed with Alco Film at the end of 1914, but recanted and signed with Paramount; sister company Life Photo Film Corp. with Roskam and Goldburg also as officers filmed dramas; Roskam resigned and was replaced by Bernard Loewenthal in 1915; sold to Twentieth Century Film Co in 1916.

**Commonwealth Film Corp. - US - 1921 -** located at 1600 Broadway, New York with Sam Zierler as president and general manager.

**Commonwealth Pictures Corp. - US - 1918-1921 -** production company formed by Hans A. Spanuth to produce Spanuth's Original Vod-A-Vil Movies (staged vaudeville acts); located at 220 S. State Street, Chicago, Illinois.

**Compagnie Belge des Films Cinematographiques (CBFC) - BELGIUM - 1919-1923 -** production company founded by Hippolyte De Kempeneer to produce comedies and dramas; studio burned down in 1923 and was not rebuilt.

**Condor Film - EGYPT - 1928-1929 -** production company formed by brothers Ibrahim and Badr Lama; studio was located in the Victoria District of Alexandria; first film is considered to be the first feature length film in Egypt; second film was stopped by censorship; closed the studio and moved to Cairo and opened under the name Lama Studio.

**Conquest Pictures - US - 1917 -** trade name used by Edison Studios.

**Consolidated Film Corp. - US - 1916 -** production company formed to produce a 16 part series titled *the Crimson Stain Mystery* directed by T. Hayes Hunter; O. E. Goebel of the St. Louis Motion Picture Co. was president and included G. B. Erb of Erbograph Co.; distribution through Metro Pictures Corp.

**Constance Talmadge Film Co. - US - 1919-1927 -** production company formed to produce films featuring Constance Talmadge.

**Continental Films, Inc. - US - 1921 -** located at 475 5th Ave., New York with Harold Bolster as general manager.

**Continental Feature Film Corp. - US - 1913-1915 -** subsidiary company of Mutual Film Corp. formed to release features produced by Reliance Film under D. W. Griffith's direction; offices located at 219 Sixth Ave, New York with W. C. Toomey was general manager.

**Continental Kunstfilm - GERMANY - 1912-1915 -** production company formed from Schmidthassler Film GmbH by Walter Schmidthassler and Max Rittberger; offices located at 235 Friedrichstrate and studio at 123 Chausseestrate (the old Deutsche Bioskop studio) in Berlin.

**Continental Photo-Play Corporation - US - 1915 -** production company with offices located at 6114 Germantown Avenue, Philadelphia, with a studio located at 20 Herman Street.

**Co-operative Cinematograph Co. - UK - 1911 -** production and distribution company.

**Copenhagen Film Co. - DENMARK - 1913-1914 -** production company with New York offices located at 712 Vanderbilt Bldg. New York.

**Coquille Film Co. - US - 1914-1915 -** production company formed April 24, 1914 with J. F. Carter; located at 1347 Moss St. New Orleans, Louisiana; films were released regionally but unable to get national distribution; bought out in November 1915, by Nola Film Co.

**Corona Cinema Co. - US - 1917 -** production company located in Los Angeles, California with F. E. Keeler as president.

**Cort Film Corporation - US - 1915 -** production company located in the Longacre Building, 1476 Broadway, New York with John Cort as president.

**Cortland Pictures Corp. - US - 1921 -** production company located at 822 Hume Mansur Bldg. Indianapolis, Indiana with offices at 117 W. 46th St. New York; Cortland J. Van Deusen was president and general manager.

**Corvin-filmgyar - HUNGARY - 1916-1928 -** production company formed by Alexander Korda in Budapest.

**Cosmo Feature Film Corp. - US - 1912-1915 -** distribution company formed in New York by Nathan Hirsch through states rights; in 1915 changed name to Pioneer Feature Film Corp.

**Cosmos Feature Film Corporation - US - 1914-1915** - production and distribution company located at 126 West 46th Street, New York.

**Cosmos Film Company - US - 1914** - production company located at 145 W. 45th Street, New York.

**Cosmofotofilm Co. - US - 1914** - distribution company formed by Paul H. Cromelin to import British films to the U.S., primarily from the London Film Co.; offices located at the Candler Bldg. 220 W. 42nd St. New York.

"Where the REAL FEATURES come from"

**Cosmograph - FRANCE - 1920-1925** - production and distribution company located at 7, Fauboug du Temple, Paris.

**Cosmopolitan Film Corp. - US - 1921** - production company located at 836-7 New York Life Bldg., Kansas City, Missouri; W. Lake Henry was president, and J. Graham Thatcher was production manager.

**Cosmopolitan Films - UK - 1913-1914** - distributor for Comet Films with offices at Film House, Gerrard St. Winchester.

**Cosmopolitan Productions - US - 1918-1938** - production company created by Randolph Hearst to promote the career of Marion Davies; distributed through Parmount until 1923; moved to Goldwyn which became MGM and then to Warner Bros in 1934; closed their doors in 1938.

**Cranfield and Clarke - US - 1924-1927** - distribution company; expanded to production in 1925.

**Creation Films, Inc. - US - 1921** - production company located at 220 S. State St. Chicago, Illinois (formerly the Kalem Studio) with B. Herbert Milligan as president and treasurer and K. Hoddy Milligan as V. P.

**Crescent Film Manufacturing Co. - US - 1913** - distribution company.

**Crescent Film Co. - US - 1908** - production company founded by Fred Balshofer and Charles O. Baumann but closed by Edison attorneys by the end of the year; merged with Empire Film Exchange, owned by Baumann and Adam Kessel, to form New York Motion Picture Co.

**Crest Picture Co. - US - 1917-1920** - production company formed by C. F. Rickey and B. W. Davies with Lyman Henry as president and William V. Mong as director general; formed to distribute by states rights; production at Monrovia, California; closed in 1920.

**Crest Pictures - US - 1917**- distribution company located in the Times Building in New York.

**Creston Feature Pictures - US - 1922** - distribution company.

**Cricks and Martin - UK - 1908-1914** - production company formed by George Cricks and John Martin to produce comedy shorts; in 1910, expanded studio at Waddon New Road in Croydon and released under trade name of Crick's Lions Head Films; in 1913, Martin left to set up

Merton Park Studio and Cricks continued production and also distributed Comet Films; offices were located at 10 Wardour St. Winchester.

**Cricks and Sharp - UK - 1901-1908 -** George Cricks and Henry Sharp formed Mitchum Studio in Surrey and produced comedy shorts; released under trade name Lions Head Films; closed in 1908 and Cricks formed Cricks and Martin Co.

**Criterion Feature Film Manufacturing Co. - US - 1914 -** distribution company located at 110 West 40th Street, New York to distribute Kennedy Feature Films.

**Cross's Pictures Ltd. - UK - 1913-1914 -** distribution company with offices at 1-2 Rupert Ct. Rupert St., Winchester.

**Crown City Film Manufacturing Co. - US - 1914-1915 -** production company formed by a group of Pasadena businessmen and located at 40 West Mountain St. Pasadena, California; produced two reel comedies under the brand Thistle Films and two reel dramas under the brand Paragon Films; distribution through Kriterion; merged to form Associated Film Service Corp. in 1915.

**Crown Features - US - 1912 -** trade name for imported films from Svenska Biografteatern.

**Crystal Film Company - US - 1912-1919 -** production company formed by Ludwig G. B. Erb (after split with Centaur Film Manufacturing Co.) to produce comedy shorts; located at Wendover and Park Ave, New York; distributed through Universal; late 1914, Erb left Universal to form United Motion Picture Producers, Inc. with distribution through United Film Service; produced films under trade name of Superba until April

1915; when United Film Service closed in June 1915, Crystal joined Combined Photoplay Producers, Inc. with Erb as president and Standard Photoplay Distributors, Inc. as distributor; later Crystal films marketed by Triumph Film Corp. through states rights; Crystal ceased operations in 1919.

**Cub Comedies - US - 1914-1917 -** trade name used by David Horsley Productions; distribution through General Film Co. until 1915 when distribution moved to Mutual Film Corp.

**Cuckoo Comedies - US - 1919 -** trade name for comedies released by Mark M. Dintenfass Productions.

**Cumberland Pictures, Inc. - US - 1922-1926 -** trade name for comedies produced by Cumberland Productions, Inc. and distributed through Arrow Pictures Corp.

**Cumberland Productions, Inc. - US - 1922-1926 -** production company releasing comedies under the trade names of Billy West Comedies, Broadway Comedies, Cumberland Pictures and Mirthquake Comedies; distribution through Arrow Pictures Corp.

**Curtiss Pictures Corp. - US - 1921** - located at Aeolian Bldg. 33 W. 42nd St. New York.

**Curwood Carver Productions, Inc. - CANADA - 1919-1921 -** production company formed by James Oliver Curwood with Ernest Shipman and H. P. Carver as general manager to produce Curwood's short stories; production in Calgary with offices at 17 W. 44th St. New York and distribution through First National.

**Cyrus J. Williams Productions - US - 1921 -** production company located at 4811 Fountain Ave. Hollywood, California with Albert H. Hayes as president and Cyrus J. Williams as secretary/treasurer and general manager; produced westerns featuring Tom Santschi and Adventures of Bill and Bob with distribution through Pathe.

Movie Posters ~ Music Posters
TV Posters ~ Celebrity Posters
Star Wars & James Bond
Harry Potter

Collectormania
17892 Cottonwood Dr
Parker, CO 80134

1-866-630-1648

questions@posterplanet.net
posterplanetfile@aol.com

## DOMINIQUE BESSON AFFICHES
220 Chemin de la Blanchère - 84270 Vedène - France
TEL : 33.613.451.355   -   FAX : 33.442.634.188
WEB : www.dominiquebesson.com
E-MAIL : info@dominiquebesson.com

CATALOGUE

ON

REQUEST

# D

**D. K. G. Films - UK - 1913 -** distributed in the U.K. by Anderson's Film Agency.

**D. N. Schwab Productions, Inc. - US -1920 -** production company located at 1600 Broadway, New York with Joseph Klein as general manager.

**D. W. Griffith Inc. - US - 1919-1921 -** production company with offices at Longacre Bldg. 1476 Broadway, New York and studio at Orienta Point, Mamaroneck, New York; D. W. Griffith was president and Albert L. Grey was V. P. and general manager.

D.W. Griffith Studio, Mamaroneck, New York

**D'Enterprises Cinematographiques - BELGIUM - 1920 -** production company formed in Bruxelles.

**Dag-Film - GREECE - 1920s -** production company; dominant Greek studio during the 1920s producing mainly historic films.

**Damfool Twin Comedies - US - 1920-1922 -** trade name of two reel comedies released by Pinnacle Productions, Inc.

**Dania Biofilm Kompagni - DENMARK - 1913-1918 -** production company located in Copenhagen.

**Daniel Carson Goodman Corp. - US - 1920-1924 -** production company.

**Danish Cinema Photo Technology Industry - DENMARK - 1907-1908 -** production company founded by Thomas S. Hermansen in May 1907; in November 1908, company incorporated and name changed to Fotorama A/S.

**Danish Film Co. Ltd.- DENMARK - 1913-1915 -** production company formed by Alex Christian and his wife Johanne Sophie Eibye; company closed because of the war.

**Danny Kaden-Film GmbH - GERMANY - 1917-1918 -** production company located in Berlin; closed due to World War I.

**Dansk Biografkompagni - DENMARK - 1914-1916 -** production company located in Hellerup.

**Dansk Filmfabrik - DENMARK - 1912-1915 -** production company located in Aarhus.

**Dansk Kino-Foto-Film Industri - DENMARK - 1904-1906 -** production company formed by Thomas Hermanson; located in Aarhus.

**Dansk Kinograf - 1913-1915 - DENMARK -** production company.

**Dansk Svensk Film - DENMARK - 1921 -** distribution company for Paramount films.

**Dart Films - UK - 1913-1914 -** production company with films distributed by Anderson's Film Agency.

**David Butler Productions - US - 1921 -** production company with Irving M. Lesser as general manager; used Brunton Studios at 5341-5601 Melrose Ave. Los Angeles, California for filming.

**David Horsley Productions - US -** [see Centaur Film Manufacturing Co; Nestor Film Co.; Centaur Film Co.; Bostock Jungle and Film Co.]

**David M. Hartford Productions - US - 1921-1927 -** production company located at 3274 W. 6th St. Los Angeles, California with Joseph Montrose as general manager; distributed by First National.

**David P. Howells - US - 1919 -** production company located at 729 Seventh Avenue, New York.

**Davis Film Co. - US - 1924-1929 -** production and distribution company; distribution arm called Davis Distributing Division.

**Davison's Film Sales Agency, Ltd - UK - 1913-1914 -** distribution company for B&C Films, Empire, Film de Paris, I. & E., Sphinx and Dart Films; offices located at 18 Charing Cross Rd. Winchester.

**De Luxe Attractions Film Co. - US - 1913-1914 -** distribution company located at 145 West 45th Street, New York.

**De Luxe Feature Co. - US - 1917 -** distribution company located at 1214 ½ 3rd Ave. Seattle, Washington with M. Rosenberg as president and general manager.

**De Luxe Feature Film Co. - US - 1913 -** distribution company located at 71 W. 23rd St., Masonic Bldg. New York; Herman Smidt was general manager.

**De Luxe Film Co. - US - 1922 -** production company with Mrs. A. B. Maescher as president and Eugene Evans as general manager; located at 1318 Vine St. Philadelphia, Pennsylvania; distributed by Arrow Film Corp.

**De Luxe Pictures, Inc. - US - 1917-1918 -** formed by Theodore C. Deitrich in November 1917 to produce films featuring Doris Kenyon with Deitrich serving as president and general manager; distributed through William Sherry Service. [see Deitrich-Beck, Inc.]

**De Recat Productions - US - 1920 -** production company formed by Emile De Recat as president; offices located at 1333 Argyle Street, Chicago, Illinois.

**Decla-Bioskop - GERMANY - 1920-1923 -** production company formed from the merger of Decla and Deusche Bioskop AG; merged with UFA in 1923 with Pommer as head of production.

**Decla-Film - GERMANY - 1915-1920 -** production company formed by Erich Pommer; in 1919, merged with Meinert Film with Rudolf Meinert becoming head of production and Erich Pommer head of distribution; in 1920, merged with Deusche Bioskop AG to become Decla-Bioskop.

**Deer Brand Film - US - 1914 -** trade name for series released by A. Blinkhorn.

**Defender Film Co. - US - 1910 -** formed by Edwin S. Porter and Joseph Engel; located at 19 Union Square, New York; desolved six months later.

**Deitrich-Beck, Inc. - US - 1919 -** formed by Theodore C. Deitrich and Arthur F. Beck in July 1919 to produce films from the novels of Louis Joseph Vance; distribution through W. W. Hodkinson Corp.

**Delac & Co. - FRANCE - 1908 -** distribution company located in Paris that distributed films of Le Film d'Art.

**Dell Henderson Productions - US - 1925-1927 -** production company formed by Dell Henderson; retired in 1927.

**DeMille Pictures Corp. - US - 1925-1929 -** production company formed by Cecil B. De Mille.

**Democracy Film Co. - US - 1919 -** formed in June 1919 to make patriotic films about black American participation in World War I; E & R Studio in Los Angeles was used for production.

**Democracy Photoplay Company - US - 1920** - production and distribution company located at 2826 Decatur Avenue, New York.

**Dependable Pictures Corp. - US - 1922** - production company.

**Det Skandinavisk-Russike Handelshus - DENMARK - 1911-1913** - production company.

**Deutsche Bioscop GmbH - GERMANY - 1899-1920** - production and distribution company located in Berlin and formed by Julius Greenbaum; initially called Bioscop GmbH until registered; in 1911, built the Babelsberg Studio to produce films featuring Asta Nielsen; in 1920, merged with Decla-Bioskop.

**Deutsche Éclair Film und Kinematographen GmbH - GERMANY - 1915-1919** - [see Decla-Film]

**Deutsche Lichtbild Gesellschaft - GERMANY - 1918-1922** - production company (translated- German photography society).

**Deutsche Universal Film AG - GERMANY - 1926-1935** - production company formed by Universal with Joe Pasternak in charge; company closed as Hitler gained more control.

**Dewesti-Filmverleih GmbH - GERMANY - 1924** - distribution company with offices located at Charlottenstr.82 Berlin SW 68.

**Di Lorenzo Films - US - 1922** - production company located at 135 West 44th Street, New York; specialized in westerns.

**Dial Film Co. - US - 1921** - production company located at 5341 Melrose Ave. Los Angeles, California with Otto Baldwin as general manager; distribution through W. W. Holdkinson.

**Diamond Dot Western Pictures - US - 1922** - trade name for western films produced and distributed by Aywon Film Corp.

**Diamond Film Co. - US - 1917-1918** - production company acquired by R. M "Diamond Rube" Chisholm as the defunct Nola Film Co.; located at 1347 Moss St. New Orleans, Louisiana in August 1917; William M. Hannon, who was the NOLA president, as V. P. began producing comedies and dramas featuring Ziegfield Follies star Diane Allen; distribution was through General Film but General Film had lost all court battles and sold to Lincoln and Parker Film, who did not pay out royalties, bankrupting Chisholm.

**Diamond Super, Ltd - UK - 1918-1922** - production company.

**Diando Film Co. - US - 1917-1919** - formed from Lasalida Films to produce films featuring Baby Marie Osborne for Pathe; W. A. S. Douglas was president and L. T. Osborne was V. P.; went out of business in 1919.

**Dierker Film Co. - US - 1921** - production company located at 1023 Van Nuys Bldg. Los Angeles, California and distributed by Producers Security Corp.

**Direct-From-Broadway Feature Film Co. - US - 1914** - production company located at 46 West 24th Street, New York with studios in New Rochelle.

**Dirigo Films, Inc. - US - 1922** - production company.

**Disney Bros. Studios - US - 1923-1926** - production company formed by Walt Disney and Roy Disney to produce Alice cartoons combining cartoons with live action; distribution by M. J. Winkler Productions; in 1926, moved to new studio on Hyperion Ave. Los Angeles and changed name to Walt Disney Studio.

**Dispatch Film Service - UK - 1921** - distribution company located at 37 Cannon St., Manchester.

**Distinctive Pictures Corp. - US - 1921** - production company located at 366 Madison Ave, New York with Henry M. Hobart as president; formed to produce films featuring George Arliss; distribution through United Artists Corp.

**Diva Pictures, Inc. - US - 1918-1920** - production company formed to produce films featuring Geraldine Farrar; distribution through Goldwyn Pictures.

**Dixie Film Co. - US - 1910** - distribution company with main office located at 722-724-726 Maison Blanche, New Orleans, Louisiana.

**Dominant Films - US - 1920** - production company specializing in two reel westerns.

**Dominant Pictures, Inc. - US - 1921** - production company with offices located at 133-135-137 W. 44th St., New York and studio at 517 W. 54th St. New York; Charles C. Burr was president and Jacques Kopfstein was general manager.

**Dominion Film Co. Ltd. - CANADA - 1917** - production company located at Maple Leaf City, Victoria, British Columbia.

**Dominion Film Co. Inc. - US - 1920** - production company located at 17 W. 44th St., New

York with Ernest Shipman as president and Stephen T. King as V. P., treasurer and general manager; produced films by Ralph Connor, James Oliver Curwood, Edgar Rice Burroughs and Myrtle Reed.

**Domino Films - US - 1913-1915 -** trade name used by New York Motion Picture Corp. until 1915 when Kessel and Bauman merged NYMPC into Triangle Films; distributed by Mutual Films, whose contract was also cancelled at the time of the merger.

**Domino Motion Picture Corporation - US - 1913 -** production company located in the Longacre Building, Broadway at 42nd Street, New York.

**Dora Film Co. - ITALY - 1909- -** production company formed in Naples by Elvira and Nicola Notari.

**Dormet Film Company - US - 1915** - production company located at Suite 1005, Candler Building, 220 West 42nd Street, New York.

**Doubleday Production Co. - US - 1920-1923 -** production company located in Los Angeles, California with some distribution through Russell-Griever-Russell.

**Douglas Fairbanks Pictures Corp. - US - 1917-1926** - production company located at 5320 Melrose Ave. Hollywood, California with Douglas Fairbanks as president and John Fairbanks as treasurer and general manager; formed to produce films featuring Douglas Fairbanks Sr.; in 1926, reorganized into the Elton Corp.

**Dra-Ko Film Co., Inc. - US - 1915 -** production company with offices located in the Commercial Trust Building, 1451 Broadway, New York and studio in Tappan, New York; George G. Wilson was president.

**Draco Film Co. - US - 1915-1916 -** formed December, 1915; located in Tappan, New York with distribution through Mutual Film Corp.

**Dramagraph Co. of America - US - 1910 -** production company with offices at Lincoln Building, No. 1 Union Square, New York and factory and studios in Edgewater, New Jersey.

**Dramascope Company - US - 1914** - production company located at 110 West 40th Street, New York.

**Dramatic Feature Film Co. - US - 1915 -** production company formed April 1915 with Frank J. Baum as president and Francis Power as head of production; distribution through Alliance.

**Drankov and Co. - RUSSIA - 1907-1917 -** [see A. Drankov & Co.]

**Drascena Productions - US - 1920-1921 -** production company located at Haas Bldg., Los Angeles, California with Charles M. Conant as president; formed to produce one, two, and five reel comedies and features.

**Drew Comedies - US - 1917 -** trade name for comedy shorts produced by Mr. and Mrs. Sidney Drew; distributed by Metro Pictures Corp.

**Dudley Motion Picture Manufacturing Co. - US - 1916 -** founded by M. B. Dudley to produce westerns in Redlands, California and released through Unity Sales Corp.

**Duke Worne Productions - US - 1926-1928 -** production company.

**Duskes Film - FRANCE - 1912-1914 -** production company with distribution through Pathes in France and through Elite Sales Agency in the U.K.

**Dustin Farnum Productions, Inc. - US - 1920-1922** - production company.

**Dyreda Art Film Corp. - US - 1914-1915** - formed in October 1914 with Frank L. **Dy**er as president, J. Parker **Re**ad, Jr. as V. P. and treasures and J. Searle **Da**wley over production; company name formed by the first 2 letters of the founders with distribution through World Film Corp until April 1915 when they switched to Metro Film Corp. In May 1915, B. A. Rolfe bought out Dyreda.

# WANTED: CONSIGNMENTS!

**Robert Edward Auctions** is currently seeking consignments for inclusion in our next auction. If you have a significant high value item or collection that you are considering selling at auction, you can't afford **NOT** to contact **Robert Edward Auctions**. For more than 30 years Robert Edward Auctions has offered an unparalleled tradition of integrity, knowledge and professionalism. **Robert Edward Auctions** offers the ultimate auction service and is exclusively geared to high quality material. Larger circulation + unparalleled knowledge and experience + lower commission rates = more money in your pocket. Robert Edward Auctions also offers: Reasonable reserves, unmatched financial security (millions in assets, NO liabilities), millions of dollars available at all times at a moment's notice for cash advances, and the most extensive list of buyers in the collecting world. **Robert Edward Auctions will put more money in your pocket**. If you have high quality material to bring to auction, Robert Edward Auctions will not only help you realize the highest possible prices for your valuable material, we provide to consignors the peace of mind that your consignments will be treated with the utmost in care, and that every aspect of the auction process will be executed with the greatest attention to every detail. If you have high quality material you think might be of interest, please call or write.

**ROBERT EDWARD AUCTIONS, LLC.**

P.O. Box 7256 • Watchung, NJ 07069
phone: 908-226-9900 fax: 908-226-9920
www.RobertEdwardAuctions.com

# E

**E & R Jungle Film Co. - US - 1912-1916** - production company formed by J. S. Edwards and John Rounan to make wild animal films; located at 1720 N. Soto St. Eastlake Park Los Angeles; Paul Machette was general manager; primary series was one reel comedies featuring chimpanzees, Sally and Napoleon.

**E. I. S. Motion Picture Corporation - US - 1917 -** production company located at 203 W. 40th Street, New York.

**E-L-K Film Co. - US - 1914 -** distribution company located at 509 Mallers Building, Chicago, Illinois with A. M. Eisner as president and general manager.

**Eagle Feature Film Company - US - 1913 -** located at 5 East 14th St, New York with Charles Streamer as general manager.

**Eagle Film Co. - US - 1916-1918 -** production company and studio located in Jacksonville, Florida; formerly Eagle Film Manufacturing and Producing Co.; produced comedies until they went bankrupt in 1918.

**Eagle Film Corp. - US - 1921 -** production company located at 914 W. Lexington St., Baltimore, Maryland with Charles A. Waldeck as president and F. J. McLaughlin as general manager.

**Eagle Film Exchange - US - 1908-1910** - distribution company with offices at 159 N. 8th Street, Philadelphia, PA and 342 Main Street, Norfolk, Virginia.

**Eagle Film Manufacturing and Producing Co. - US - 1915-1916** - located at 109 North Dearborn St., Chicago, Illinois with William J. Dunn as general manager; distribution through Unity Sales Corp; in June 1916, moved to Florida and changed name to Eagle Film Co.

**Earle Williams Productions - US - 1921 -** production company.

**East Coast Productions, Inc. - US - 1922-1925 -** distribution company.

**East India Feature Film Company - US - 1913-1914 -** distribution company located at 225 W. 26th Street, New York.

**Eastern Film Co. - US - 1915-1916 -** production company formed by Frederick S. Peck as president, Benjamin L. Cook as V. P. and Elwood F. Boswick as general manager; located at 17 McKinley St., Providence, Rhode Island; films released under the trade name of Pelican Films.

**Eastern Film Corporation -** production company located at 220 W. 42nd Street, New York.

**Ebony Comedies - US - 1918-1922 -** trade name for one reel and multi-reel black cast comedies released by Ebony Film Corp.

**Ebony Film Corp. - US - 1915-1922 -** production company located in the Transportation Building in Chicago, Illinois; formed to produce one reel black comedies featuring Luther Pollard and released under the trade name of Ebony Comedies through General Film; started making one reel comedies with all black casts, but after some success, expanded to multi reels with black and white casts; moved production to Fort du Lac, Wisconsin; company went out of business in 1922. **NOTE:** some contradictions as Ebony Film Corp was white owned featuring Luther Pollard while three years later records indicate that Luther Pollard was part owner of Ebony Pictures. They were associated and closed at the same time but not enough information to indicate how.

**Ebony Pictures Corporation - US - 1918-1922 -** production company founded by L. J. Pollard and Bob Horner to produce black comedies; filming in Oshkosh, Wisconsin; later built a studio in Fond du Lac, Wisconsin.

**Ec-Ko Film Co. - UK - 1913-1915 -** production company formed to produce comedy shorts; in 1915, changed name to Homeland Films.

**Éclair American Co. - US - 1910-1916 -** production and distribution subsidiary of French company Societe Francaise des

Films et Cinematographes Éclair and located in Fort Lee, N.J.; moved to California in 1912 and joined with Universal Film; in 1914, studio had fire that did major damage; many employees left to newly formed World Film; in 1915, studio name changed to Ideal.

**Éclair Film Co. - UK - 1913-1914** - distributor of American Standard and Savoia Films; offices at 12 Moor St. Winchester.

**Eclair Film Company - US - 1910-1912** - distribution company with offices located at 31 East 27th Street, New York.

**Éclair Films - FRANCE/US - 1910-1916** - trade name for films produced by Éclair and distributed by Éclair Film Co.

**Eclair-Universal - US - 1912-1913** - trade name used for Éclair films distributed through Universal.

**Eclectic Films Co - US - 1912-1915** - distribution company formed by Ferdinand Wolff who imported European films located at 145 West 45th St. New York; in 1914, started production jointly with Pathe Freres to produce the Pearl White serial; serial was presented in Hearst newspapers with a massive 147 episodes produced; in January 1915, Eclectic Films and Pathe Freres merged to create Pathe Exchange, Inc.

**Eclipse Film Service - UK - 1912-1914 -** distribution company with offices located at 58 Victoria St. Manchester.

**Eclipse Films - FRANCE - 1918 -** distribution company with offices located at 94 Rue S. Lazare in Paris.

**Eclipse Films - BELGIUM - 1928-1930 -** distribution company of imported films.

**Edgar Comedies - US - 1921 -** trade name for two reel comedies featuring Johnny Jones and distributed by Goldwyn Pictures Corp.

**Edgar Lewis Productions, Inc. - US - 1918-1921 -** production company located at 1119 Westchester Place, Hollywood, California; distribution through William L. Sherry Service.

**Edison Manufacturing Co. - US - 1891-1911 -** production company owned by Thomas Edison and reorganized as Thomas A. Edison, Inc. in 1911.

**Edna Schley Productions - US - 1921 -** production company with offices at 6372 Hollywood Blvd. Hollywood, California and studio at 1116 Lodi St. Hollywood; Edna Schley was president; produced two reel comedy-dramas distributed through Western Pictures Exploitation Co.

**Educational Film Exchanges, Inc. - US - 1914-1939 -** distribution company founded by Earle (E.

W.) Hammons to distribute Mermaid Comedies, Pat Sullivan Comics, Christie Comedies, C. L. Chester Comedies, Torchy Comedies, Kinograms, Bruce Scenics, Vanity Comedies, Mack Sennett, et. al.

**Educational Films Corp. of America - US - 1914-1927 -** production and distribution company located at Penn Terminal Bldg. 270 7th Ave., New York; E. W. Hammons was president and general manager and G. A. Skinner as V. P.

**Educational Pictures, Inc. - US - 1927-1939 -** reorganization of Educational Films Corp. by E. W. Hammons; Hammons tried to move to feature films by forming Grand National Pictures but went bankrupt.

**Edward Dillon Productions - US - 1922-1923 -** production company with distribution through Truart Film Corp.

**Edward A. Salisbury - US - 1915 -** production company located in the Knickerbocker Hotel, New York.

**Edward Sloman Productions - US - 1922 -** production company located at 4534 Sunset Boulevard, Los Angeles, California.

**Edward Warren Productions - US - 1917-1919 -** production company located at 1482 Broadway, New York with H. Z. Levine as general manager.

**Edwin Carewe Productions, Inc. - US - 1920-1929 -** production company

**EGM Co. - UK - 1913-1914 -** production company released under the trade name of Anderson Films; in 1914 expanded to distribution; changed name to Anderson Vay Hubert & Blumberg Ltd.

**Egyptian Cinematographic Institute - EGYPT - 1932-1933** - production company formed by Mohamed Bayoum, the first Egyptian owned production company; studio located at 39 Missalla St. in Alexandria; blosed the following year due to financial problems.

**Eichberg Films - GERMANY - 1920-1938 -** production company formed by Richard Eichberg in Berlin; French distribution through Pax Film and Swedish distribution through A-B Films.

**Eiko Film Company of America - 1912-1927 -** distribution company located at 220 West

42nd Street, New York; distributed for Eiko Film GmbH of Germany with W. H. Rudolph as general manager.

**Eiko Film GmbH - GERMANY - 1912-1927** - production and distribution company.

**El Dorado Feature Film Co. - US - 1915** - production company with studio and offices located at 40 West Mountain Street, Pasadena, California.

**El Dorado Productions - US - 1928-1929** - production company.

**El Paso Feature Film Co. - 1914** - production company owned by Dr. Charles A. Pryor; released Great Mexican War with several battle scenes and then arrested.

**Electragraff Co. of Philadelphia - US - 1910** - production company located at 2556 North 24th St., Philadelphia, Pennsylvani; formerly known as Motograff Co. of Philadelphia.

**Elfelt Productions - US - 1923-1926** - [see Clifford S. Elfert Productions.]

**Elge Films - FRANCE - 1912-1915** - trade name used for Gaumont Films; named for his initials L. G. (Leon Gaumont)

**Elite Sales Agency Ltd. - UK - 1912-1914 -** distribution company located at 1 Shaftsbury Ave. Gloucester Mansions, Westminster; distributed for Continental, Duskes, Eiko, Skandinavisk, Elite and BB.

**Elk Photo Plays - US - 1914-1921 -** distribution company.

**Ella Wheeler Wilcox Photoplays, Inc. - US - 1917 -** production company located at 729 Seventh Avenue, New York.

**Ellbee Pictures Corporation - US - 1925-1929** - production and distribution company located at 1540 Broadway, New York.

**Elmer J. McGovern - US - 1920 -** production company formed by Elmer J. McGovern; located at 130 West 46 Street, New York.

**Elton Corp. - US - 1926-1932 -** formed to replace the Douglas Fairbanks Pictures Co. to produce films featuring Douglas Fairbanks, Sr.; Elton was his middle name.

**Emelka-Konzern - GERMANY - 1919-** production company formed in Grunwald by Peter Oster Mayr who expanded in a studio; official starting name was Munich Lichtspielkunst AG, but abbreviated as MLK which turned into Em el ka; converted to sound in 1930, but filed for bankruptcy in 1932; acquired and became the Bavaria Film AG; after numerous changes over the years, it is currently Bavaria Film GmbH.

**Emerald Motion Picture Co. - US - 1917 -** production company located at 1717-1729 N. Wells St. Chicago, Illinois; merged into Reelcraft Pictures.

**Eminent Authors Pictures, Inc. - US - 1919-1921 -** production company formed by Samuel Goldwyn with Rex Beach as president and included Gertrude Atherton, Rupert Hughes, Leroy Scott, Basil King, Gouverneur Morris, and Mary Roberts Rinehart; distribution was through Goldwyn Distributing Corp.

**Emory Johnson Productions - US - 1922-1926 -** production company.

**Empire All Star Corp. - US - 1917-1918 -** production company formed with James M. Sheldon as president.

**Empire Cine Supplies - UK - 1913-1914 -** distribution company with offices at 11 Pelham St., Nottingham with branches in Cardiff and Swansea.

**Empire Feature Film Co. - US - 1916-1917 -** production company formed by Henry Kabierske to use the studios of Monrovia Feature Film Co. in Monrovia, California; purchased 40 acres to build their own studios but went bankrupt in 1917.

**Empire Film Exchange - US - 1906-1909 -** distribution company owned by Adam Kessel and Charles O. Baumann who then formed New York Motion Picture Co.

**Empress Films - US - 1915 -** trade name used by American Gaumont for their one reel comedies; distributed through United Film Service.

**Encore Pictures - US - 1923-1926 -** production company with distribution through Associated Exhibitors.

**Enlightment Photoplays Corp - US - 1917 -** production company located at 220 West 42nd Street, Suite 1005, New York with Henry J. Brock as president.

**Enterprise Distributing Corp. - US - 1916-1939 -** distribution company formed to re-distribute low budget films through states rights.

**Epic Film Attractions - US - 1924** - distribution company located at 808 S. Wabash Avenue, Chicago, Illinois.

**Epoch Producing Corp. - US - 1915** - production and distribution company.

**Equality Photo-Play Corporation - US - 1920** - distribution company located at 145 West 45th Street, New York with Antonio Morino as president.

**Equitable Film - FRANCE - 1916** - distribution company with offices at 416 Rue Saint Menora, Paris.

**Equitable Film Producing Co., Inc. - US - 1913-1914** - production company located at 145 West 46th Street, New York; successors to New York Film Co.

**Equitable Motion Pictures Corp. - US - 1915-1919** - formed in June 1915 to produce films for World Film Corp.; Arthur Spiegel was president and Lewis J. Selznick was V. P.; offices located at 517 W. 54th St. New York; Equitable formed Triumph Film Corp as a subsidiary in Sept. 1915; Equitable acquired by World Film in 1916 in a stock buyout; distribution in France through Productions Reunies.

**Equity Pictures Corp. - US - 1919-1924** - production company located at 33 W. 42nd St. New York with Joseph J. Schnitzer as president; formed to produce films featuring Clara Kimball Young; films produced at the Garson Studios located at 1845 Glendale Ave. in Los Angeles, California.

**Equity Pictures - US - 1920-1921 -** states right distributor for Indiana & Illinois; located at 110 South State Street, Chicago, Illinois.

**Equity Pictures Corporation - US - 1920-1924 -** distribution company located at 723 7th Avenue, New York.

**Erbograph Co. - US - 1916-1917 -** production company located at 203 W. 146th St., New York; Ludwig G. B. Erb was president and Benjamin Goetz was secretary/treasurer; films released through Art Dramas, Inc.; distribution moved to Metro Pictures Corp. until they closed in 1917.

**Erda-Film Produktions GmbH - GERMANY - 1928-1929 -** production company located in Berlin.

**Erka-Prodisco - FRANCE - 1919-1921 -** distribution company with offices at 38th Av Rue, de la Republique, Paris.

**Ermine Productions - US - 1924-1925 -** production company specializing in westerns

**Ermolev Co. - RUSSIA - 1915-1919 -** [see I. Ermol'ev Co.]

**Ernest Shipman and Associates - US - 1913-1924 -** production and distribution company with offices located at 6 W. 48th St. New York; in 1921 moved to 17 W. 44th St. New York; production through separate corporations including James Oliver Curwood Productions, Ralph Connor Productions, Canadian Photoplays Ltd., Winnipeg Productions Ltd., Renco Film Co. Inc., Ultra Film Co., Pena Menichelli Productions, Dominion Film Co., Inc., Legend Film Productions, Inc., Catherine Curtis Corp. and Northern Pictures Corp. Ltd.; some distribution was through states rights while others were released through First National Pictures and W. W. Hodkinson Corp.

**Ernst Hofmann-Film - GERMANY - 1919 -** production company located in Berlin.

**Erste Ostereichische Kinofilms-Industrie - AUZ - 1910-1912 -** production company founded by Anton Kolm, Luise Kolm and Jacob Fleck; started with documentaries and then moved to fiction film production; changed name of studio to Wiener Kunstfilm.

**Eskay Harris Feature Film Co. - US - 1915 - 1922 -** production company which evolved into primarily redistributed of films.

**Essanay Film Co. - UK - 1913-1914 -** distribution arm for Essanay Films with offices at 148 Charing Cross Rd. Winchester.

**Essanay Film Manufacturing Co. - US - 1907-1918 -** production company located at 1333 Argyle St. in Chicago; named for the initials of George K. Spoor and Gilbert A. "Bronco Billy" Anderson (S & A) in 1912; Anderson was a western actor from the 1903 western, *The Great Train Robbery* and Spoor was owner of the Kinodrome Circuit and needed film production for his theaters; opened a studio at 501 Wells St. in Chicago; in 1909, Essanay moved to new studios in Niles, California with distribution through the General Film Co. until 1915 when they switched to V-L-S-E; in 1915, Essanay signed Charlie Chaplin but did not renew his contract the following year; in 1916, Spoor bought out Anderson, but by 1918 they closed their doors; Essanay production was bought out by Victor Kremer.

**Estee Studios - US - 1918-1919 -** production company with Eugene Spritz as president; located at 561-562 125th St., New York.

**Eugenic Film Co. - US - 1917 -** production and distribution company.

**European Feature Films - US - 1914 -** production company located at 110 West 40th Street, Room 1803, New York with Jacques Greenzweig as general manager.

**European Motion Picture Co. - UK - 1928 -** distribution company and exporter of European films to the UK.

**Eva Tanguay Films - US - 1916-1917 -** production and distribution company located at Long Acre Building, Broadway and 42nd Street, New York; formed to produce and distribute films featuring Eva Tanguay.

**Ewing Motion Picture Co. Ltd. - US - 1912 -** distribution company located in Baton Rouge, Louisiana with Solon Farrenbacher as president.

**Exactus Photo-film Corp. of Palo Alto -** production company formed August 28, 1914 specializing in educational films; in 1916, some assets were auctioned off and the remaining taken over by the Palo Alto Film Co.

**Excelsior Feature Film Co. - US - 1914-1915 -** production company formed with Harry Handworth as president and William A. Williams as V. P.; offices located at 110 west 40th Street, New York and studio in Lake Placid; distribution was through Alco Film Corp. until late 1914 when it was moved to Alliance Films Corp.; stopped production in 1915.

**Exceptional Pictures Corporation - 1921-1922 -** production company with distribution through Apollo Trading Corp., Apollo Films, Ltd., "His Nibs" Syndicate, Inc. and American Releasing Corporation.

**Exclusive Features, Inc. - US - 1914-1921** - located at 126 W. 46th St. New York with Joseph Goldstein and J. Weinberg.

**Exclusive Supply Co. - UK - 1913-1914** - distribution company located at Gerard St., Winchester and New Street, Birmingham.

**Exclusive Supply Corp. - US - 1913-1914** - distribution company formed in 1913 to replace the Film Supply Corp. of America, distributor for Mutual Film Corp.; offices were located at 220 West 42nd Street, New York; Herbert Blache was president, I. C. Oes was V.P., Harry R. Raver was Secretary/Treasurer and Joseph R. Milesw was general manager; distributed All Star Feature, Gaumont, Italia, Lewis Pennant, Lloyd Films, Ramo Films and Solax films; closed in October 1914.

**Exhibitors Film Corp. - US - 1928-1929** - production company specializing in westerns.

**Exhibitors Mutual Distributing Corp. - US - 1918** - distribution company formed when Affiliated Distributors Corp. took control of Mutual Films in November 1918 by buying 51% of the stock; moved headquarters to Grand Rapids, Michigan with the intent of dividing the U.S. into five regions to book films directly from the producer to the exhibitor; Robertson Cole Co. signed a long term contract to furnish films.

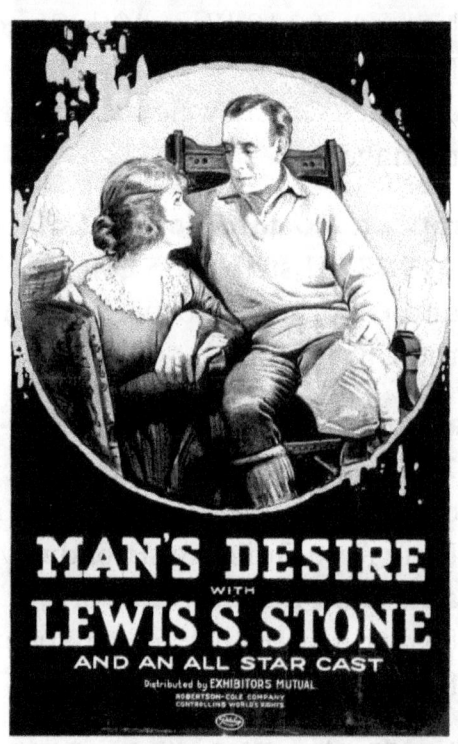

**Explorers Films Ltd - UK - 1924** - distribution company specializing in documentaries of scientific explorations

**Export & Import Film Co. - US - 1918-1923** - distribution company located at 729 7th Ave., New York with Ben Blumenthal as president, L. Auerbach as V. P.; handled rereleases, i. e. Charlie Chaplin.

**Express Film Service Ltd. - UK - 1913-1914 -** distributor with offices at 11 Denman St. Winchester.

**Extra-Film Genina - ITALY - 1922** - production company located in Rome.

# F

**F-4 Picture Corp. - US - 1918 -** production company.

**F. B. Warren Corp. - US - 1921-1922 -** distribution company located at 1540 Broadway, New York with branch offices all around the U.S.

**F. E. Moore - US - 1913 -** distribution company located at 1212 Times Building, New York.

**F. E. R. T. - ITALY - 1919-1924 -** production studio established in Turin by Enrico Fiori that was independent from the Italian Cinematographic Union (UCI); studio was acquired by Societa Anonima Stefano Pittaluga in 1924.

**F. O. Nielsen - US - 1915 -** production company located in the Schiller Building, Chicago, Illinois and in the Candler Building in New York.

**F. Ray Comstock Photoplay Co. - US - 1916 -** production company.

**Fables Pictures, Inc. - US - 1920-1922 -** production company with Amadee J. Van Beuren as president and general manager; offices located at 1562 Broadway, New York; distribution through Pathe. [see Adventure Films, Inc.; AyVeeBee Film Corp; V. B. K Film Corp; Timely Topics Inc.; Timely Films Inc.]

**Fairmount Film Co. - US - 1917 -** production company.

**Falstaff Comedies - US - 1915 -** trade name used by Thanhouser Film Corp.

**Famous Artists Corp. of America - US - 1927 -** production and distribution company for All Star Negro Motion Pictures and Famous Negro News; offices located at Widener Bldg. Philadelphia, Pennsylvania.

**Famous Negro News - US - 1927 -** [see Famous Artists Corp. of America]

**Famous Pictures - UK - 1918 -** production company formed by Edwin H. Wright with the purchase of the British Empire Film studio at Whetstone.

**Famous Players Film Co. - UK - 1912-1916 -** distributors of Famous Players Films with offices at 84 Charing Cross Rd. Winchester.

**Famous Players Film Co. - US - 1912-1916 -** formed by Adolph Zukor in 1912 with offices located at 213-229 W. 26th Street, New York; merged with Jesse Lasky's Feature Play Co. to form Famous Players-Lasky Corp.

**Famous Players Film Service - CANADA - 1916- -** distribution company with offices located in Toronto; states rights distributor of Christie's Comedies et al for Toronto, Montreal, St. John, Winnipeg, Calgary, and Vancouver.

**Famous Players-Lasky Corp. - US - 1916-1927 -** production company merged July 19, 1916, a month after the takeover of Paramount Pictures with offices located at 485 5th Ave. New York and 1520 Vine St. Hollywood, California with Adolph Zukor as president, Jesse L. Lasky as V. P. and Cecil B. De Mille as general manager; distribution through Paramount Pictures.

**Famous Players-Mary Pickford Co. - US - 1916 -** production company featuring Mary Pickford with distribution through Paramount.

**Fanark Pictures Corporation - US - 1920 -** production company located at 40 W. 32nd Street, New York with D. J. H. Levett as president.

**Farra Feature Productions - US - 1922 -** production company with Charles Farra as president; specialized in westerns.

**Favorite Players Film Co. - US - 1914-1915 -** formed by Carlyle Blackwell in August 1914; offices located at 110 West 40th Street, Suite 1003, New York; initially distributed by Alco Film Corp; in October, Blackwell changed to Alliance Films Corp.; company closed April 1915 and Blackwell joined Jesse L. Lasky Feature Play Co.

**Favorite Players Film Corporation - US - 1920 -** states rights distributor for Illinois, Indiana and Wisconsin; offices located at 63 East Adams Street, Chicago, Illinois.

**Feature and Educational film Co. - US - 1911 -** production and distribution company with main offices located at 112 Prospect Avenue, Cleveland, Ohio; E. Mandelbaum was president

**Feature Film Manufacturing Company - US - 1913 -** distribution company located at 405 Eleventh Street, N.W., Washington, D.C.

**Feature Films Ltd - UK - 1913-1914** - distribution company with offices located at Regent Street, Blackburn.

**Feature Photoplay Company - US - 1912** - distribution, import and export company located at 145 West 45th Street, New York with H. A. Lande as general manager.

**Feature Photoplay Company - US - 1912-1914** - production company located at 220 West 42nd Street, Candler Building, New York.

**Feature Productions, Inc. - US - 1925-1926** - production company formed by Art Finance Corp. to produce Rudolph Valentino films; absorbed by Art Cinema Corp in 1926.

**Features Ideal - US - 1913-1915** - distribution company located at 227 West 42nd Street, New York.

**Federal Photoplays - US - 1914-1915** - production company in Rocky Glen, Pennsylvania; merged with Metro Pictures in 1915.

**Federal Photoplays of California - US - 1921** - production company located at 5341 Melrose Ave. Los Angeles, California and offices at 25 W. 45th St. New York owned by Benjamin Hampton and Hewlings Mumpers; produced features for Zane Grey Pictures and Great Authors Pictures.

**Federated Chester Comedies - US - 1921** - trade name for a series of comedies featuring Snooky the Humanzee, produced by C. L. Chester and distributed through Federated Film Exchanges

**Federated Film Exchanges of America, Inc. - US - 1921 -** distribution company located at 220 West 42 Street, New York with J. L. Friedman as president and George H. Wiley as general manager; distributed for several independents including C. B. C. and C. L. Chester.

**Fenning Film Service - UK - 1913-1914 -** distribution company with offices at 3 Kingly St. Winchester and 86 Great Clyde St., Glascow.

**Fernand Weill - FRANCE - 1915-1939 -** production and distribution company with offices located at 9.B des Filles du Calvaire in Paris; French distributor for Chaplin films through Production Reunies (his company?); moved to Himalya Films (also his company?) in 1918; expanded to production into the 1930s. **NOTE:** posters show tag as Fernand Weill while legal announcements show as M. Fernand Weill.

Etab^ts FERNAND WEILL
9.B des Filles du Calvaire _ PARIS

**Fert Studios - ITALY - 1919-1924 -** [see F.E.R.T.]

**Fiction Pictures, Inc. - US - 1915 -** production company and studio founded by Louis Joseph Vance; distribution through Universal; ceased business and sold the studio to Famous Players Film Co. in June, 1915

**Fidelity Pictures Co. - US - 1921 -** located at 117 W. 46th St., New York with William G. Smith as general manager.

**Filmag - AUSTRIA - 1918-1920 -** production company.

**Film A. B. Liberty - SWEDEN - 1922 -** distribution company for Paramount films

**Film Ambrosio - ITALY -** [see Ambrosio Film Co.]

**Film-Art Productions, Inc. - US - 1921 -** production company located in the Bank of Italy Bldg., Fresno, California with L. O. Stephens as president, William F. Dunn as secretary and B. D.

Biggerstaff as treasurer and general manager; produced two reel and five reel features.

**Film Arts Corp. - US - 1915-1921 -** production company formed Sept. 4, 1915 by Harry E. Aitken to produce D. W. Griffith films distributed by Triangle Film Corp; studio was located at 4500 Sunset Blvd. in Hollywood with an east coast studio at 537 Riverdale Ave. in Yonkers (old Reliance Studios); in 1917, Thomas H. Ince became the controlling director; by 1921, the studios had become the Arthur H. Gooden rental studios.

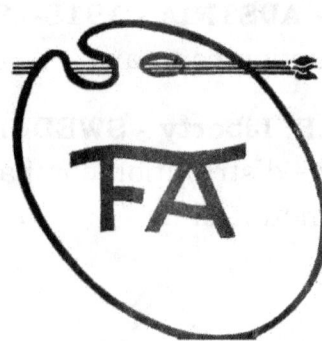

**Film Attractions Co. - US - 1914 -** production company located at 1482 Broadway, New York.

**Film Booking Offices of America, Inc. [FBO] - US - 1922-1928 -** distribution arm of Robertson-Cole Co. with offices at 723 7th Avenue, New York; part of the merger in 1928 to form RKO.

**Film Booking Offices Ltd. - UK - 1923 -** distribution arm in the UK.

**Film Centralen Palladium - DENMARK - 1922-1929 -** distribution company for Palladium films and Svensk Industri.

**Film Classic Exchange - US - 1927** - distribution company specializing in rereleases.

**Film Clearing House - US- 1918-1919 -** distribution company formed May 6, 1918 by Colonel Julian Ruppert (owner of NY Yankees) as a different type of distributor; bought and remodeled the Kleine exchanges and then took over distribution for Blackton Productions, Bacon-Backer, and William L. Sherry Service; instead of sales reps, they used Independent Sales Corp.; in September 1919, merged with Independent Sales Corp et al to form Hallmark Pictures Corp.

**Film Company of Ireland - IRELAND - 1916-1920 -** production and distribution company formed by Henry M. Fitzgibbon and James Mark Sullivan in Dublin.

**Film d'Art Corporation - US - 1917 -** production and distribution company located at 47 West 42nd Street, New York with John D. Perry as president, S. H. Wells as V. P., and William Wells as secretary/treasurer; studio located at Box 1, Malden, Massachusetts and released as Perry Pictures.

**Film d'Arte Italiana - ITALY - 1909-1924 -** production company and studio subsidiary of Pathe; formed to provide film production for French distribution, specializing in historical dramas.

**Film Distributors League - US - 1915-1916 -** production company with distribution through Triangle Film and states rights.

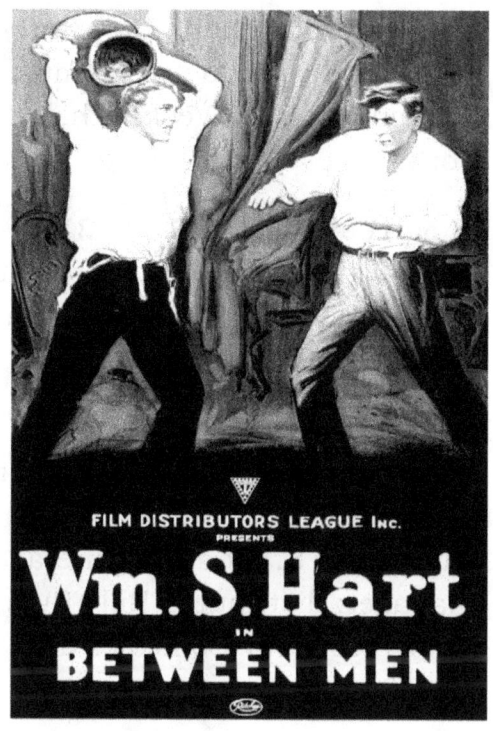

**Film Frolic Pictures Corp. - US - 1920 -** production company formed by Flora Finch; located at Apollo Hall, 1383 Broadway, New York.

**Film Import & Trading Co. - US - 1908 -** distribution company located at 143 East 23rd Street, New York; distributed for Williamson, Eclair and Society Italian Cines.

**Film-Centralen - DENMARK - 1926 -** distribution company for Metro Goldwyn films with offices in Copenhagen.

**Film-Lore Productions Co., Inc. - US - 1919** - production company located at 18-20 West 34th, New York.

**Film Market, Inc. - US - 1921** - distribution company located at 1482 Broadway, New York with Robert W. Priest as president.

**Film Sales Co. - US - 1921** - distribution company located at 158-160 W. 45th St., New York with Harry S. Stone as general manager; distributed Billy Ruge Comedies, Jolly Comedies and Film Special Comedies.

**Film Society General - ARGENTINA - 1909-1928** - distribution company formed by Julian Ajuria to import, translate and distribute international films; in 1915, frustrated by the way Argentina was portrayed in imported films, Ajuria moved to production to try to make Argentine films more positive.

**Film Special Comedies - US - 1921** - trade name for one reel comedies released through Film Sales Co.

**Film Supply Company of America - US - 1911-1913** - distribution company for Ammex and New York Motion Picture after their fight with Universal and before they went to Mutual.

**Film Triomphe - FRANCE - 1921-1927** - distribution company located at 33, rue de Surene, Paris.

**Filmbryan S. B. D. - SWEDEN - 1920-1924** - distributor that also released U.S. imports.

**Filmfabriek Hollandia - NETHERLANDS - 1912-1919** - production and distribution company formed April 9, 1912 by Maurits Binger; initially filmed outside until a studio was built in 1913; World War I cut production drastically and after the war, Binger had financial trouble; in 1919, Binger signed to supply film production to British distributor Smith's Film Sales and changed name of the company to Anglo-Hollandia Film Co.

**Filmfabrikken Danmark - DENMARK - 1912-1919 -** production company featuring Emilie Sannom.

**Filmfabrikken Skandinavien - DENMARK - 1912-1917 -** production company formed from Biorama and expanded into importing films for distribution.

**Filmindustri Inc Skandia - SWEDEN - 1918-1919 -** production company formed by the merger of Pathe Freres Sweden and Hasselblad Film Co; following year merged again with Svenska Bio to form Svenska Filmindustri.

**Films Abel Gance - FRANCE - 1920-1927 -** production company featuring Abel Gance material.

**Films Albatros - FRANCE - 1922-1940 -** production company located in Montreuil in the old Pathe studio building; Alexandre Kamenka was general manager.

**Films Barcelona - SPAIN - 1906-1910 -** production company formed in Barcelona by Fructuos Gelabert.

**Films Cuesta - SPAIN - 1905-1914 -** production company formed by Antonio Cuesta in Valencia.

**Films Diamant - FRANCE - 1921-1934 -** production company.

**Films Lloyds, Inc. - US - 1914 -** [see Lloyds Films, Inc.]

**Films Ltd. - UK - 1913-1914 -** distributor with offices in Winchester, Liverpool, Newcastle, Cardiff, Belfast and Dublin.

**Films Renoir - FRANCE - 1925-1926 -** production company with offices located at 15 W. Matignon in Paris.

**Films Valetta - FRANCE - 1913-1921 -** production and distribution company; also distributed Pathe films.

**Filmzentrale - GERMANY - 1923 -** production company.

**Fim Film - NETHERLANDS - 1926-1933** - distribution company located in Amsterdam.

**Fine Art Pictures, Inc. - US - 1920- 1921** - distribution company located at 1457 Broadway, New York with Murray W. Garsson as president and Charles F. Schwerin as general manager; moved to 130 W. 46th St. New York in 1921.

**Fine Arts Pictures Co. - US - 1915-1919** - production company located in Los Angeles to produce films for Triangle; after Triangle closed, Fine Arts expanded to distribute their own films.

**Fine Arts Pictures, Inc. - US - 1921** - production company and studio located in Jacksonville, Florida and offices at 130 W. 46th St. New York with Murray W. Garsson as general manager.

**Fireside Productions, Inc. - US - 1922-1923** - production company formed to produce Fisher's Boarding House series.

**Fireproof Film Co. - US - 1917-1918** - production company located in Rochester, New York; acquired in 1918 by "Pat" Powers to produce 3-D talking films.

**First Biorama Co. - AUSTRALIA - 1900-1902** - formed as part of the Limelight Division of the Australian Salvation Army and headed by Joe Perry; other Biorama companies were formed to continue making Salvation Army films.

**First Division (FD) - US - 1925-1937** - production company but soon expanded into distribution by states rights; included Chadwick Pictures.

**First National Exhibitors' Circuit, Inc. - US - 1917-1919** - distribution company formed by 26 theater chains; offices at 6-8 W. 48th St.m New York with Robert Lieber as president, Samuel Katz as V. P., and Harry O. Schwalbe as secretary/

treasurer; in 1919, changed name to Associated First National Pictures.

**First National Pictures, Inc - US - 1924-1929** - was created by name change from Associated First National Pictures when they started producing films; in 1928, Warner Bros bought controlling interest and finished buy out in 1936; from 1941 to 1958, most Warner Bros. films bore the combined trademarks "A Warner Bros.-First National Picture."

**First Sign Film Co. - RUSSIA - 1915-1916** - production company created by Vladimir Aleksandrovich Sashin-Fydorov; filmed behind the theater but closed due to illness.

**Fischer Features - US - 1919-1921** - [see A.H. Fischer Features, Inc]

**Flamingo Film Co. - US - 1914-1915** - formed October 1914 with Frederick Upham Adams as president, A. H. Sawyer as secretary and A. H. Hallett as V. P. and general manager; offices in the Meece Building at 48th St. and Broadway, New York.

**Flora Finch Film Corp. - US - 1917** - production company located at 729 7th Avenue, New York.

**Florence Vidor Productions - US - 1922** - production company featuring Florence Vidor (King Vidor's wife).

**Florida Film Corporation - US - 1918-1919** - production company located at 22 West 9th St., Jacksonville, Florida; studios at Klutho Studios, Jacksonville, Florida.

**Flying A Films - US - 1915** - trade name used by American Film Co.

**Folly Films - US - 1912-1915** - production company formed by Fred Evans and Joe Evans in Phoenix, Arizona.

**Fordart Films, Inc. - US - 1918 -** trade name for Francis Ford Producing Co.

**Fort Dearborn Photoplays Co. - US - 1917 -** production company located in Chicago, Illinois with Frederick Russell Clark.

**Forum Films, Inc. - US - 1917 -** distribution company located at 1905 Times Building, New York.

**Forward Film Distributors, Inc - US - 1921 -** distribution company located at 110 W. 40th St., New York with J. Joseph Sameth as president and M. Warschauer as V. P.

**Foster Photoplay Co. - US - 1910-1919 -** production and distribution company formed by William Foster in Chicago, Illinois; considered one of the first black owned production companies.

**Fotorama A/S - DENMARK - 1908-1940 -** production company formed from Danish Cinema Photo Technology Industry on November 18, 1908 by Thomas S. Hermansen with studios in Aarhus and Kinografen; in 1911, expanded to distribution and also distributed for Nordisk Films.

**Four Star Productions - US - 1919 -** trade name for Artco Productions, Inc.

**Fox Film Corp. - US - 1915-1935 -** formed February 1, 1915 from Box Office Attractions Co. after making their first film production and building a permanent studio in California; Fox leased the old Selig studio in Edendale while their studio was being built at 1417 N. Western Ave. Hollywood, California; offices were located at 10th Ave and 55th St., New York with William Fox as president and Winfield R. Sheehan as general manager; in 1919, Fox began making newsreels as Fox News and opened offices in Berlin, Dublin, London, Paris, and Rome; in early 1920s, began acquiring theaters and in November 1925 formed Fox

Theater Corp.; in 1925, acquired the rights to the Case-Sponable sound system and renamed it Movietone; in 1927, acquired the U.S. rights to the German Tri-Ergon sound system and released talking Newsreels; in 1929, Fox borrowed $40 million and purchased Loew's. Inc. but before he could take control, he was in a bad car accident; during his hospitalization, the stock market crashed and basically bankrupted him.; in 1930, he was ousted and control of the company was shuffled through several people who lost massive amounts of money; on May 29, 1935, Fox Film merged with Twentieth Century Pictures and the name changed to 20th Century-Fox Film Corp. on August 15, 1935. [See Twentieth Century Pictures and 20th Century-Fox Film Corp.]

**France Films Inc. - US - 1917 -** production company located in Suite 608 Candler Building, 220 W. 42nd Street, New York.

**Frances Edmonde Productions - US - 1919-1920** - production company located at 1676 Arlington Ave., Los Angeles, California.

**Francis Ford Producing Co. - US - 1918 -** production company formed April 1914 by Frances Ford to produce films for the states rights market; offices located at 1476 Broadway, New York; leased space from Christie Studios in Hollywood and released under the trade name Fordart Films.

**Franco-American Film Co. - US - 1911-1912 -** distribution company for imports.

**Franco-British Film Co. - UK - 1912 -** production company for a series featuring George Treville.

**Franco-Film - FRANCE - 1920-1934 -** production and distribution company located in Paris with distribution offices in Belgium.

**Frank A. Keeney Pictures Corp. - US - 1918 -** production company formed January 1918 by Frank A. Keeney, vaudeville chain owner, to produce films featuring Catherine Calvert; offices were in the Putnam Building at 1493 Broadway, New York; used Pathe studios for filming; distribution through William L. Sherry Service.

**Frank Lloyd Productions, Inc. - US - 1920-1942 -** production company with distribution through First National Pictures - Warner Bros.

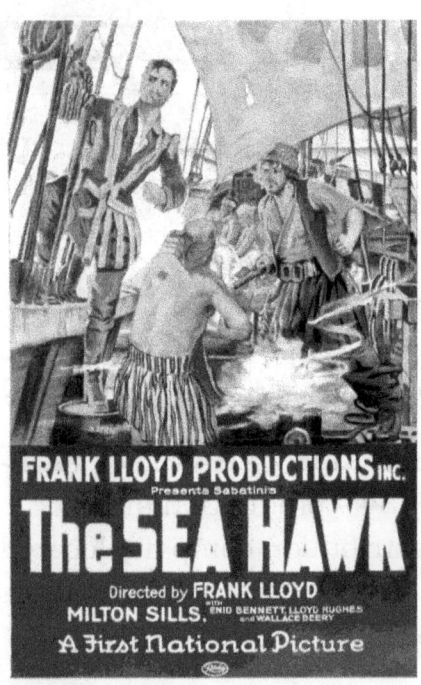

**Franklin Feature Film Co. - US - 1913 -** distribution company located at 803 James Building, Chattanooga, Tennessee.

**Frazee Films Productions - US - 1918 -** production company formed July 1918 by Edwin A. Frazee for underwater filming techniques; studio was in Boyle Heights, Los Angeles; distribution through Ernest Shipman.

**French American Film Co. - US - 1912 -** states rights distribution company located at 403 Times Building, New York.

**French Official War Films - US - 1915 -** production and distribution company located at 110 West 40th Street, Suite 1503, New York.

**Frieder Film Corporation - US - 1917 -** distribution and production company located at 215 W. Randolph St, Chicago, Illinois with studios in Lankershim, California.

**Frivol Film Co. - US - 1921 -** production company using Victor Studios at 645 W. 43rd St New

York; distributed through Clark-Cornelius Corp.

**Frohman Amusement Corp. - US - 1914-1915** - founded November 1914 by Gustave Frohman, William L. Sherrill and S. H. Boynton with Frank Norcross as general manager; distribution through World Film Corp.

**Frontier - US - 1913-1914** - trade name for films produced by St. Louis Motion Picture Co. for Universal in 1913-1914.

**Frontier Features, Inc. - US - 1921** - production company located at 729 7th Ave., New York; Anders Randolf was president and Floyd T. Buckley was general manager; distribution through Jans Pictures Inc.

**Fukuhodo - JAPAN - 1910-1912** - production company.

---

**FILM/ART**
Original Film Posters

Hollywood, CA

323.363.2969

filmartgallery.com

**channingposters**

ORIGINAL MOVIE POSTERS, LOBBY CARDS, AND AUTOGRAPHED ITEMS

CHANNING THOMSON
P. O. BOX 330232
SAN FRANCISCO, CA 94133-0232

Email: channinglylethomson@att.net
ebay: http://stores.ebay.com/CHANNINGPOSTERS

# G

**G & J Photoplay Co. - US - 1921 -** production company.

**G. A. S. Films - UK - 1897-1914 -** trade name for films produced by George Albert Smith.

**G. Melies - US -** [see Star Films - Gaston Melies]

**G. P. C. - FRANCE -** [see Grandes Productions Cinematographiques]

**G. Serra Ltd. - UK - 1913-1915 -** distribution company formed by Guido Serra Cassano with offices at 22 Denman St. Westminster; distributed for Cines, Celio and Splendor.

**Gail Kane Productions - US - 1918-1919 -** production company for films featuring Gail Kane.

**Gale Henry Comedies - US - 1921 -** trade name for a series of two reel comedies featuring Gale Henry and distributed by Reelcraft Pictures Corp.

**Garrick Studios - US - 1917 -** production company located in Jacksonville, Florida.

**Garrison Film Co., Inc. - US - 1914 -** production company located at 1402 Broadway, Room 740, New York.

**Garson Studios, Inc. - US - 1919-1924 -** production company owned by Harry Garson and located at 1845 Glendale Ave., Los Angeles, California; produced films primarily featuring actress Clara Kimball Young; distributed by Equity Pictures Corp.

**Gaumont British Picture Corp. - UK - 1898-1941 -** production company formed in 1898 as British subsidiary of the French Gaumont Film Co.; distributed under the Gaumont and Elge trade names; in 1915, Gaumont built the Lime Grove Studio complex, the largest studio in the UK; in 1922, Isidore Ostrer acquired controlling interest and broke Gaumont-British away from parent company; in 1924, Gainsborough Studios was built to produce the "B" films for Gaumont; in 1927 merged with Ideal Film Co.; in 1941, Rank Organization bought out Gaumont British, including Lime Grove Studios and Gainsborough Studios.

**Gaumont Company, Ltd - US - 1912-1915 -** distribution branch of the French film company with studios in Flushing, New York; Gaumont started production in the U.S. in 1913 with Herbert Blache, (husband of Alice Guy Blache) as V. P. and U. S. rep; company became known as American Gaumont and distributed through Exclusive Supply Corp. (of which Blache was president); in 1915, started releasing one reel comedies under Empress trade name and in October 1915, moved distribution to Mutual Film Corp.; Gaumont had production studios in Flushing, New York and Jacksonville, Florida; released films under the trade names of Rialto Star Features and Casino Star Comedies; in 1918, moved to states rights distribution.

**Gaumont Film Co. - FR - 1897-current -** Gaumont Film Co. was founded by Leon Gaumont and is the first and oldest continuously operating film company in the world; began producing short films in 1897 to promote camera-projector; Leon Gaumont's secretary, Alice Guy Blache, created the first stories on film and became the industry's first female director; Guy became Head of Production for Gaumont from 1897 to 1907; Alice Guy Blache and her husband Herbert came to the U.S. to open the American Gaumont [see Gaumont Company; Exclusive Supply Corp.; Solax Film Corp.; Blache Films]; from 1905 to 1914, its Cite Elge studios at La Villete, France, were the largest in the world; Gaumont (along with Pathe) dominated the motion-picture industry in Europe until the outbreak of World War I in 1914; Gaumont established offices and studios in numerous countries and is still in operation.

**Gaumont Film Service - UK - 1906-1914** - distribution company with offices at 6 Denman St., Winchester and branches at Manchester, Liverpool, Glascow, Newcastle, Birmingham and Cardiff.

**Gaumont Metro Goldwyn - FRANCE - 1925-1927 -** distribution company in Paris for Metro Goldwyn and Metro Goldwyn Mayer films

**Gavin Production Co. - US - 1921 -** production company located at 611 Union League Blvd. Los Angeles, California with William Watts as president and W. H. Kollman as V.P; produced western shorts featuring John S. Gavin and released through Plymouth Corp.

**Gayety Comedies - US - 1919-1920 -** trade name used for comedy shorts produced by Christie Film Co. featuring comedian George Ovey.

**Gaylord Lloyd Comedies - US - 1921 -** trade name for a series of comedies released by Hal Roach Studios.

**Gem Film - CZECHOSLOVAKIA - 1929 -** production company formed by Gustav Machaty.

**Gem Motion Picture Co. - US - 1911-1913 -** production company formed by Marion Leonard and her husband, director Stanner E. V. Taylor; produced films featuring Marion Leonard, who replaced Florence Lawrence as the Biograph Girl, considered the first female star to own their own production company; acquired by Rex Motion Picture Co.

**Gendov-Film - BULGARIA - 1915-1937** - production and distribution company formed by Vasil Gendov.

**Gene Gauntier Feature Players Co. - US - 1912-1915** - production company formed in December 1912 by ex-Kalem actress Gene Gautier; offices located at 515 West 54th Street, New York, with filming in Jacksonville, Florida for the first half of 1913 and then moved to Ireland; distribution was through Warner Bros. and internationally by Warner's Features; in 1915, company closed when Gautier's husband Jack J. Clark went to work for Universal.

**General Cinematography Agency - UK - 1913-1914** - distribution company with offices at 74 Shaftesbury Ave. Winchester.

**General Enterprises, Inc. - US - 1916-1917** - distribution company formed by Harry G. Kosch as president, Arthur H. Sawyer and Herbert Lubin in New York to distribute films by states rights for the New England territory; offices located at 1476 Broadway New York.

**General Film Agency Ltd. - UK - 1912-1916** - distribution company formed by Harry Battersby, Norman Hart, Leopold Sutto, Mary Harriott Swan, Thomas James West, and Ernest Seville Williams; located at 58 Dean St. Winchester and 76 Talbot St. Dublin; distributed for Milano, Roma, Gem, Ramo, Vera and Carrick.

**General Film Co. - US - 1910-1917** - distribution company for Edison's Trust companies; in 1917, Trust was declared illegal and the company sold to Lincoln & Parker Film Co.

**General Film Company of Australasia - AUSTRALIA - 1912-1913** - production company formed from the merger of Amalgamated Pictures, West's Pictures and Spencer's Pictures; in January 1913, merged with Greater J. D. Williams Amusement Company to become Australasian Films and called "The Combine."

**General Film Publicity & Sales Co. - US - 1912** - production company located at 145 West 45th Street, New York with H. A. Spanuth as president.

**General Film Renters - UK - 1919-1922** - distribution company formed by Denton Hardwicke in January 1919 to export British films; in November 1920, acquired G. B. Samuelson; in February 1922, acquired by British Super Films.

**General Film Supply Co. - US - 1920** - production company.

**General Films - US - 1913** - trade name used by Melies Films.

**Genina Film - ITALY - 1921-1929** - production company formed by Augusto Genina and closed when he moved to France.

**Georg Kleinke - GERMANY - 1912** - distribution company located in Berlin SW, Friedrichstrasse.

**George B. Seitz, Inc. - US - 1921** - production company located at 1990 Park Ave., New York; George B. Seitz was president and general manager; distribution through Pathe.

**George Beban Productions - US - 1922-1926** - production company formed by George Beban; operated until his wife died at which time he retired and closed the company.

**George Clark Productions - UK - 1919-1924** - production company formed to make comedy shorts featuring Guy Newall; George Clark was president; acquired by British Lion after quota legislation.

**George H. Hamilton, Inc. - US - 1922** - production and distribution with offices at 729 Seventh Ave. New York.

**George H. Wiley, Inc. - US - 1923 -** distribution company located at 220 W. 42nd Street, New York.

**George Kleine Attractions - US - 1913 -** distribution company located at 166 N. State Street, Chicago, Illinois.

**George Kleine Optical Company - US - 1907-1919 -** distribution company located at 63 E. Adams St. Chicago, Illinois with offices at 110 W. 40th St. New York; one of the founders of the Kalem Company and member of the Motion Pictures Patents Co.; known for importing and distributing international films in the U.S.

**George Prince Film Service - UK - 1913-1914 -** distribution company with offices located at 124 Dale St. Liverpool.

**Georgia Hopkins Picture Co. - US - 1921 -** production company.

**Gerald F. Bacon Productions - US - 1920-1921 -** production company located at Fulton Theater Bldg., Broadway and 46th St., New York.

**German-American Cinematograph and Film Co. - US - 1904 -** production company formed by Eberhard Schneider and located at 175 E. 96th St. New York.

**German Biograph - GERMANY -** [see Deutches Biograph]

**Germanic Official War Films, Inc. - US - 1917 -** production company located at 729 Seventh Avenue, New York.

**Gerrard Film Company Limited - UK - 1915-1916 -** distribution company located at 13, Gerrard Street, London.

**Gibraltar Pictures - US - 1920 -** production company located at 135 West 44th Street, New York.

**Gillespie Brothers & Co. - US - 1919 -** distribution company located at 220 West 42nd Street, New York.

**Glasgow Film Co. - UK - 1913-1914 -** distribution company with offices at 4 Howard St., Glasgow.

**Globe Feature Film Corporation - US - 1914 -** production company located at 110 West 40th Street, New York.

**Globe Feature Picture Booking Co. - US - 1915 -** states rights distributor.

**Globe Film Co. Ltd. - UK - 1909-1916 -** distribution company formed by Gerald Michael Bishop, Harold Roswell Bishop, George Howard Cricks, George William Holdsworth and Frederick William Stephens with James Charles Squier as general manager; offices located at 8 Cecil Court Westminster; in May 1910, took over Hepworth studios and expanded to offices at 81-81 Shaftsbury Ave in 1911.

**Globe Productions Corp. - US - 1921 -** production company and studio located at 44th St. Studio, New York; formed to produce films featuring May Murray and released through Associated Exhibitors.

**Gloria American Co - US - 1913-15 -** distribution company located at 110 W. 40th Street, New York.

**Gnome Motion Picture Company - US - 1910 -** production company with offices and studios located at S.W. Corner, Park & Tremont Aves, Bronx, New York.

**Gold Medal Photo Players - US - 1917 -** production and

distribution company located at 729 Seventh Ave., New York.

**Gold Seal Film Corp. - US - 1920** - produced comedy shorts under trade name Joy Comedies and distributed through Awyon Film.

**Golden Eagle Features - US - 1916-1917** - trade name for features released by Frohman Amusement Corporation and distributed by International Film Service.

**Golden Gate Film Exchange - US - 1912** - distribution company located at 166 Golden Gate Avenue, San Francisco, California with Sol Lesser as manager.

**Golden Rooster Plays - US - 1916** - trade name for high quality productions by Balboa and distributed through Pathe.

**Golden State Motion Picture Company of California - US - 1913** - production company formed by James K. Hackett with Ernest Shipman and H. M. Russell; distributed through the states rights market.

**Goldstone Productions - US - 1921-1925** - production company formed by Philip Goldstone.

**Goldwyn-Bray Comics - US - 1921** - trade name for one reel cartoons produced by Bray and released by Goldwyn Pictures Corp.

**Goldwyn Distributing Corp. - 1916-1924** - distribution arm of Goldwyn Pictures Corp.

**Goldwyn Pictures Corporation - US - 1916-1924** - production company and studio founded by Samuel Goldwyn with offices at

469 5th Ave. New York and studio in Culver City, California; Samuel Goldwyn was president, Frank Godsol and Francis A. Sudger were V.P.s; Goldwyn left the company in 1922 but the studio continued due to its association with Cosmopolitan; in1924, Goldwyn Pictures merged with Metro Pictures to form Metro-Goldwyn.

**Golgate Feature Service - US - 1913-1914 -** distribution company located in 614 Candler Building, New York with offices around the U.S.; Sol L. Lesser was president and general manager.

**Goodall's Pictures Ltd - UK - 1913-1914 -** distribution company with offices at Albion St. Cleckheaton.

**Goodman Films - US - 1920-1924 -** production company formed by Daniel Carson Goodman.

**Gordon Boney Attractions - US - 1927 -** distribution company through states rights for black films in Georgia, Florida, North Carolina and South Carolina.

**Gorman Film Mfg. Co., Inc. - US - 1914 -** production company located at 1402 Broadway, New York with Jack Gorman as general manager.

**Gosfotokino - RUSSIA - 1923-current -** [see Goskino]

**Goskino - RUSSIA - 1923- current** - production company and studio; named was changed to Gosfotokino in late 1923, Armenkino in 1928 and eventually to Armenfil'm.

**Gosvoenkino - RUSSIA - 1923-1928 -** production company formerly known as Goskino; in 1928, name was changed to Armenkino.

**Gotham Film Co - US - 1914 -** production company located at 145 West 45th Street, New York.

**Gotham Film Company - US - 1915-1916 -** production company formed April 24, 1915 with Marshall W. Taggart as president; studio was located at 237 Lafayette St. New York and offices at 1600 Broadway, New York; distribution through Reel Photoplay Co.

**Gotham Productions - US - 1926 -** production company distributed by Lumas Film Corporation.

**Governor's Boss Photo Play Co. - US - 1915 -** production company located in the Times Building, New York with J. Huyler Ellison as president.

**Graf Productions, Inc. - US - 1922-1923 -** production company formed by Max Graf; distribution through Metro Pictures Corp.

**Grafton Film Publishing Co. - US - 1916-1917 -** distribution company formed by Edward L. Grafton to distribute for Monrovia Feature Film Corp. and Empire Feature Film Co.

**Grand Feature Film Co. - US - 1915 -** distribution company located in Kansas City, Missouri, with Nate Block as president.

**Grand-Asher Distributing Corp. - US - 1923-1924 -** distribution company formed by Harry Asher to distribute Grand-Asher Films; located at 15 W. 44th Street, New York.

**Grand-Asher Films - US - 1923-1924 -** production company formed by Harry Asher; located at 1432-38 Gowers St., Los Angeles, California; distributed through Grand-Asher Distributors.

**Grandes Productions Cinematographiques - FRANCE - 1920-1926 -** distribution company located in Paris; expanded to production in 1923.

**Graphic Film Corp. - US - 1917-1922 -** production company formed December 3, 1917 by Ivan Abramson after leaving Ivan

Film Production Co.; Abramson was president and general manager; offices located at 729 Seventh Ave. New York; used Estee studio at 209 E. 124th St. New York for filming.

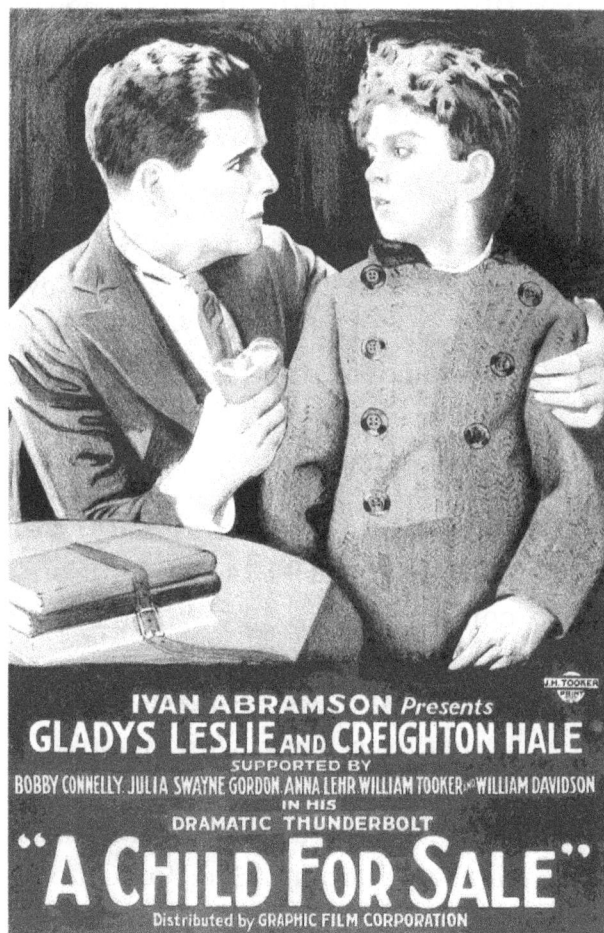

**Graphic Film Exchange - US - 1917-1922 -** distribution company for Graphic Film Corp.

**Great Authors' Pictures, Inc - US - 1919 -** production company formed by Benjamin Hampton and George H. Perry; featured films by well-known authors with no "stars"; offices located at 5341 Melrose Ave. Los Angeles, California; distribution by W. W. Hodkinson through Pathe.

**Great Northern Films Co. - US - 1908-1916 -** distribution company founded January 1908 as the American branch of Nordisk Film Co. of Denmark; in 1911, became separate import company with offices located at 110 West 40th Street, New York and headed by Ingvald C. Oes; became Great Northern Special Feature Film Co.

**Great Northern Special Feature Film Co. - US - 1914-1921 -** distribution company formed from Great Northern Film Co.; located on the Tenth Floor, Candler Building, New York.

**Great Players Feature Film Corp. - US - 1914** - production company located in the Longacre Building, Room 909, New York.

**Great Western Film Co. - US - 1910** - production company in San Francisco, California.

**Great Western Motion Picture Co. - US - 1913-1914** - production company with distribution by Warner Bros. through Warner's Features.

**Great Western Pictures Corp. - US - 1921** - production company located in Los Angeles, California, with Emmett Dalton as general manager.

**Great Western Producing Co. - US - 1919-21** - production company with offices located at 1600 Broadway, New York and studio at 6100 Sunset Blvd. Hollywood, California; owned by Weiss Brothers with Julius Stern as president and general manager; produced Elmo Lincoln films for Universal and Numa Pictures Corp.

**Greater America Films - US - 1921** - located at 1520 Broadway, New York with Clifford Slater Wheeler as president and Robert N. Marx as secretary/treasurer and general manager.

**Greater New York Film Rental Co. - US - 1904-1913** - distribution company formed by William Fox to supply his own theaters; located at 116-118 East 14th Street, New York; won lawsuit against General Film Co. in 1912; changed name and started film production. [See Box Office Attraction Film Rental Co]

**Greater Stars Productions, Inc. - US - 1920** - distribution company located at 537 South Dearborn Street, Chicago, Illinois for states rights in Indiana and Illinois territories.

**Greene's Feature Photo Plays, Inc. - US - 1913-1914** - distribution company located at 110 W. 40th Street, New York.

**Greens Film Service - UK - 1913-1914** - distribution company with offices located at 833-901 Gallowgate, Glascow.

**Greiver Distributing Corporation - US - 1918-1920** - distribution company located at 207 So. Wabash Avenue, Chicago, Illinois; changed name and location in 1921 to Greiver Productions.

**Greiver Productions - US - 1920** - distribution company formed from Greiver Distributing Corp. and located at 831 So. Wabash Avenue, Chicago, Illinois.

**Guaranteed Pictures Co. - US - 1918-1938** - distribution company formed by Samuel Goldstein and Mortimer D. Sackett in New York specialized in European imports and reissues. In 1938, they changed to become Commonwealth Pictures.

**Gumps - US - 1921** - trade name for a series of one reel comedies released by Celebrated Players Corp.

**Guy Croswell Smith, Ltd. - US - 1919** - distribution company located at 807 Longacre Building, New York.

**Guy Empey Productions - US - 1919-1920** - production company located at 220 West 42nd Street, New York with Arthur Guy Empey as president and James F. Shaw and F. C. Richardson as officers.

---

**Where can you go to get instant access to:**

- 50,000 production codes
- 25,000 NSS codes
- 18,000 trailer codes
- 1000s lithography plate #s
- 100s artist signatures
- studio logos and info
- int'l censorship and markings
- advance research and **more**

**ONLY when you become a LAMP Member**
LearnAboutMoviePosters.com

# H

**H. A. Molzon Co.** - US - 1910-1914 - states rights distributor for major titles of the time.

**H. A. Spoor** - UK - 1909-1910 - distribution arm for Essanay films with offices at 5 New Compton St. Holborn; December 1909 moved to 4 Rupert St.

**H. Grossman** - US - 1917 - distribution company located at 729 7th Avenue, New York.

**H. Winik Co.** - UK - 1913 - distribution company.

**Hal Roach Studios, Inc.** - US - 1919-1963 - production company formed in 1919 with Hal E. Roach as president and Warren Doane as V. P. and general manager; built their own studio at 8822 West Washington Blvd. in Culver City; produced a wide variety of comedy shorts and features.

**Hall Room Boys Photoplays** - US - [see C. B. C. Film Sales Corp.]

**Hallmark Pictures Corp.** - US - 1919-1920 - distribution company formed September 1919 by Film Clearing House, Independent Sales Corp, Film Finance Corp., Hobart Henley Productions, Inc. and Charles Miller Productions; most notable for the *Trail of the Octopus* serial released under the trade name Famous Directors' Pictures series; in 1920, took over Triangle Distributing Corp. and soon afterwards was taken over by Robertson-Cole.

**Ham Comedy Co. - US - 1916-** - production company headed by Lloyd V. Hamilton; formed to produce comedy shorts for Kalem; sometime referred to as the Kalem-Ham Comedy Co.

**Hamilton Film Corp. - US - 1916-1917** - production company released through Triangle Film Corp.

**Hamilton-White Comedies, Inc - 1921-1923** - production company located at 4534 Sunset Blvd. Los Angeles, California; formed to produce comedies released under the trade name of Mermaid Comedies featuring Lloyd Hamilton; distributed through Educational Film.

**Hank Mann Co. - US - 1921 -** production company located at 1439 Beechwood Dr. Hollywood, California with Morris Schlank; distributed by Arrow Film Corp.

**Hap Film - NETHERLANDS - 1916-1923** - distribution company located in Amsterdam.

**Happy Jack Comedies - US - 1920-1921** - trade name for comedy shorts produced by Jack MacCullough Co.

**Harcol Film Co. - US - 1916-1930s** - production company formed in September 1916 with the acquisition of Pickwick Film Co.; Abe Harrison, Jr. was president; offices located at 241-253 Broadway St., New Orleans, Louisiana; created newsreels for Pathe and events for regional theaters.

**Harmony Film Co. Inc. - US - 1921** - production company located at 405 Courier Bldg., Los Angeles, California with George Edwards Hall as president and general manager; formed to produce westerns for distribution through Sunny West Co.

**Harold Lloyd Comedies - US - 1921** - trade name for a series of comedies released by Hal Roach Studios.

**Harold Lloyd Film Corp. - US - 1924-1939** - production company formed by Harold Lloyd with William R. Fraser as secretary and John L. Murphy as general manager; maintained offices and filmed at the Hollywood General Studios.

**Harper Film Corporation - US - 1916 -** distribution company located at the Times Building, New York with J. Parker Read, Jr. as general manager.

**Harry Berg Productions - US - 1917 -** production company located at 729 Seventh Avenue, New York.

**Harry Garson Productions - US - 1919-1925 -** production company formed by Harry Garson with offices at 1845 Allesandro Street, Los Angeles, California and 512 Fifth Avenue, New York; distribution through Metro Pictures Corp.

**Harry J. Brown Productions - US - 1925 -** production company formed by Harry J. Brown.

**Harry Levey Productions - US - 1920 -** production company located at 230 West 38th Street, New York.

**Harry McRae Webster Productions, Inc. - US - 1918-1919 -** production company located in the Brokaw Building, 42nd St. & Broadway, New York.

**Harry Raver, Inc. - US - 1918-1921 -** production company formed from Raver Film Corp. with Harry Raver as president; located at 1400 Broadway New York; distribution through states rights.

**Hasselblad Film Co. - SWEDEN - 1915-1918 -** production company formed in Gothenburg to meet the demand of the war; Georg af Klercker was general manager; in 1918, merged with Pathe Freres Sweden to form Filmindustri Inc Skandia.

**Hawk Film Co. - US - 1917 -** production company located at 1600 Broadway, New York.

**Haworth Pictures Corp. - US - 1918-1920 -** production company formed March 1918 by Sessua Hayakawa to produce better quality Japanese-American films; located in the H. W. Hellman Bldg. in Los Angeles, California; distribution by Robertson-Cole; closed in 1920 and Hayakawa created Hayakawa Feature Play Co.

**Hayakawa Feature Play Co. - US - 1921 -** production company formed by Sessua Hayakawa in 1921 after the closing of Haworth Pictures Corp.; absorbed by Robertson-Cole in 1922 when they started their own film production.

**Hearst News - US - 1919-1929 -** production company formed to produce newsreels by Hearst International News Service for distribution by Universal and called International News; Universal began producing their own in 1929-1967 called the U-I Newsreel.

**Hector Film Corp. - US - 1914 -** production company formed by Hector J. Streyckmans featuring Beulah Paynter; located at Suite 308, Times Building, 42$^{nd}$ and Broadway, New York.

**Helen Gardner Picture Players - US - 1913-1914 -** production company featuring Helen Gardner; Charles L. Gaskill was general manager; distribution by Warner Bros. through Warner's Features.

**Helgar Corporation - US - 1913 -** distribution company located at 472 Fulton Street, Brooklyn, New York.

**Hemmer Superior Productions, Inc.** - US - 1920 - production company located at 137 W. 48th Street, New York.

**Henderson's Film Service** - UK - 1913-1914 - distributor with offices at Irving House, Newcastle and 94 Wardour St., Winchester.

**Henry Ginsberg Distributing Corp.** - US - 1924-1925 - distribution company for Banner Productions; offices located at 729 Seventh Avenue, New York.

**Henry Lehrman Comedies** - US - 1920- - production company formed April 17, 1920; A. L. Barnes was general manager; specialized in comedy shorts.

**Henry Lehman Productions** - US - 1919- production company formed March 21, 1919 by Henry Lehman after leaving Fox Film. [see L-KO Motion Picture Kompany]

**Hepwix Productions** - UK - 1899-1907 - trade name for films produced by Hepworth and Company.

**Hepworth American Film Corporation** - US - 1913-1915 - production company located at 110-112 West 40th Street, New York, with Albert Blinkhorn as president.

**Hepworth and Co.** - UK - 1899-1907 - production company formed by Cecil Hepworth and his cousin Monty Wicks; used their studio known as Walton-on-Thames; released films using trade name Hepwix Productions; studio destroyed by fire in 1907 and rebuilt as Hepworth Film Manufacturing Co.

**Hepworth Film Manufacturing Co.** - UK - 1908-1923 - production and distribution company for Hepworth and Turner Films with offices located at 2 Denman St. London; moved to Walton-on-Thames during the war; went bankrupt in 1923.

**Hepworth Film Manufacturing Co. - US - 1913-1914** - the U.S. distribution arm for Hepworth Film with Albert Blinkhorn as president; distribution through Blinkhorn's company Vivaphone Film & Sales Corp.

**Hepworth Picture Plays Ltd. - UK - 1919-1923** - special feature projects released by Hepworth after the World War I.

**Herald Film Corp. - US - 1915-1916** - distribution company with offices located at 126-130 W. 46th St., New York, with L. Rosengarten as president.

**Herald Film Corp. - US - 1921-1922** - production company

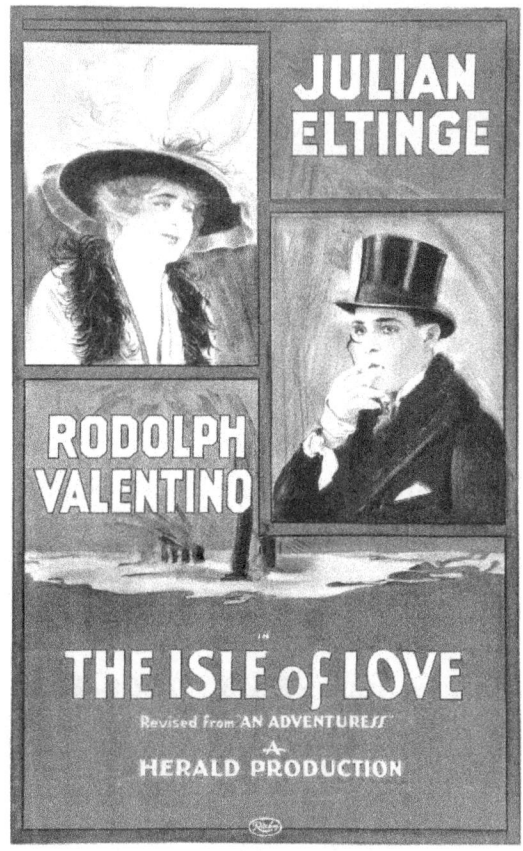

**Herbert Brenon Film Corp. - US - 1916-1918** - production company located at Hudson Heights, New Jersey; distributed by Lewis J. Selznick Productions, which became Select Pictures in 1917.

**Hermann Film Corp. - US - 1921** - production company located at 2435 Wilshire Blvd., Santa Monica, California with E. P. Hermann as president, Francis J. Heney as V. P. and J. Livingston as secretary/treasurer; produced six reel comedies and dramas.

**Hi Mark Productions - US - 1912-1928** - production and distribution company located at 220 W. 42nd St., New York.

**Hiawatha Films - US - 1916** - production company specializing in western dramas distributed by Unicorn Film Service.

**Hibbert's Pictures - UK - 1913-1914** - distributor of Hepworth Films with offices at 10 Dixon St. Glascow.

**High Grade Feature Film Company - US - 1914** - distribution company located at 220 West 42nd Street, Suite 602-4, New York.

**Hiller & Wick - US - 1917** - distribution company with offices at 924 Longacre Building, New York; handled Haworth reissues.

**Himalaya Film Co. - FRANCE - 1918-1929** - distribution company formed to distribute Chaplin films in France; managed by Fernand Weill; originally located at Fernand Weill offices but moved to 17 Rue de Choisseul in Paris. [see Fernand Weill]

**Hippo Film Co. US - 1916** - production company using the trade name Hippo Comedies; distributed by Unicorn Film Service.

"Propose or Die."

**Hippodrome Film Company, Inc. - US - 1916** - distribution company located at Room 501, 110 West 40th Street, New York with H. S. Clark as general manager.

**Hispano Film - SPAIN - 1906-1918** - production company formed as subsidiary of Pathe with Ricardo Banos as general manager.

**Historical Feature Film Co. - US - 1914-1917** - production company located at 105 West Monroe Street, Chicago, Illinois.

**Historic Features, Inc. - US - 1917** - distribution company located at 200 Fifth Avenue, New York.

**Historical Film Corp. of America - US - 1913-1919** - production company formed in April 1913 specializing in historical and educational films; offices were in London and One Madison Ave. New York; studio was on East 23d St. with Eustache Hale Bennett as general manager and Garfield Thompson as director.

**Hobart Bosworth, Inc. - US - 1913-1916** - production company formed by Frank A. Garbutt, Joseph Garbutt, H.T. Rudisill and Hobart Bosworth; distributed by Bosworth-Paramount; located at 648 South Olive Street, Los Angeles, California; acquired by Morosco and Pallas Pictures in 1916.

**Hodkinson Corporation - US - 1917-1924** - distribution company formed by W. W. Hodkinson after being ousted from Paramount; Hodkinson formed several companies including Hodkinson Corp.; later reorganized as Producers Distributing Co. [see W.W. Hodkinson Corp]

**Hoffman Foursquare Pictures - US - 1917** - trade name for films produced by M. H. Hoffman, Inc. [see M. H. Hoffman, Inc.]

**Hokke-do Studio - JAPAN - 1912-1918** - production studio built by Yokota & Co. in Kyoto; after the merger of Yoshizawa Shoten, Yokota Shokia, Fukuhodo and M.

Pathe late in 1912, the studio was renamed Nikkatsu Kansai Studio; produced over 400 films before it closed in 1918.

**Holland Film Manufacturing Co. - US - 1914-1915** - production company formed by Herbert B. Holland and featuring Maude Fealy; offices were located at 105 Lawrence Ave, Roxbury district, Boston, Massachusetts; in 1915, went bankrupt and everything sold at auction.

**Hollandia Film Factory - NETHERLANDS - 1912-1923 -** [see Filmfabriek Hollandia]

**Hollywood Comedies - US - 1923-1924** - trade name for comedies released by L. K. C. Productions, Inc.

**Hollywood Pictures - US - 1925-1930** - production company.

**Hollywood Producers - US - 1926-1927** - production company.

**Holman Day Productions - US -** production company located in Augusta, Maine to produce Holman Day stories; released through Associated Exhibitors.

**Holmes Producing Corp. - US -** production company formed to produce films featuring Helen Holmes.

**Holy Land Exhibition Co., Inc. - US - 1914 -** distribution company located at 32 Union Square, New York.

**Homeland Films - UK - 1915-1916** - production company formed from Ec-Ko Film Co. to produce one, two and three reel comedies including a series called Kinekature Komedies featuring Lupino Lane and Violet Blythe (his wife); studio located at Kew Bridge closed due to World War I.

**Hope Hampton Productions, Inc. - US - 1920** - production company located at Loew Bldg., Broadway and 45th New York, with Jules Brulatour and Hope Hampton; distributed through Metro Pictures Corp.

**Horizon Pictures, Inc - US - 1921-1922** - distribution company located at Times Bldg., New York with Franklyn Backer as president.

**Horsley Manufacturing Co. - US - 1907-1908 -** production company formed by David Horsley in Bayonne, New Jersey; constantly attacked by Edison, in 1908, changed the name of the company to Centaur Film Manufacturing Co. [See Centaur Film Manufacturing Co.; Nestor Company]

**Hotex Film Manufacturing Corp. - US - 1914** - production company formed by King Vidor, John Boggs and Ed Sedgwick in

Galveston, Texas; distribution through Sawyer, Inc. but Sawyer went bankrupt at the end of the year, also bankrupting Hotex.

**Houdini Pictures Corp. - US - 1921-1923 -** production company formed by Harry Houdini and located at 220 W. 42nd Street, New York.

**Howard Productions - US - 1923** [see Samuel Goldwyn, Inc]

**Howells Films - US - 1919 -** trade name for films released by David P. Howell.

**Hudson Film Service Co. - US - 1915 -** distribution company located at 141 West 44th Street, New York.

**Hudson Bay Travel Series - US - 1921 -** trade name for one reel scenics released by Educational Film Corp.

**Hugo Ballin Productions, Inc. - US - 1920-1923 -** production company located at 366 5th Ave., New York with Hugo Ballin as president; distributed through W. W. Hodkinson.

**Hukuhou-do - JAPAN - 1912 -** production company formed by the Fukuhodo theater chain but quickly merged with Yoshizawa & Co, M-Pathe, and Yokota & Co. to form Nihon Katsudo Film, Inc., which was known as Nikkatsu. [see Yoshizawa & Co. - Yokota & Co. - M. Pathe Co.]

**Humanology Film Producing Co. - US - 1913 -** production company formed in 1913 and located in Medford, Massachusetts; Jack Rose was president; distribution through United Film Service.

**Humboldt Film GmbH - GERMANY - 1921-1932 -** production and distribution company located at Friedrichstr 235 in Berlin.

**Hunt Miller Western Production, Inc. - US - 1925 -** production company featuring Tom Foreman and two reel comedies; state rights distribution through Miller and Steen Distributors Inc.

**Hunt Stromberg Productions - US - 1922-1923 -** production company with distribution through Metro Pictures Corp.

# I

**I. Ermol'ev Co - RUSSIA - 1915-1919** - production company formed from Pathe Russia when they left during World War I, by Ermolev, who had been general manager there; Iakov Protazanov was head of production and distribution was through Pathe; closed during revolution in 1919.

**Ideal Film Co. - UK - 1911-1927** - distribution company formed by Simon Gelburg, Harry Rosenbaum, Simon Rosenbaum and Sara Wolgemouth using the trade name Ideal Films; expanded into production in 1915 with offices at 45 Gerard St. Winchester and branches in Glascow, Birmingham, Leeds, and Manchester; in 1927, merged into Gaumont British.

**Ideal Films, Ltd - US - 1915** - production company formed from Éclair with distribution through Associated Film Sales.

**Iliodor Picture Corporation - US - 1917** - production company located at 729 7th Avenue, New York, with distribution through states rights.

**IMP Films - US - 1909-1913** - trade name produced by Independent Moving Pictures Co.; distributed through Universal and their international distributors.

**Impartial Film Agency - UK - 1913-1914** - distribution company with offices at 40 Gerard St. Winchester.

**Imperial Animated Picture Co. - UK - 1913-1914 -** distribution company with offices at Hustlergate, Bradford.

**Imperial Comedies - US - 1915 -** trade name for a series of comedies produced by Fox Film.

**Imperial Film Co. of Canada - CANADA - 1918-1919 -** production company located in Calgary with William R. Marshall as general manager.

**Imperial Film Co., Ltd - US - 1913 -** production company located in St. Louis, Missouri; produced westerns distributed by Warner's Features.

**Imperial Film Exchange - US - 1910 -** distribution company located at 144 North 12th St., Philadelphia, Pennsylvania.

**Imperial Film Mfg. Co. - US - 1917 -** production company located at 956 Edgecomb Place, Chicago, Illinois.

**Imperial Films Co. - UK - 1913-1921 -** distribution company formed by Paul Kimberley as the distribution arm for Thanhouser Films; released in the UK under the trade names of Imperial Films, Princess Films and Falstaff Films; offices were located at 100 Charing Cross Rd in Westminister and then at 166-168 Shaftsbury Ave. Holborn from 1915 until February 1917; tmoved to 167-169 Wardour St. Westminister until their close in 1921.

**Imperial Productions, Inc. - US - 1921 -** located at 112 W. 44th St. New York; Joseph J. Goldstein was president and Jesse J. Goldburg was V. P. and general manager.

**Independent Distributors of America - US - 1921 -** distribution company located at 130 W. 46th St., New York; formed by Herman Rifkin, Maurice Fleckles and Ben Friedman to re-distribute Triangle Films and productions of Hamilton Film Co.

**Independent Feature Film Co. - CANADA - 1914 -** distribution company opened by M. Kashin with offices at 10 Victoria St., Montreal.

**Independent Film - UK - 1913-1914 -** distribution company with offices located at 99a Charing Cross Rd. Winchester.

**Independent Films Assoc. - US - 1920-1921 -** distribution company located on the Sixth

Floor, Consumers Building, Chicago, Illinois with Eddy Eckles as general manager; exclusive distributors of all Pinnacle Productions.

**Independent Moving Pictures Co., Inc. (IMP) - US - 1909-1913 -** production company formed by Carl Laemmle and Robert Cochrane to produce films for independent exhibitors; merged with several other companies to form Universal Pictures. [See Laemmle Film Service, Universal Pictures]

**Independent Pictures Corporation - US - 1923-1925 -** distribution and production company located at 1540 Broadway, New York, with Jesse J. Goldburg as president.

**Independent Sales Corp - US - 1918-1919 -** distribution company formed May 6, 1918 by Colonel Julian Ruppert (owner of NY Yankees) as the marketing arm of Film Clearing House; in September 1919, merged with Film Clearing House to become Hallmark Pictures Corp.

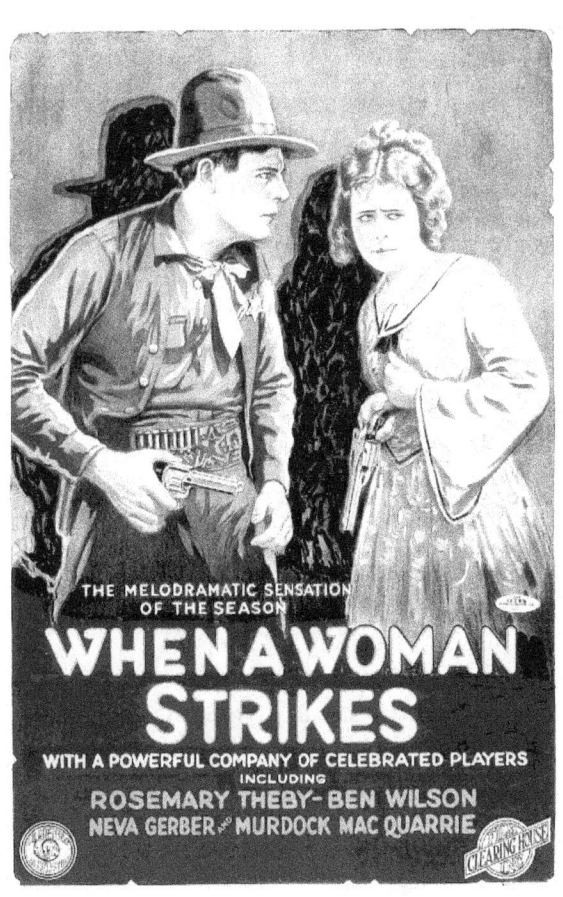

**Indo-British Film Co. - INDIA - 1918 -** production company formed by Dhirendranath Ganguly in Calcutta.

**Inkwell Studios - US - 1927-1929 -** production company formed from Out of the Inkwell Films, Inc. by Max and Dave Fleischer to produce animated comedy shorts.

**Inspiration Pictures, Inc. - US - 1921-1931 -** production company located at 565 5th Ave. New York with Charles H. Duell as president and J. Boyce Smith, Jr. as V. P.; produced films featuring Richard Barthelmess; by mid 1920s, Walter Camp, Jr. became president; distribution went through United Artists, First National, Metro Pictures and Paramount.

**Instituto Nazionale LUCE - ITALY - 1925-current -** distribution company formed from L'Unione Cinematografica Educativa (LUCE) when it was nationalized; controlled by the state and over all documentaries, newsreels and educational films in Italy; Italian law required all theaters to show a LUCE film before any feature film.

**Inter-Continent Film Co. - US - 1914 -** distribution arm for the Verafilm Co. of Rome but exported to Japan; offices located at the World's Tower Bldg at 110-112 W. 40th St., New York.

**Inter Ocean Film Co. Ltd - UK - 1917 -** distribution company for VIM Comedies and Supreme Comedies.

**Inter-Ocean Film Corp. - US - 1917-1921 -** distribution company located at Inter-Ocean Bldg., 220 W. 42nd St., New York with Henry J. Brock as president, Paul H. Cromelin as V. P. (later becoming president), George W. Newgrass as V. P., Fred Newman as secretary/treasurer and Samuel A. Herzog as general manager; exported US films; offices in London and Paris.

**Inter-Ocean Photoplays, Ltd. - UK - 1922 -** distribution company for American films in the UK, such as Arrow Films; offices at 162 Wardour St., London.

**International Cine Corp. Ltd. - UK - 1913-1914 -** distribution company for IMP Films; offices at 17 Gerrard St., Winchester.

**International Film Traders, Inc. - US - 1912 -** distribution and import company located at 5 West 14th Street, New York.

**International Film Service Co., Inc. (IFS) - US - 1914-1922 -** distribution company formed by Randolph Hearst after the success of *Perils of Pauline*; sponsored and distributed other films; in 1916, began opening exchanges in cities where Hearst newspaper was strong to release their own newsreels; in January 1917, began distributing through Pathe exchanges and formed Hearst-Pathe News; in 1919, moved distribution to Famous Players-Lasky Corp.; offices located at 127th St. and 2nd Ave., New York, with William Randolph Hearst as president and George B. Van Cleve as V. P. and general manager; closed in 1922.

**International Higher Culture Films, Inc. - US - 1921 -** production company located at 815-17 Union League Bldg. Los Angeles, California with A. L. Tull as president and R. S. Marsh as V. P.; produced six reel features

**International Moving Picture Co. - US - 1911 -** production company founded May 23, 1911 in Long Beach, California as a joint U.S. and Japanese venture with films made in both countries; studio owned by John Bowers, a local photographer and headed by Ichiro Asia who was a Japanese citizen living in Long Beach; later that year, John Bowers was shot and killed in a love triangle dispute and the studio closed.

**International Photoplay Corp. - US - 1921-1930 -** production company located at 3501-13 N. Kenton Ave. Chicago, Illinois with John Wojtalewicz as president and general manager; produced one and two reel comedies featuring Art Bates and Lou Tops.

**International Projecting and Producing Company - US - 1909 -** distribution company for international independent films; located in the Schiller Building, Chicago, Illinois.

**Interstate Feature Film Co. - US - 1915** - production company formed by a group of businessmen in Middletown, Connecticut with Kenneth MacDougall as general manager; produced feature films starring Snyder Shields; distribution through Picture Playhouse Film Co.

**Interstate Film, Inc. of New York - US - 1920** - merged with Reelcraft Pictures.

**Invicta Film Co. - UK - 1912-1915** - distribution company with offices located at 7 Rupert Court Westminster; moved to 75 Shaftsbury Ave.; distributed for Gem, Victor and Bison.

**Invincible Photoplays - US - 1921** - located at 516 5th Ave., New York with Arthur Reeves as general manager.

**Ipek Film - TURKEY - 1928** - production company opened by the Ipekci Brothers.

**Iris Film - CZECHOSLOVAKIA - 1921-1926** - distribution company.

**Irish Film Company of America - US - 1919** - production company formed by Francis J. Flynn; located at 95 Milk Street, Boston, Massachusetts; produced Irish films in America.

**Iroquois Films - US - 1920** - production distributed through Metro Pictures Corp.

**Itala Film Company - ITALY - 1908-1914** - production company formed from Carlo Rossi & Co. and located in Turin, Italy

**Itala Film Co. of America - US - 1912-1914** - distribution arm of Itala Film; located at 220 West 42nd Street, New York with Harry R. Raver as general manager.

**Italian American Film Corp. - US - 1914** - production company located in the Fitzgerald

Building, 1482 Broadway, New York.

**Italian-American Film Corp. - US - 1921 -** distribution company located at 403 Douglas Bldg., Los Angeles, California; A. Guard Hill was president and general manager.

**Italian Cinematographic Society (SITCIA) - EGYPT - 1917-1918 -** production company formed by Umberto Dores to make Egyptian films using Egyptian actors; located at 2 El Saraya St. Hadra, Alexandria; closed the following year when Banco di Roma seized the assets.

**Ivan Abrahamson Productions - US - 1921 -** production and distribution company located at 130 West 46th St. New York.

**Ivan Film Productions, Inc. - US - 1914-1917 -** production company founded by Ivan Abramson and located at 126 W. 46th St.; produced films for distribution through states rights; in 1917, Abramson left to form another company (Graphic Film Corp.) and I. E. Chadwick; became president.

---

**PROTECT YOUR POSTERS**

with
MAILING TUBES
from

**Erdie Industries, Inc.
1205 Colorado Avenue
Lorain, Ohio 44052
1-800-848-0166
www.erdie.com**

# J

**J. & N. Tait - AUSTRALIA - 1902-1920 -** production company formed by John and Nevin Tait; in 1905, produced *The Kelly Gang*, which was the first feature length film in the world; young brother Frank Tait was added to the company and a separate company, Amalgamated Pictures Ltd. was formed for distribution; in 1920, J & N Tait merged with J. C. Williamson Film Co., a subsidiary of J. C. Williamson, Ltd., with the Tait Brothers as management.

**J. C. Williamson Co. - AUSTRALIA - 1900-1909 -** production and distribution of newsreels and factuals released under the trade names of Bio-Tableau and Anglo American Bio-Tableau.

**J. C. Williamson Film Co. - AUSTRALIA - 1920-1938 -** production company formed by merger of J & N Tait and film division of J. C. Williamson, Ltd., Tait brothers were managers.

**J. C. Williamson, Ltd. - AUSTRALIA - 1909-1920 -** production company formed to work with their opera and vaudeville companies; in 1920, merged with J & N. Tait to form J. C. Williamson Film Co., a subsidiary of J. C. Williamson, Ltd. [see J & N Tait - J. C. Williamson Film Co.]

**J. C. Williamson Picture Corp. of New Zealand - New Zealand -** production company subsidiary of J. C. Williamson, Ltd.

**J. F. Brockliss, Ltd. - UK - 1911-1914 -** distribution company for Brightonia Films, Champion, Star and IMP Films with offices at 4 New Compton St. Winchester and in Paris.

**J. Frank Hatch Enterprises - US - 1919 -** production company located in the Longacre Building Room 912, 42nd Street and Broadway, New York.

**J. H. Hoffberg Co. - US - 1924-1940 -** distribution and import company formed by Jack H. Hoffberg in New York; in 1940, name changed to Hoffberg Productions; remained operational until 1970.

**J. L. Frothingham Productions - US - 1921 -** production company located at 5341 Melrose Ave. Los Angeles, California; J. L. Frothingham was president and Edward Sloman was head of production; distribution through Associated Producers.

**J. Parker Read Jr. Productions - US - 1921 -** production company utilizing the Ince Studios; J. Parker Read, Jr. was president and George D. Read was general manager; distribution through Associated Producers.

**J. Searle Dawley Productions - US - 1919-1926 -** production company.

**J. W. Film Corporation - US - 1922 -** distribution company located at 126 W. 46th Street, New York with C. J. Weinstock as president and E. S. Manheimer as general manager.

**Jack MacCullough Co. - US - 1920-1921 -** production company and studio located at 1825-31 Warren Ave. Chicago, Illinois; Jack MacCullough was president and Otto F. Wegner was secretary and general manager; produced five reel features, series and Happy Jack Comedies; used Ebony Studio for filming.

**Jacobs Photoplays - US - 1917-1919 -** [see A.H. Jacobs Photoplays, Inc.]

**Jacquelin Film Co. - US - 1921 -** production company in Chicago, Illinois with W. H. Engleman as general manager; used the Reelcraft Studios.

**James Keane Feature Photoplay Productions - US - 1916-1921 -** production company in Fairfax, California; reorganized from United Keanograph Film Manufacturing Co.; ceased operation in 1921.

**James Oliver Curwood Productions, Inc - 1920-1921 -** production company formed by James Curwood and Ernest Shipman to produce James Curwood material; distribution through First National Pictures. [see Ernest Shipman and Assoc.]

**Jamieson Film Co. - US - 1916-1972** - production company formed in Dallas, Texas to produce westerns; appears to have gone dormant in the 1920s; assets were acquired in 1972 by Masters Film Co. of Houston.

**Jans Pictures, Inc. - US - 1920-1926** - distribution company for Jans Productions, Inc. with Maurice Broskie as general manager.

**Jans Productions, Inc. - US - 1920-1926** - production company founded by Herman F. Jans to produce dramas in 1920; offices located at 729 7th Ave. Suite 1005-6, New York; used a studio in Fort Lee, New Jersey for filming; distribution through Jans Pictures, Inc. and international distribution through Export Import Film Co.

**Japanese-American Film Co. - US - 1914- -** production company created in October 1914 by Japanese businessmen to improve the quality of Japanese American films; K. Numamoto was president; distribution by Sawyer, Inc.

**Jawitz Pictures Co. - US - 1921 -** distribution company for Italian imports.

**Jaxon Film Co. - US - 1918 -** located at 220 W. 42nd St. New York with F. A. Tichenor as general manager; released under the trade names of Jaxon Comedies and Jaxon Films.

**Jesse D. Hampton Productions - US - 1918-1921 -** production company located at 7100 Santa Monica Blvd., Hollywood, and studios located at 1425 Fleming Street, Los Angeles, California; Jesse D. Hampton was owner and general manager.

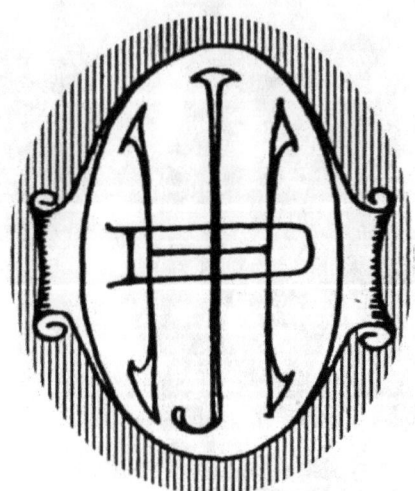

**Jesse L. Lasky Feature Play Co., Inc - US - 1914-1916 -** production company formed by Jesse L. Lasky with offices located at Long Acre Theater, W. 48th Street, New York; Samuel Goldfish was general manager and Cecil B. DeMille was director general.

**Jester Comedy Co. - US - 1917-1918 -** production company formed by William Steiner to make two reel comedies featuring Fernandez Perez as Twede-Dan; offices and studios located in Cliffside, New Jersey.

**Jewel Productions, Inc - US - 1917-1919 -** production company formed August 26, 1917 with Harry M. Berman as president and Leon J. Bamburger as general manager; located at 405 Mecca Building, New York; in June 1919, consolidated with Universal and used the trade name of Universal-Jewel.

**Jimmy Aubrey Comedies - US - 1921 -** trade name for two reel comedies produced by Vitagraph Studios.

**Jimmy Callahan Comedies - US - 1921 -** trade name for two reel comedies produced by Callahan Film Co. and distributed through Film Market, Inc.

**Joan Film Sales Co. - US - 1921 -** located at 33 W. 42nd St., New York, with Nat Rothstein as manager.

**Jockey Film Co. - US - 1916 -** production company for comedy shorts using the trade name Jockey Comedies; distributed by Unicorn Distribution.

**Joe Horwitz Productions - US - 1920-1921 -** production company for states rights distribution; located at Columbia Theatre Building, New York; moved to the Loew Annex Bldg. at 160 W. 46th St., New York.

**John M. Stahl Productions - US - 1921 -** production company located at 3800 Mission Road, Los Angeles, California with Louis B. Mayer as president; distributed by First National.

**John W. Noble Production - US - 1917 -** production company located at 1457 Broadway, New York.

**Joker Comedies - US - 1914-1915 -** trade name for one reel comedies released through Universal.

**Jolly Comedies - US - 1921 -** trade name for one and two reel comedies released through Film Sales Co.

**Joseph M. Schenck Productions - US - 1921 -** production company featuring Norma Talmadge, Constance Talmadge and Buster Keaton; located at 318 E. 48th St. New York.

**Joseph W. Farnham - US - 1916 -** distribution company located at Room 7220, West 42nd St., New York.

**Joy Comedies - US - 1920 -** trade name for one and two reel comedies produced by Gold Seal

Film Corp. and distributed by Awyon Film.

**Joy Film Distributors, Inc. - US - 1921 -** distribution company located at 117 W. 46th St., New York.

**Judy Film Co. - US - 1916 -** production company for comedy shorts released under the trade name of Judy Comedies; distributed through Unicorn Films.

**Jump Imperial Pictures Ltd. - UK - 1921-1922 -** distribution company.

**Jungle Film Co. - US - 1913 -** distribution company located at 1600 Broadway, New York; distributed for E & R Jungle Film Co.

**Juno Comedies - US - 1914-1915 -** trade name used for comedy shorts by Sunshine Film Corp.

**Jury Metro Goldwyn Ltd. - UK - 1926-1928 -** distribution company.

**Jury's Imperial Pictures Ltd. - UK - 1909-1914 -** production and distribution company formed by William Frith, Alfred Moul, James Charles Squier and William Jury; offices located at 142 Long Acre, Westminster; released under the trade name Jury's Exclusive Productions.

**Juvenile Film Corp. - US - 1915-1921 -** distribution name for Juvenile Photo Play Co.

**Juvenile Photo Play Co. - US - 1915-1921 -** production company for children's films by James A. Fitzpatrick; offices located at 310 Sloan Bldg. Cleveland, Ohio with Jacques Bergh as president.

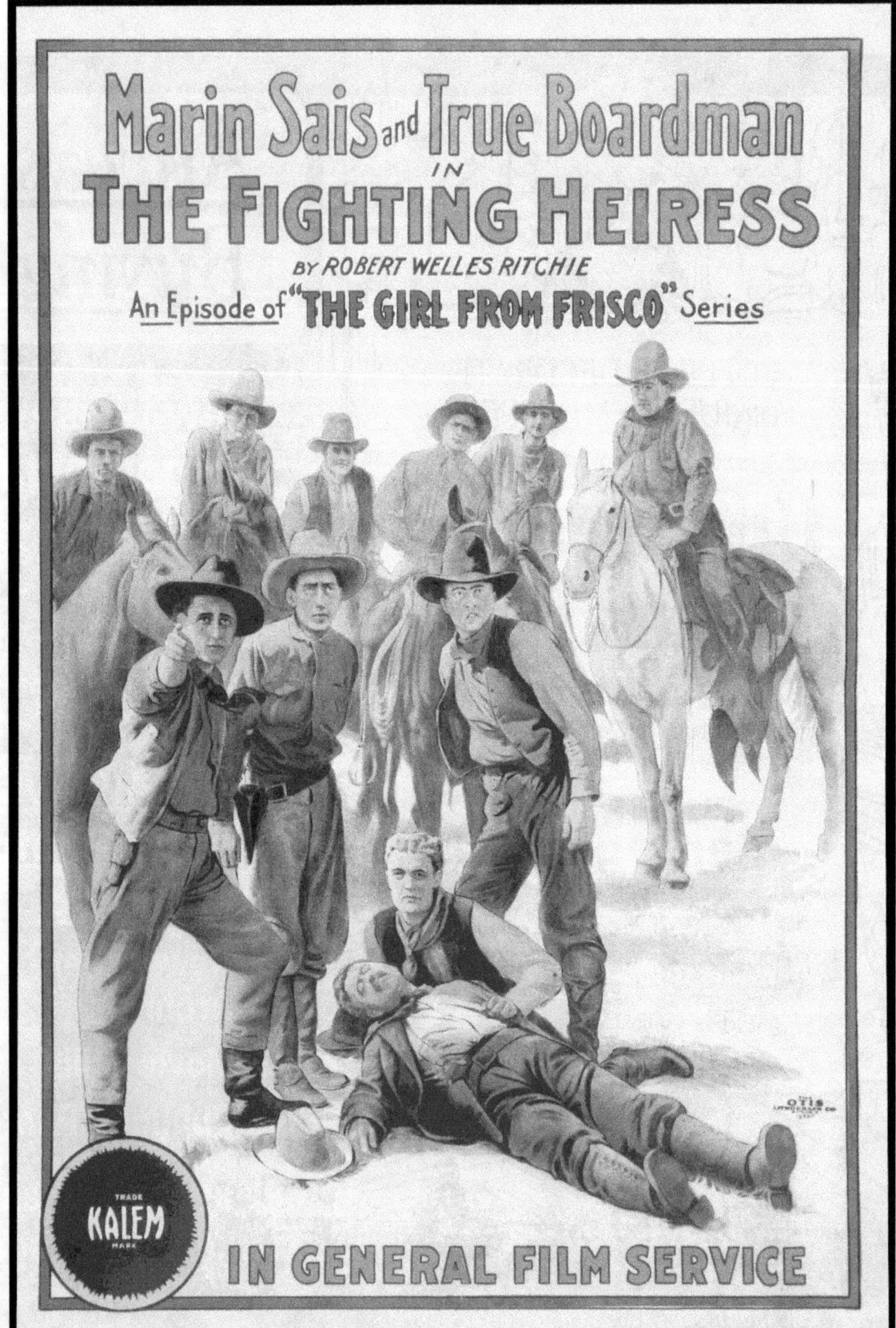

# K

**K & K Productions - US - 1921 -** production company located at 6070 Sunset Blvd. Hollywood, California; formed by I. W. Norcross and George W. Roach with Al Smith as production manager to produce childrens comedies; distributed by Olympia Productions.

**K & R Film Co. - US - 1915 -** formed in April 1915 by R. R. Roberts, Pierce Kingsley, and Frances Kell with Leon Victor as general manager; offices located in the Putnam Bldg at 1493 Broadway, New York.

**K. C. Booking Co, Inc. - US - 1914** - distribution company located at 126-132 West 46th Street, New York with Ira H. Simmons as general manager; imported films from Ambrosia Co. of Italy, Kinetophote Film Corp. and Hollandia Film Co.

**K-E-S-E Service - US - 1915-1917 -** distribution company for **K**leine, **E**dison, **S**elig, and **E**ssanay.

**Kahn Kid Komedies - US - 1924 -** production company formed by Ivan Kahn to produce short comedies featuring children.

**Kaiser Film Company - US - 1914-1915** - production company located at 110 W. 40th Street, New York.

**Kalem Film Manufacturing Co. - US - 1907-1919** - production company formed by George **K**leine, Samuel **L**ong and Frank **M**arion; company name was created from the first initial of each last name (K - L - M); located at 131 W. 24th St., New York; boasted numerous firsts, i.e., first to create a stock company, first to use the actors names, and first to test literary rights in court; filmed in New Jersey and Florida and sent film crews to Ireland and Palestine; established a California studio in Glendale on December 11, 1910; built a studio in Cliffside, New Jersey that was used from 1912-1915; distributed through General Film until 1916 when they stopped production; sold to Vitagraph in 1919.

**Kalem-Ham Comedy Co. - US -** [see Ham Comedy Co.]

**Katherine MacDonald Pictures Corp. - US - 1919-1921 -** [see Ambassador Pictures, Inc.]

**Kay-Bee - US -1912-1918 -** production company formed by Adam Kessel and Charles Baumann as a subsidiary of New York Motion Picture Co. after they left Universal; (Kay Bee was for **K**essel and **B**aumann).

**Kemal Film Co. - TURKEY - 1922-1923** - production company (first private production company in Turkey) opened by the Seded Brothers; closed the following year.

**Kemble Film Corporation - US - 1916** - production and distribution company located at 587 Fulton Street, Brooklyn, New York.

**Kendall Chambers Corp. - US - 1921 -** formed by Messmore Kendall and Robert W. Chambers; located at Capitol Theatre Bldg., Broadway and 51st St., New York.

**Kennedy Features Inc. - US - 1914** - production company formed by Aubrey M. Kennedy and Irving Ackerman to produce feature films; offices located at 110 W. 40th St., New York, in the World's Tower Bldg.; distribution through Criterion Feature Film Manufacturing Co.

**Kerman Film Exchange - US - 1924** - distribution company for New York and New Jersey by states rights; located at 729 Seventh Street, New York.

**Kessel-Baumann Picture Corp. - US** - production company formed by Adam Kessell and Charles Baumann; instrumental in the formation of Universal Film in 1912 but pulled out and left Laemmle to become president; became part of Triangle films with Aitken and released using several trade names - Bison (before Universal), 101-Bison (after Universal), Broncho, Domino, Kay-Bee Films, Keystone, and Tri-Stone films for Triangle rereleases.

**Keystone Film Co. - 1912-1917 -** production company formed by Adam Kessel, Charles O. Baumann and Mack Sennett with offices located at 150 East 14th Street, New York and studios at 1712 Allesandro Street in Edendale, California; produced comedy shorts distributed by Mutual Film Corp. (1912-1916), Triangle Film Corp. (1916-1917) and Triangle Distributing Corp. (1917); company sold to Triangle Film Corp. in June 1917.

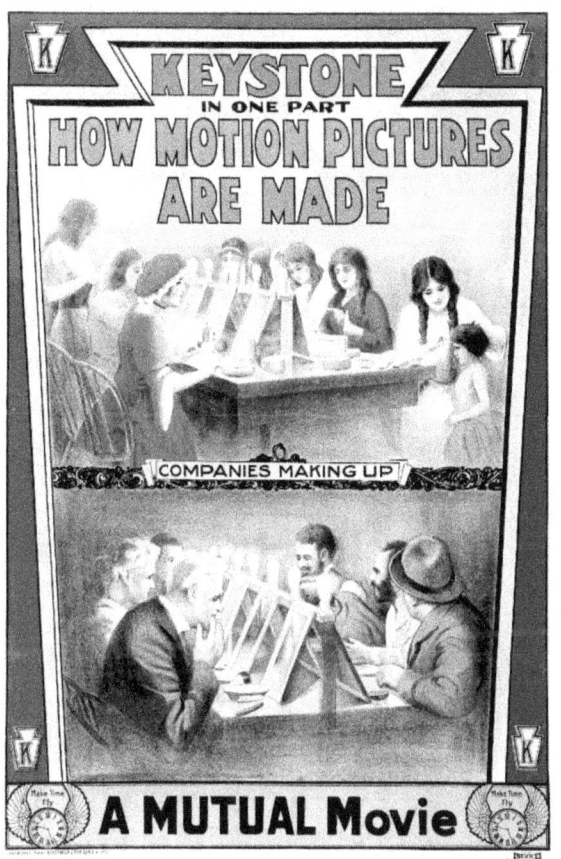

**Khanzhonkov Co. - RUSSIA - 1908-1917 -** [see A. Khanzhonkov Co.]

**Kinema Exclusives - UK - 1915 -** distribution company located at 30 Gerrard St. Westminster.

**Kinematograph Trading Company - UK - 1912-1914 -** distribution company formed by Robert Bailey Chattey, Constance Parfrey, Emma Poole and George Poole with offices at 55-59 Shaftesbury Ave. Westminster.

**Kineto Company of America, Inc. - US - 1920-1921 -** production company with offices located at 71 W. 23rd St., New York, and studio at Irvington-on-Hudson, New York; Charles Urban was president, M. E. A. Tucker was secretary and F. R. Minrath was treasurer.

**Kineto Film Exchange - US - 1912** - distribution company located at 32 Union Square, New York.

**Kineto Ltd. - UK - 1907-1910 -** distribution company formed by Frederick Gardner Clark and Charles Urban with John Avery as general manager; offices located at 80-82 Wardour St., Westminster; distributed for Kalem and Urban Science.

**Kinetograph Co. - US - 1913 -** distribution company formed by J. J. Kennedy and P. L. Waters on Feb. 9, 1913 with branches in New York, Atlanta and New Orleans; acquired by General Film Co.

**Kinetophote Film Corp. - US - 1914 -** distribution company with Ira H. Simmons as general manager; imported and distributed for Ambrosia Co. of Italy and Hollandia Film Co.; formed sister company, K. C. Booking Co, Inc., to handle U. S. distribution.

**Kinetrol Film Agency Ltd. - UK - 1913-1916 -** distribution company formed by Frederick Josiah Harrington and Henri Valeriani; offices locate at 132 Charing Cross Road Westminster.

**King-Bee Films Corp. - US - 1917 -** production company formed by Louis B. Burstein to make Billy West Comedies; offices located at Suite 924, Longacre Building, 42nd Street and Broadway, New York, with studios in Jacksonville, Florida.

**King Cole Comedies - US - 1916 -** trade name for one-reel comedies featuring William (Smiling Bill) Parsons and distributed through Pathe Exchange, Inc.

**King Vidor Productions - US - 1920-1922** - production company with offices and studio at 7100 Santa Monica Blvd. Hollywood, California; distributed through First National.

**Kinofa - CZECHOSLOVAKIA - 1908-1914** - first production company in Czechoslovakia founded by Antonin Pech; produced newsreels, nature films and comedy shorts; had some international success but ended due to the World War I.

**Kinografen - DENMARK - 1906-1913** - production company formed by Alex Christian and Peter Elfelt; films distributed in United States by Box Office Attraction Film Rental Company.

**Kinograph Company of America - US - 1912-1913** - distribution and import company located at 145 W. 45th Street, New York, for films made by Kinograph Co. of Copenhagen.

**Kinograph Company of Copenhagen - DENMARK - 1912** - production company located in Copenhagen, Denmark.

**Kinosev - RUSSIA - 1917-1925** - production studio in Leningrad; reorganized in 1925 as Sovkino.

**Kipling Film Exchange, Inc. - US** - distribution company for Richard Kipling Enterprises; formed by Richard Kipling, R. A. Sullivan and S. J. Sullivan; located at 802 S. Olive St. Los Angeles, California.

**Kitty Gordon Co. - US - 1916-1917** - production company with distribution by Lewis J. Selznick Productions; became Select Pictures in 1917.

**Klaw & Erlanger - US - 1913-1916** - production company with distribution through General Film Company.

**Kleine-Edison Feature Service - US - 1915-1916 -** distribution company formed in June 1915 to distribute films by the two companies but was replaced starting September 2, 1916 by Kleine-Edison-Selig-Essanay Service; distributed through the George Kleine exchanges.

**Kleine Optical Co. - US - 1907-1928 -** primarily a distributor of European films and a member of the Edison Trust.

**Klever Komedies - US - 1916-1919** - trade name used by New York based Klever Pictures, Inc.

**Klever Pictures, Inc. - US - 1916-1919 -** production company located in New York; produced comedies featuring Victor Moore with Jackson and Chester M. Vonde directing; released under the trade name, "Klever Komedies"; filmed at 29 E. 9th St. Jacksonville, Florida.

**Klimax Pictures - US - 1921 -** states rights distribution company located at 17 East Seventh Street, Chicago, Illinois.

**Klotz & Streimer, Inc. - US - 1917** - distribution company located at 126 West 46th Street, New York.

**Kluthe Studios - US - 1917 -** production company located at 30 W. 9th St. Jacksonville, Florida.

**Knickerbocker Star Features - US - 1915-1917 -** production company formed May 1915 with Stanner E. V. Taylor as head of production and located in Flushing, New York; offices locatedat 326 Lexington Ave., New York and distribution through General Film Co.; in February 1917, taken over by Balboa Amusement; trade name continued as a section of Balboa Amusement Producing Co. and released through General Film Co.

**Ko-Ko Films - US - 1915 -** production company located at One Wall Street, New York.

**Komedia Filmi - FINLAND - 1926-1927 -** production and distribution company formed by German cinematographer Jager; distributed German Ufanamet films to Finland.

**Kosmik Films, Inc. - US - 1912 -** production company distributed through George Kleine.

**Kosmofilm - POLAND - 1912-1914 -** production company formed in Warsaw by Henryk Finkelstein and Samuel Ginzberg to produce Yiddish films; in 1914, absorbed by Sfinks Studio.

**Krackerjack Komedies, Inc - US - 1921 -** production company located at Knickerbocker Theatre Bldg. 116 W. 39th St., New York, with Frederick A. Blumberg as president and James A. Montalbano as V. P. and treasurer; produced two reel comedies.

**Kremer Films - US -** [see Victor Kremer Film Features]

**Kriterion Film Corp. - US - 1914-1915 -** distribution company formed November 1914 by C. H. Ayres, E. H. Reilly and H. F. Rhatigan for Alhambra Motion Picture Co., Crown City Film Manufacturing, Liberty Film Co., Mica Film Co., Monarch Producing Co., Monty Films, Nash Motion Picture Co., Inc., Navajo Film Manufacturing, Robin's Photoplays, Inc., Santa Barbara Motion Picture Co.; offices located at 1600 Broadway New York; distributed approximately 21 films per week as a package called Kriterion Program; mid 1915, Associated Film Service Corp. began distributing their films.

**Kulee Features - US - 1915-1916 -** production and distribution company that handled some of Photo Drama material.

# L

**L. Gaumont and Co. - FRANCE** [see Gaumont Film Co.]

**L. K. C. Productions, Inc. - US - 1923-1924** - production company for Hollywood Comedies distributed by Selznick Distributing Corp.

**L-KO Motion Picture Kompany - US - 1914-1919** - formed by Henry M. Lehrman [Lehrman-Knock Out] on July 14, 1914 with studios at Sunset Blvd. and Gower St. in Hollywood; filmed comedies distributed through Universal; Lehrman left the studio in 1917 and joined Fox Film to produce the Sunshine Comedies.

**L-Ko Pictures Co. - US - 1920-1921** - distribution company located at 1600 Broadway, New York, with Julius Stern as president, Abe Stern as V. P. and Louis Jacobs as general manager; rereleased Lehrman Knock Out comedies.

**L. L. Hiller - US - 1919** - distribution company located in the Longacre Building, 42nd & Broadway, New York.

**L. Lawrence Weber & Bobby North - US - 1922** - production and distribution company located at 1600 Broadway, New York.

**L. Lawrence Weber Photo Dramas, Inc. - US - 1921** - production company located at Longacre Theatre, 48th St. and Broadway, New York; L. Lawrence Weber was president, Lee Shubert was V. P. and Bobby North was secretary/treasurer and general manager; produced feature films.

**L'Unione Cinematografica Educativa (LUCE) - ITALY - 1924-1925** - production company formed by the state to provide documentaries and educational films; in 1925, name changed to Instituto Nazionale LUCE.

**Labadie-Detroit Motion Picture Co. - US - 1915-1916** production company formed by Oliver Ladadie and located on Labadie Island, Kent Lake in New Hudson, Michigan.

**Lacal Productions - US - 1921** - production company located at 224 O. T. Johnson Bldg. Los Angeles, California; formed by M. A. Robin, R. C. Wilson and Frank Thorwald to make two reel westerns.

**Laclede Western Features - US - 1913-1914** - trade name for westerns produced by Lloyd Films, Inc.

**Lady Mackenzie Film Company - US - 1915** - distribution company located at 1004-7 Candler Building, 220 West 42d Street, New York.

**Laemmle Film Service - US - 1909-1913** - distribution company founded in Chicago and Minneapolis by Carl Laemmle and Robert Cochrane; merged with other companies to become Universal.

**Lafco Comedies - US - 1917** - trade name for one reel comedies produced by La Salle Film Co. and distributed by Mutual.

**Lama Studio - EGYPT - 1930-1953** - production company formed by brothers Ibrahim and Badr Lama as a re-formation of their company, Condor Films, from Alexandria to Cairo.

**Lariat Co. - US - 1914-1916** - trade name for films produced by Pike's Peak Film Co. and distributed by United Film Service

**Lariat Productions - US - 1925** - production company specializing in westerns. (no affiliation with Lariat Co.)

**Larry Semon Comedies - US - 1921** - trade name for comedy shorts featuring Larry Semon and distributed by Vitagraph Co. of America.

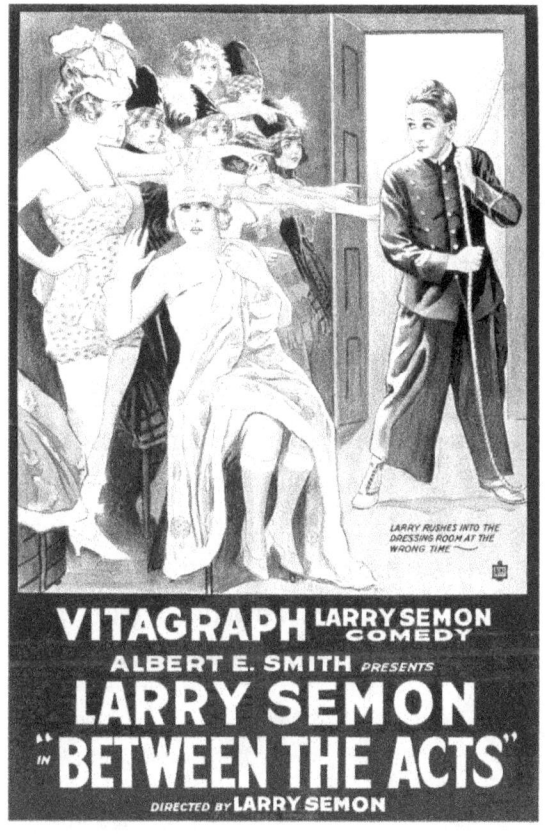

**Lasalida Films, Inc. - US - 1917 -** production company formed in April 1917 producing Baby Marie Osborne films; W. A. S. Douglas was V. P. and general manager; distribution through Pathe Exchanges; closed end of 1917 when Douglas and Baby Osborne's father opened a new studio, Diando Films, to produce their films.

**LaSalle Film Co. - US - 1917 -** production company located at 1450 Dayton St. Chicago, Illinois with B. F. Lewis as president; formed to produce one reel comedies for Mutual called Lafco Comedies; used studios in Hollywood and then moved to Culver City.

**Lascelle Co. - US - 1921-1927 -** production company formed by Ward Lascelle.

**Lasky Pictures - US - 1913-1914 -** production company founded in 1913 by Jesse Lasky, Samuel Goldfish and Cecil B. DeMille; - merged in 1914 with Adolph Zukor to form Famous Players-Lasky.

**Laugh-o-Gram Films, Inc. - US - 1922-1923** formed by Walt Disney and Ub Iwwerks on May 23, 1922 in Kansas City, Missouri; produced animated shorts for the Newman Theatre Co.; Disney left in 1923 for Hollywood to form Disney Bros. Studio.

**Lawrence Weber Photo Dramas, Inc.** - US - 1921 - [see Apollo Trading Corp.]

**Le Film d'Art** - FRANCE - 1908-1909 - production company formed by Paul Laffitte and located in Paris.

**Lea Bel Co.** - US - 1914-1917 - production company located at 912 Schiller Building, Chicago, Illinois.

**Leading Players Film Corporation** - US - 1913-194 - distribution company located at the Leavitt Building, 126-130 W. 46 Street, New York.

**Leah Baird Productions** - US - 1920-1923 - production company located at Ince Studio, Culver City, California.

**Lederer's Celebrities Film Co.** - US - 1913-1914 - production company formed by George W. Lederer with distribution through Warner Bros.-Warner's Features.

**Lee-Bradford Corp.** - US - 1924-1925 - production and distribution company formed in New York by Arthur A. Lee and F. G. Bradford to produce a series of comedies under the trade name of Lightning Comedies; imported British films for distribution through states rights; Bradford died in 1925; Lee closed Lee-Bradford Corp. and opened AmerAnglo Corp.

**Leeds Film Supply - UK - 1913-1914** - distribution company with offices located at 9 Wellington St. Leeds.

**Legend Film Productions - US - 1920-1921** - production company located at 47 West 42nd Street, Suite 305, New York; formed by Ernest Shipman to produce two reel comedies. [see Ernest Shipman and Associates]

**Leningradkino - RUSSIA - 1920s-current** - production company formed from Kinosev which had opened in 1917; name changed several times and finally in 1934, the name was changed to Lenfilm which still remains.

**Leofilm - POLAND - 1924-1929** - production company formed in Warsaw by Leo Forbert, who also owned the largest processing lab in Poland.

**Leonce Perret Productions - US - 1921** - production company located at 220 W. 42nd St., New York.

**Les Artistes Associes S. A. - FRANCE - 1921-1960s+** - distribution arm for United Artists with offices at 20 Rue D'Aguesseau, Paris; used the old U/A coffin logo.

**Les Films Celebres - FRANCE - 1918** - distribution company with offices located at 36 Rue de Mont-Thabor, Paris.

**Lester Cuneo Productions - US - 1921** - production company for films featuring Lester Cuneo and distributed through Capitol Film Co.

**Lew Cody Films Corp. - US - 1919** - production company located in Glendale, California.

**Lewis J. Selznick Enterprises, Inc. - US - 1916-1917** - distribution company formed April 1916 by Lewis Selznick after he left as V.P. and general manager of World Film Corp.; offices located at 126 W. 46th Street, New York; Selznick took Clara Kimball Young from World Film and created her own Clara Kimball Young Corp. with himself as president of CKY Corp.; distribution of her films was through Lewis J. Selznick Inc.; also distributed for Herbert Brenon Film Corp., Kitty Gordon Co. and Norma Talmadge Film Corp.; opened film exchanges all over the country owning 50% of each exchange (and 50% local); in August 1917, Adolph Zukor acquired controlling interest and had the name of the company changed to Select Pictures Corp.; moved filming to the Lasky studio but left Selznick as president; in April 1919, Selznick bought out Zukor's interest for over $1 million, leaving Selznick strapped and Zukor cash rich. Select Pictures went bankrupt in 1923.

**Lewis Pennant Features - US - 1913-1914** - distribution company.

**Liberty Film Co. - US - 1914-1915** - production company located in San Mateo, California with S. Lindblom as president; distributed through Kriterion; merged to form Associated Film Service Corp. in 1915.

**Liberty Film Exchange - US - 1908-1909** - distribution company located at 12 N. 13th Street, Philadelphia, Pennsylvania.

**Liberty Motion Picture Co. - US - 1914** - production company formed July 1914 in Germantown, Pennsylvania with John Oxford as president and Howard G. Bobb as general manager; distribution through Sawyer, Inc.; in November 1914, reorganized, moved to San Mateo California and changed name to Liberty Film Co.

**Life Photo Film Corp. - US - 1914-1916** - production company located in Grantwood, New Jersey with Edward M. Roskam as president and Jesse J. Goldburg as secretary and general manager; initially distributed through states rights; briefly signed with Alco Film at the end of 1914, but recanted and signed with Paramount; had sister company, Commercial Motion Pictures Co., that filmed sports events with Roskam and Goldburg also as officers; in 1915, Roskam resigned and was replaced by Bernard Loewenthal; sold to Twentieth Century Film Co. in 1916.

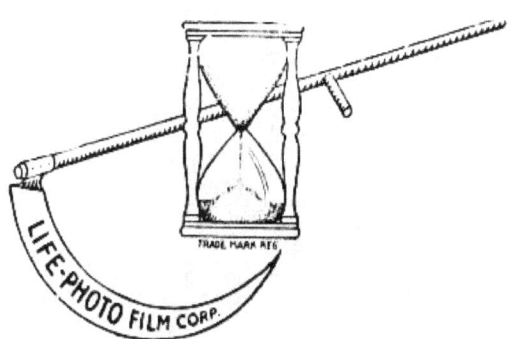

**Lightning Comedies - US - 1925-1926** - trade name for comedy series produced by Lee-Bradford Corp.

**Lillian Walker Pictures Corp. - US - 1918-1919** - production company located at 501 Fifth Ave., New York, with Lester Park as president.

**Lily Film Co - US - 1916** - production company with distribution through Unicorn Distributors.

**Lincoln & Parker Film Co. - US - 1914-1918** - production and distribution company located at Worcester, Massachusetts with F. H. Lincoln as president and J. H. Parker as treasurer; Edison's son was on the board; acquired Edison's plant and studio in 1918.

**Lincoln Motion Picture Co., Inc. - US - 1914-1921** - production company formed in Los Angeles by Noble Johnson and George P. Johnson to produce black race films; distribution in the Midwest (primarily Nebraska); in 1920, Johnson became an actor for Universal Studios and James Smith became president and Harry A. Grant became general manager; distribution by states rights; closed in 1921.

**Lions Head Films - UK - 1901-1913** - trade name for Cricks and Sharp from 1901-1908; trade name continued when the studio name was changed to Cricks and Martin from 1908-1913.

**Live Wire Comedy - US - 1926-1930** - trade name for comedies produced by William M. Pizor.

**Livingston Productions - US - 1921** - located at 2435 Wilshire Blvd., Santa Monica, California.

**Lloyd Carleton Productions - US - 1920-1925** - production company located at 6070 Sunset Blvd., Hollywood, California; distribution through Selznick.

**Lloyd Films - US - 1913-1914** - production company located at 220 W. 42nd St., New York, with Charles Abrams as general manager; released under trade name Laclede Western Features; distributed through Exclusive until they closed in 1914.

**Lloyd-Rowan Features - US - 1913** - distribution company located at Plymouth Hotel, 38th Street, New York.

**Loew Metro Goldwyn - BELGIUM - 1927** - distribution arm for MGM.

**Lois Weber Productions - US - 1916-1921** - production company located at 4634 Santa Monica Blvd., Los Angeles, California, with Lois Weber president and William H. Carr general manager; distribution through Famous Players-Lasky.

**London - US - 1913-1921** - trade name for films released by London Film Co., Ltd.

**London and Country Film Service - UK - 1913-1914** - distribution company with offices located at 104 Wardour St. Winchester.

**London Cinematograph Co. Ltd - UK - 1909-1910** - distribution company formed by Roland George Hill, Sydney Boyle Lawrence, Frederick Arthur Charles Mouillot, Sydney George Vernham, William MacLean Borradaile, and George W. Jones as general manager; offices located at 154 Charing Cross Road Westminster; distributed for Theo, Pathe and Bison.

**London Film Co., Ltd. - UK - 1913-1921** - production and distribution company located in London with films released under the trade name of London; distributor for Lagium Films with offices at St. Margarets, Twickenham.

**London Independent Film Trading Co. - UK - 1913-1920** - distribution company formed by George Bingham, Enrique Carreras, Carlos Jauralde, Santiago Laborda, James Charles Squier and Aurelio Valls with offices at 10 Little St. Holborn.

**Lone Star Co. - US - 1915-1917** - production company formed in San Antonio, Texas by Patrick Sylvester McGeeney; distributed through Mutual Film. In 1917, they reorganized as Shamrock Photoplay Corp.

**Lone Star Film Productions - US - 1921** - production company with offices at 1745 Glendale Blvd. Hollywood, California; W. J. Forrester was president and W. J. Miller was V. P.; produced five reel westerns featuring Ranger Bill Miller.

**Lone Star Corporation - US - 1916-1917** - production company formed by the Mutual Film Corporation solely to make Charlie Chaplin films with studio located at 1025 Lillian Way, Hollywood, California.

**Louis B. Mayer Productions, Inc. - US - 1918-1926** - production company with offices at 6 W. 48th St., New York, and 3800 Mission Road, Los Angeles, California with Louis B. Mayer as president and general manager; distribution through First National.

**Louis Jacobson Enterprises, Inc. - US - 1921** - located at 110 W. 42nd St., New York

**Lubin Co. - UK - 1912-1916** - distribution arm in the UK for Lubin Films with offices at 4 New Compton St. Holborn.

**Lubin Manufacturing Co. - US - 1897-1918** - production and distribution company formed by Sigmund Lubin in Philadelphia, Pennsylvania; expanded with studios in Florida, Nassau, Los Angeles, Phoenix, New Orleans, and Coronade, California; built largest enclosed studio in the country on a 500 acre estate Lubin purchased from John Betz in Philadelphia in 1912; in April 1915, joined with Vitagraph, Selig and Essanay to form V-L-S-E Distributors; in 1918, studios were acquired by Vitagraph except for the Phildelphia studio which became Betzwood Film Co. and was operated by his son-in-law, Ira M. Lowry.

**Lucernafilm - CZECHOSLOVAKIA - 1914-1949** - production company founded by Vaclav Havel Prague.

**Lucky Cat Films - UK - 1919-1922** - trade name for comedy shorts featuring Guy Newal and produced by George Clark Productions.

**Lule Warrenton Photoplays - US - 1917** - trade name for films distributed by Warrenton Photoplays Film Distributing Co.

**Lumas Film Corp. - US - 1924-1929** - production company located at 1650 Broadway, New York. with Sam Sax as president.

**Luna Film Co. - UK - 1913-1915** - production and distribution company formed by Raoul Paul, Horace Chabauty, Lucien Georges Ergot and Sydney George Vernham with offices at 63 Leigham Court Road, Streatham.

**Luna Films - US - 1913-1918** - trade name used by Albuquerque Film Company and distributed through United Film Service.

**Luna-Film - BELGIUM - 1925** - distribution company located in Bruxelles.

**Lupu Pick Produktion - GERMANY - 1919-1930** - production company in Berlin.

**Lux Films - FRANCE** [see Societe Lux]

**Lyyra Filmi - FINLAND** (before independence) **- 1914-1916** - production company formed by Hjalmar V. Pohjanheimo to produce short comedies and art films; closed by Russian decree as this was part of Russia until the independence in 1917.

# M

**M. Baer and Co. - UK - 1913-1914** - distribution company with offices located at 28 Gerrard St. Winchester.

**M. Fernand Weill - FRANCE - 1915-1939** - [see Fernand Weill]

**M. H. Hoffman, Inc. - US - 1917-1924** - production and distribution company located at 729 Seventh Ave., New York, and distributed under trade name of Hoffman Foursquare Pictures.

**M. J. Winkler Productions - US - 1922-1926** - distribution company formed by Margaret Winkler with offices at 220 W. 42nd St. New York; distributed animated comedy shorts for Fleischer's Out of the Inkwell, Pat Sullivan and Walt Disney; distribution through states rights or to larger distributors such as Universal or FBO.

**M. P. Sales Agency - UK - 1913-1914** - distribution company for Aquila Film, Biograph Brightonia, Cabot, Comet, Film d'Art, F.P.P., Geem, Milano, Pilot, Roma, Searchlight, Shamrock, Kalem, Special, Welt and Solax Films with offices at 86 Wardour St. Winchester.

**M. Pathe Co. - JAPAN - 1905-1912** - production company formed by Umeya Shokichi without any association with Pathe or Yokota; in 1912, merged with Yokota & Co., Yoshizawa & Co., and Hukuhou-do to form Nihon Katsudo Film, Inc., which was known as Nikkatsu.

**Mabel Normand Feature Film Co - US - 1916-1918** production company formed in April 1916 by Mack Sennett and Adam Kessel, Jr., featuring Mabel Normand; located in the Loneacre Bldg.. New York.

**Mac Dons Cartoons, Inc. - US - 1922** - production company of cartoon shorts and distributed through Educational Films.

**Mac Lean Productions - UK - 1924** - production company formed by Hugh Mac Lean and located in London.

**Mac Manus Corporation - US - 1919** - production company located at No. 2 West 47th St., New York.

**Macauley Photoplays, Inc. - US - 1919-1921** - production company with offices at 516 Fifth Ave., New York and I. W. Hellman Bldg., Los Angeles, California; C. R. Macauley was president and general manager.

**Mack Sennett Productions - US - 1918-1928** - production company located at 1712 Glendale Blvd, Los Angeles, California; specialized in comedies.

**Mack Swain Comedies - US - 1921** - trade name for two reel comedies featuring Mack Swain and distributed by Herald Productions.

**Macnamara Feature Film Co., Inc. - US - 1914** - production company formed by Walter Macnamara and located at 126 W. 46th Street, New York.

**Madoc Sales Co. - US - 1923-1925** - distribution company located in New York specializing in westerns.

**Magnet Comedies - US - 1914-1915** - trade name for comedy shorts produced by Sunshine Film Corp.

**Magnet Film Co. Ltd - UK - 1913-1914** - distribution company with offices at 9 St. Martin's Court, Winchester that distributed films of stage plays.

**Magnet Film Releasing Co. - US - 1914** - distribution company with offices located at 110 W. 40th Street, New York.

**Maguire & Baucas, Ltd - UK - 1895-1897** - distribution company opened in London by Frank Maguire and Joseph Baucas to distribute Edison films and equipment; in 1896, added Lumiere films and in 1897, Charles Urban took control and changed the name to Warwick Trading Co.

**Majestic Motion Picture Co. - US - 1911-1917** - production company formed September 1911 by Harry E. Aitken and Roy Aitken to produce Mary Pickford films with her husband Owen Moore and Thomas D. Cochrane; offices were located at 145 W. 45th St. New York; distribution through Mutual Film Corp.; Pickford returned to Biograph the following year; in 1914, moved to 4500 Sunset Blvd. with Reliance Motion Picture to be supervised by D. W. Griffith; called Reliance-Majestic Studios until 1915 when considered part of Fine Arts and distribution moved to Triangle; Majestic Motion Picture Co. was officially sold to Triangle Film Corp. in 1917; also had a studio in Jacksonville, Florida.

**Mandarin Film Co. - US - 1917 -** production company formed in Oakland, California in 1917 with Marion E. Wong as president; produced films showing Chinese in a more positive light.

**Manhattan Film Rental Company - US - 1908 -** distribution company located at 120 East 23rd Street, New York, with C. B. Purdy as general manager.

**Maoriland Films - NEW ZEALAND - 1921-1922 -** trade name used by New Zealand Moving Picture Co. Ltd.

**Mappemonde Film - FRANCE - 1925 -** distribution company for Palladium Films.

**Marguerite Clark Productions - US - 1921 -** production company located at 807 E. 175th St., New York; produced films featuring Marguerite Clark and distributed through First National Pictures.

**Marine Film Co. - US - 1917 -** production company formed in Hollywood in 1917 with M. Phillip Hansen as general manager and Henry Otto as production manager; used the old Kalem studios for production.

**Mario-Cartoons - UK - 1914-1915 -** trade name for a series of marionette cartoons produced by Bamforth and Co.

**Marion Davies Film Corp. - US -** [see Cosmopolitan Pictures]

**Marion Fairfax Productions - US - 1921 -** production company located at 6642 Santa Monica Blvd. Hollywood, California with Marion Fairfax as president and John Jasper as general manager.

**Marion H. Kohn Productions - US - 1920 -** production company located at 1600 Broadway, New York with distribution through Goldwyn.

**Marion Leonard Film Co. - US - 1913-1914 -** production company headed by S. E. V. Taylor and distributed by Warner Bros. - Warner's Features.

**Mark M. Dintenfass Productions - US - 1919-1922** - production company located at 220 W. 42st Street, New York; produced Cuckoo Comedies.

**Marnell & Keen - US - 1914 -** production company formed by David Marnell and Morris Keen; specialized in westerns.

**Mars Comedies - US - 1914-1915 -** trade name used for comedy shorts produced by Sunshine Film Corp.

**Marshall Neilan Productions, Inc.** - production company located at 6642 Santa Monica Blvd., Hollywood, California; Marshall Neilan was president and L. L. Baxterw as general manager; distribution through First National.

**Martin and Sanders - UK - 1913-1914** - distribution company with offices at 20 Charing Cross Rd., Winchester.

**Martin Johnson Film Co. - US - 1921** - production company with distribution through Robertson Cole.

**Martin's Feature Films - UK - 1913-1915** - distribution company with offices located at 28 Gerrard St., Winchester.

**Mary Pickford Film Corp. - US - 1916-1921** - production company created in August 1916 to produce films featuring Mary Pickford; Adolph Zukor was president and Charlotte Pickford (Mary's mother) was treasurer; distribution was through newly formed Artcraft Pictures Corp. to distinguish them from standard Paramount Pictures releases.

**Mary Pickford Co. - US - 1919-1921** - production company formed to separate Pickford productions from the Mary Pickford Film Corp. which was controlled by Adolph Zukor and Charlotte Pickford (Mary's mother); offices located at 5341 Melrose Ave. Los Angeles, California; Charlotte Pickford Smith was general manager; distribution was through United Artists.

**Mascot Film Co. - UK - 1913-1914** - distributor with offices at Greek St., Winchester.

**Mascot Pictures Corp. - US - 1927-1935** - production company formed by Nat Levine to produce western serials featuring John Wayne, Rin-Tin-Tin et al; early 1930s, expanded to feature films; in 1935, merged with Monogram and Consolidated Laboratories to form Republic Pictures.

**Masko Film Co. - US - 1912-1914 -** production and distribution company located at 145 West 45th Street, New York.

**Master Drama Features Inc. - US - 1917** - production company located at 1473 Broadway, New York.

**Master Films - UK - 1917-1923 -** production company with Harry B. Parkinson as general manager; filming was done at Weir House, Teddington with distribution through British Exhibitors Films and later by Butchers.

**Master Pictures, Inc. - US - 1921 -** production company located at 135 W. 44th Street, New York, with C. C. Burr as president; produced "Torchy Comedies" distributed by Educational Film Exchanges.

**Mastercraft Photo-Play Corp. - US - 1918 -** formed in Boston, Massachusetts with F. Eugene Farnsworth as president and Isaac Wolper as general manager.

**Masterpiece Film Attractions - US - 1918 -** distribution company with B. Amsterdam as general manager with offices located at 1225 Vine St. Philadelphia, Pennsylvania.

**Masterpiece Film Distributing Corp - US - 1920** - distribution company located at 207 South Wabash Ave., Chicago, Illinois with Phil H. Solomon as manager; distributed through states rights for Illinois, Indiana and Wisconsin.

**Masterpiece Film Manufacturing Co. - US - 1913-1914** - formed by Harry Aitkens with offices located at 1111 Van Nuys Building, Los Angeles, California; distributed through Reliance until late 1914 when Aitkens combined his companies to create Mutual Films.

**Mastodon Films, Inc. - US - 1922-1923** - formed by C. C. Burr to produce Burr Scenics with offices located at 135 W. 44th St. New York and studios on Long Island; distributed by states rights and also distributed for All Star Comedies, Earl Hurd Comedies, and Torchy Comedies.

**Matty Roubert Comedies - US - 1921** - trade name for two reel comedies featuring Matty Roubert produced by Matty Roubert Productions and distributed by Reelcraft Pictures Corp.

**Matty Roubert Productions, Inc. - US - 1920** - production company located at 1457 Broadway, New York.

**Maurice Tourneur Productions - US - 1918-1924** - production company located at Longacre Building, 42nd & Broadway, New York; productions filmed at the Ince Studios and distributed by Associated Producers.

**Max Cohen - US - 1917** - distribution company located at Suite 707, 729 Seventh Ave., New York.

**Max Glucksmann Cinamatography - ARGENTINA - 1900-1940s** - production and distribution company formed by Max Glucksmann, the first production company to film documentaries in Argentina; Eugenio Py headed production; Glucksmann's brother Jacobo came to the U.S. to export films to Argentina; opened over 100 theaters across Argentina, Uruguay and Chile with Gluckmann's brothers overseeing most of them; dominated the newsreel industry there until Glucksmann's death in 1946.

**Max Linder Productions - US - 1921** - production company located at Universal City, California with Max Linder as general manager and distribution through Robertson Cole.

**Mayfair Film Corporation - US - 1917** - production company with offices located at 10 Wall Street,

New York, and studios at 515-517 West 54th Street, New York with M. A. Schlesinger as president.

**Mayflower Photoplay Corp. - US - 1919 -** production company formed in Boston, Massachusetts with Isaac Wolper as president; produced Allan Dwan and Emile Chautard productions and distributed through Realart Pictures Corp.

**Mayflower Picture Corp. - US - 1921 -** production company located at 5341 Melrose Ave., Los Angeles, California with Richard McFarland as general manager.

**McCarthy Picture Corp. - US - 1921 -** production company located at 500 Markham Bldg., Hollywood, California, with J. P. McCarthy as president.

**McClure Pictures, Inc. - US - 1917** - production company located at 25 W. 44th Street, New York, with Frederick L. Collins as president; distribution through Triangle Films.

**Mecca Feature Film Co., Inc. - US - 1913 -** distribution company located at 126 W. 46th St., New York, with David Greenebaum as president and William Kessel as general manager.

**Medusa Film - ITALY - 1915 -** production company located at lungo Tevere Castello 3, Rome.

**Meinert Film Gesellschaft - GERMANY - 1918-1919 -** production company formed by Rudolf Meinert; merged with Decla Film in 1919 with Meinert becoming head of production.

**Melies Films - US - 1913 -** distribution and production company located at 204 E. 38th Street, New York; distributed under trade name of General.

**Melies Manufacturing Co. - US - 1908 - 1911 -** production company formed by Gaston Melies and located in Chicago, Illinois; in 1909, studio moved to Fort Lee, N. J.; in 1910, moved to San Antonio, Texas and called the Star Films Ranch where they began producing westerns; in 1911, name was changed to Star Films American Wild West Productions and moved to Santa Paula, California. [see Star Films; Star Films American Wild West Productions]

**Mena Film Co. - US - 1921 -** located at Fountain and Berando Sts., Hollywood, California with E. W. Kuehn as president and G. C. Driscoll and R. R. Hollister as officers.

**Menchen Film Co. Ltd. - UK - 1915 -** distribution company located at 20 Frith St., Westminster, with Joseph Menchen as president and general manager.

**Mercury Film Service - UK - 1919-1926 -** production and distribution company located at Film House, Mill Hill, Leeds; distributed for Arrow Pictures.

**Merit Film Corp. - US - 1916-1922** - located at 130 W. 46th St., New York with I. E. Chadwick as V. P.

**Mermaid Comedies - 1921-1923** - trade name for Jack White comedy shorts produced by Astra Film Corp and distributed through Educational Film Corp.

**Mesco Pictures - US - 1921** - production and distribution company formed to produce and distribute Jesse James films by his son Jesse E. James.

**Meteor Film - UK - 1913-1914** - distribution company formed by Frank Cross, William Albert Habberfield, Joseph Oakley and Henry Wood with offices at 15-16 Brewer St. Winchester.

**Metro Goldwyn Pictures Co. - SWEDEN - 1924** - distributor for Metro Goldwyn films.

**Metro-Goldwyn Pictures Corp. - US - 1924** - production and distribution company formed with the merger of Metro Pictures and Goldwyn Pictures; following year became Metro-Goldwyn-Mayer.

**Metro-Goldwyn-Mayer Pictures Corp. - US - 1925-current** - production and distribution company formed from the merger of Metro-Goldwyn Pictures Corp. with Louis B. Mayer Pictures.

**Metro Pictures Corp. - US - 1915-1924** - distribution company formed March 5, 1915 with Richard Rowland as president and Louis B. Mayer as secretary; re-organization of Al Lichtman's Alco Pictures which had formed a year earlier and was distributing films for All Star Feature Corp.; became distributors for Amalgamated Producing Co., C. E. Shurtleff Inc., Comique Film Corp., Consolidated Film Corp., Drew Comedies, Dyreda Art Film Corp., Erbograph Co., Graf Productions, Inc., Harry Garson Productions, Hope Hampton Productions, Inc., Hunt Stromberg Productions, Inspiration Pictures, Inc., Iroquois Films, Murray W. Garsson Productions, Nazimova Productions, Inc., Quality Pictures Corp., Popular Plays and Players, Quality Film Productions, Quality Pictures Corp., Rolfe Photoplays, Inc., S-L Productions, Samuel Zierler Photoplay Corp., Sawyer Lubin Productions, Serial Producing Corp., Solax Films, Thomas H. Ince Corp., Tiffany Film Corp., Yorke Film Corp., and Columbia

Pictures Corp.; moved into production with feature films released under the trade name of Screen Classics, Inc.; in 1918, overpaying for screen rights caused Mayer to leave the company and move to California to start his own production company; Solax left creating some financial problems; in 1920, Marcus Loew's bought Metro Pictures to provide films for his theater chain and established their offices at Loew Bldg. Broadway and 45th St. New York and studio at 900 Cahuenga St. Hollywood, California; merged with Goldwyn films in 1924 to form Metro-Goldwyn.

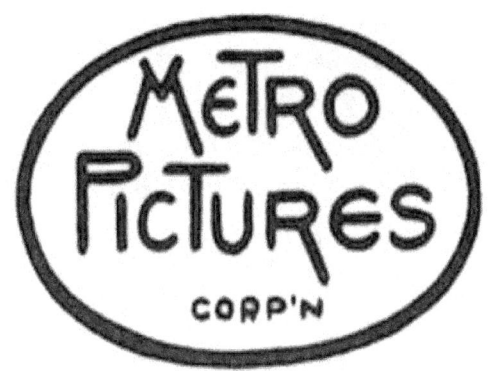

**Metropolitan Film Co. - UK - 1913-1914** - distribution company formed by Tom Musson, Emma Poole, George Poole, and Thomas Walter Saint with offices at 6 Greek St. Winchester; in July 1914 offices burned down and never reopened.

**Metropolitan Film Co. - US - 1914** - formed February 1914 with Hans Bartsch as president; offices located on the 6th Floor, World Tower Bldg, 110 West 40th Street, New York.

**Mexican War Film Corporation - US - 1914** - distribution company through states rights; located at 71 West 23rd Street, Room 1205, New York.

**Mezhrabpom-fil'm - RUSSIA - 1928-1936** - production company formed from Mezhrabpom-Rus; name was changed in 1936 to Rotfil'm (Red Front Studio); closed in 1937.

**Mezhrabpom-Rus - RUSSIA - 1923-1928** - production company operated by the state after creation of the Soviet Union; Iakov Protazanov, former production head for Pathe Russia, was brought back from exile and appointed as head of production; name changed in 1928 to Mexhrabpom-fil'm.

**Mica Film Corp. - US - 1913-1914** - production company formed by C. H. Ayres; located at 220 West 42nd Street, New York; merged to form Kriterion Film Corp. in 1914, which merged to form Associated Film Service Corp. in 1915.

**Micheaux Film and Book Co. - US - 1918-1928** - production company formed when Oscar Micheaux could not get his book, The Homesteader, made into a film by Lincoln Motion Picture Co.; Micheaux produced, directed and worked in almost every position; travelled from theater to theater marketing his films; went bankrupt in 1928 but was re-incorporated in 1930 as Micheaux Film Corp.

**Micheaux Film Corp. - US - 1928-1951** - production company owned by Oscar Micheaux with offices located at 538 S. Dearborn St. Chicago, Illinois; W. R. Cowan was V.P and S. E. Micheaux was secretary/treasurer and general manager; produced five and seven reel black race films until 1940; continued distributing until Micheaux died in 1951.

**Midget Comedies - US - 1921** - trade name for comedy shorts featuring Eddie Frank and Jimmy Roson; distributed by S-E Enterprises.

**Midgar Features - US - 1913** - production company located at 135 West 44th Street, New York.

**Milano Films - ITALY - 1909-1913** - production and distribution company formed SAFFI-Comerio in Milan and owned by Luca Comerio and Adolfo Croce.

**Miles Bros - US - 1907-1908** - production and distribution company with offices at 10 E. 14th Street, New York, Hub Theatre, Boston, Massachusetts; and 790 Turk St., San Francisco, California.

**Miller and Steen Distributors Inc. US - 1925-1926** - distributor of the Hunt Miller Western Productions featuring Tom Foreman and 2 reel comedies.

**Milo Motion Picture Corp - US - 1917** - production company located in Baltimore, Maryland.

**Mina Films - US - 1914-1916** - trade name used by Centaur

Film Co.; name was the winning name in a contest that Horsley held and meant, "Made in America"; distribution was through General Film Co. until 1915 when Horsley cancelled their contract and moved to Mutual Film Corp.; some dispute was there as the brand name stayed at General Film for a while.

**Minerva Film Co. - UK - 1920-1921** - production company formed on the closing of British Actors Film Co. by A. A. Milne, Leslie Howard, Nigel Playfair, C. Aubrey Smith and Adrian Brunel; produced comedy shorts.

**MingXing Film Co. - SHANGHAI - 1922-1925** - production company formed by Zhang Shichuan, Zheng Zhengqiu, Zhou Jianyun and Runje Shaw.

**Mirror Films, Inc. - US - 1915** - production company formed October 1915 with Clifford B. Harmon as president and Capt. Harry L. Lambart in charge of production; studios were a converted casino and dance hall located in Glendale, Long Island, with offices at 16 E. 42nd St. New York.

**Mirth Comedies - US - 1921** - trade name for two reel comedy shorts produced by Mirth Motion Pictures and distributed by Reelcraft Pictures Corp.

**Mirth Motion Pictures, Inc. - US - 1921** - production company located at 145 W. 45th St., New York, with E. J. Carpenter and Travers Vale.

**Mirthquake Comedies - US - 1925-1926** - trade name for comedies produced by Cumberland Productions and distributed by Arrow Pictures Corp.

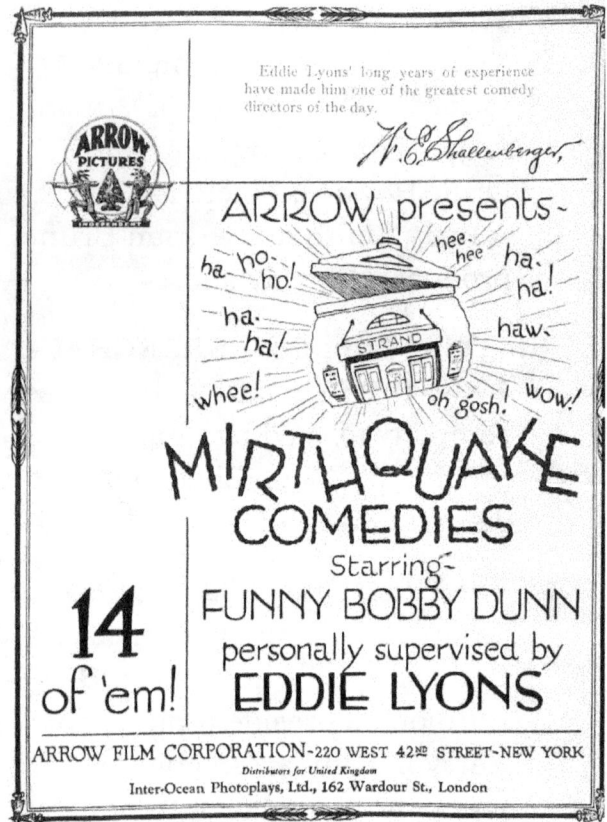

**Misr Co. - EGYPT - 1925 -** production company, the first Egyptian owned film studio in Egypt and backed by the Egyptian government.

**Mission Film Corp. - US - 1918 -** production company formed to produce a series of films featuring child actress Gloria Joy with distribution through Pathe Exchange.

**Mittenthal Film Co. - US - 1913-1916 -** production company formed in May 1913 by the Mittenthal brothers; produced feature films under the trade name of Mittenthal Features; Theodore Marston was president and Chester De Vond was production manager; offices were located at 1402 Broadway St., New York, and studios were the Pilot Studios in Yonkers; distribution by Warner Bros through Warner's Features; in December 1914, began producing single reel films under the trade name Starlight which were distributed by United Film Service.

**Mohawk Film Company, Inc. - US - 1912-1914 -** production company located in the Times Building, New York.

**Molina Film Corp. - US - 1921 -** located in Anaheim, California and formed by Leon J. Mook, Walter F. Rippe, Max Royer, Wilbur Miller, Richard Melrose, Marie Faraud, and John W. Wilcox.

**Mona Darkfeather Productions - US - 1921 -** production company to produce one reel Indian dramas distributed by C. B. Price, Inc.

**Monarch Exclusive Film Co. - UK - 1913-1914 -** distribution company formed by Lewis Cohen and Philip Glenswick with offices at 18 Cecil Court, Winchester.

**Monarch Photo Play Co., Inc. - US - 1915 -** production and distribution company located in Room 1408 Times Building, New York, with Bob Russell as president.

**Monarch Producing Co. - US - 1914-1915** production company formed by Harry Harvey and distributed through Kriterion; merged to form Associated Film Service Corp. in 1915.

**Monarch Production Co. - US - 1924 -** production and distribution company located in New York specializing in black films.

**Monmouth Film Corp - US - 1916-1917 -** production company located in the Brokaw Building, New York, with Harry McRae Webster as president and Julies Burnstein as general manager.

**Monogram Films - US - 1924-1925 -** production company with Dwight Leeper as president; specialized in westerns; **(NOTE:** not to be confused with Monogram Pictures which was formed in 1931 and not a silent studio.)

**Monopol Film Co. - UK - 1913-1914** - distributor with offices at 49 Greek St., Winchester.

**Monopol Film Co. - US - 1911-1913** - distribution company located at 111 East 14th Street, New York, with P. P. Craft as general manager; moved to 145 W. 45th St., New York with Isadore Bernstein as general manager; acquired by Pat Powers in September 1913.

**Monrovia Feature Film Co. - US - 1916-1917** - production company formed in Monrovia, California with R. M. Francisco as president; distribution through Grafton Film Publishing Co.; declared bankruptcy October 1917.

**Monty Films - US - 1915** - production company with distribution through Kriterion.

**Monty Banks Comedies - US - 1921** - trade name of comedies starring Monty Banks; distributed by Federated Films Exchanges of America.

**Moore Films - US - 1913** - production company.

**Moore's Film Exchange - US - 1910** - distribution company formed by Tom Moore; located at 434 Ninth St., Northwest, Washington, D.C.

**Moranti Comedies - US - 1921** - trade name for comedy shorts released by Reelcraft Pictures Corp.

**Morosco Better Pictures - US - 1921** - [see Oliver Morosco Productions, Inc.]

**Morris R. Schlank Productions - US - 1921** - production company featuring Hank Mann films and Spotlight Comedies; located at 1439 Beachwood Dr., Los Angeles, California; distribution through Arrow Film Corp.

**Moss Films - US - 1915-1918** - trade name for films released by B. S. Moss Motion Picture Corp.

**Motion Picture Distributing and Sales Co. - US - 1910-1912 -** distribution company formed April 1910 by New York Motion Picture Co. and Independent Motion Picture Co. (IMP); in July 1910, Associated Independent Manufacturers merged by including Nestor, Thanhouser, Éclair, Capitol, Great Northern and Lux; Carl Laemmle was president, Pat Powers was V. P., Charles O. Baumann was treasurer and Herbert Miles was secretary; distributed for Ambrosio, Atlas, Bison, Capitol, Carson, Centaur, Champion, Cines, Columbia, Defender, Éclair, Electrafraff, Film d'Art, Gaumont, Great Northern, IMP, Itala, Kinograph, Lux, Motograph, Nestor, Powers, Reliance, Rex, Solax, Thanhouser, and Yankee; organization came to an end mid 1912 and split into three pieces forming Film Supply Co. of America, Mutual Film Corp. and Universal Pictures.

**Motion Picture Theatre Owners of America - US - 1917-1925 -** distribution company located in Chicago, Illinois.

**Motograff Co. of Philadelphia - US - 1910 -** production company located at 2556 North 24th Street, Philadelphia, Pennsylvania; May 1910, company name changed to Electragraff Co. of Philadelphia.

**Motograph Company of America - US - 1910 -** production company with offices located at 202 N. Calvert Street, Baltimore, Maryland and studios at Dupont Park.

**Motograph Film Co. - UK - 1913-1914 -** distribution company formed from the acquisition of Francis-Claire & Bamberger Enterprises by Joseph Jay Bamberger, Jocelyn Brandon, Samuel Cohen, S. L. Francis-Clare, J. B. Johnson and Hedley

Llewelyn of Milano Films; offices located at Upper St. Martin's Lane, Holborn, Winchester.

**Motoy Comedies - US - 1917** - trade name for comedies released by Toyland Films, Inc.

**Movca Film Studios - US - 1916** - production company of comedy cartoons located in San Francisco with distribution through Herald Film Corp.

**Movie Chats - US - 1917** - trade name for a series produced by Charles Urban and distributed through W. W. Hodkinson.

**Mt. Olympus Distributing Corp. - US - 1921** - distribution company located at 110 W. 40th St., New York, and distributed for Atlas Film Co. of America.

**Multnomah Film Co. - US - 1919** - formed by Raymond Wells and located in Portland, Oregon.

**Mundstuk Features - US - 1912-1914** - distribution company located in the Longacre Building, 42nd Street and Broadway, New York.

**Muriel Ostriche Comedies - US - 1921** - trade name for two reel comedy shorts featuring Muriel Ostriche and released by Arrow Film Corp.

**Murray W. Garsson Productions - US - 1920-1924** - production company formed by Murray W. Garsson with offices at 522 Fifth Ave., New York; distribution through Metro Pictures Corp.

**Mustang Films - US - 1915- 1916** - trade name used by American Film Co.

**Mustang Films - US - 1920s-1927** - production company distributed through several distributors.

**Muswell Hill - UK - 1901-1908** - production company.

**Mutt and Jeff, Inc. - US - 1916** - production company to produce Mutt and Jeff cartoons by Bud

Fisher with offices at 207 S. Wabash in Chicago, Illinois and 1600 Broadway, New York; distribution through states rights.

**Mutual Exclusive Film Co. - UK - 1913-1914** - distribution company with offices at 28 Gerrard St. Winchester.

**Mutual Film Corp. - US - 1912-1918** - distribution company located at 71 West 23rd Street, New York; formed March 1912 by Harry Aitken, et al to consolidate and compete with the Motion Picture Distributing and Sales Co.; located at 60 Wall St. New York and distributed for American Film, Comet, Crystal Photoplays, Éclair, Empire All Star, Gail Kane Productions, Gaumont, Great Northern, Haworth, Keystone, Komic, Lux, Majestic, New York Motion Picture, Reliance, Signal, Solax, Thanhouser, Vogue and William Russell Productions; in May 1915, Aitken left with Kessel and Baumann of New York Motion Picture to form Triangle Film Corp. with D. W. Griffith, Thomas Ince and Mack Sennett; John R. Freuler replaced Aitken as president of Mutual with J. C. Graham as general manager; Mutual signed Centaur Film, Bostock Jungle and Film Co, and Charlie Chaplin as new additions; Mutual had four subsidiary studios operating in California: American Film Co., Lone Star Film Co., Signal Film Corp. and Vogue Films Inc.; Chaplin produced 12 films at the Lone Star studio and left to go to First National; Freuler resigned in May 1918 and was replaced by James M. Shelton; November 1918, Affiliated Distributors Corp acquired controlling interest and merged to become Exhibitors Mutual Distributing Corp.

# N

**N. C. M. P., Inc. - US - 1915 -** [see Natural Color Moving Picture Inc.]

**Napoleon and Sally Comedies - US - 1914-1921 -** trade name for one reel comedy shorts featuring Napoleon and Sally the chimpanzees; originally released through E & R Jungle Film Co. and later re-released through Reelcraft Pictures Corp.

**Napoleon Film Co. of America - US - 1914 -** distribution company located at 68 W. Washington Street, Chicago, Illinois.

**Nash Motion Picture Co., Inc. - US - 1914-1915 -** production company with distribution through Kriterion; part of merger to form Associated Film Service Corp. in 1915.

**National Bioscope and Film Co. - UK - 1909 -** distribution company located at 12 St. Martin's Court, Westminster.

**National Cinematograph Co. - UK - 1909-1910 -** distribution company located at 55 St. Martin's Lane Westminster.

**National Drama Corp. - US - 1915-1916 -** production company formed by Thomas Dixon; located at 1480 Broadway, New York, with P. D. Gold, Jr. as president and Dixon as head of production.

**National Exchanges, Inc. - US - 1921-1922 -** distribution company located at 398 Fifth Avenue, New York, with Hunter Bennett as general manager.

**National Film Corp. - US - 1917-1923 -** [see National Film Corp. of America]

**National Film Corp. of America - US - 1915-1923 -** production company formed by William Parsons to promote his "Smilin' Bill" Parsons comedies; 1918 to 1921, released a series of Clover Comedies, Hall Room Boys comedies, Capital Comedies; started the Tarzan of the Apes franchise with distribution through Goldwyn, Pioneer and W. W. Hodkinson; acquired by R. E. Frey and moved to 1116 Lodi St. Hollywood, California, after Parsons died in 1919; company name appears shortened in all advertising to National Film Corp.; closed in 1923.

**National Film Distributing Co - US - 1911-1912** - distribution company located at 34 and 36 W. Houston Street, New York; distributed for National Film Manufacturing and Leasing Company; also imported European films; later that year, moved into permanent facilities located at 145 West 45th St., New York and issued a new logo.

**National Film Mfg. & Leasing Co., Inc. - 1911-1912** - distribution company located at 12 East 15th Street, New York.

**National Film Corp. - US - 1915 -** [see National Pictures Co.]

**National Picture Theatres, Inc. - US - 1919-1920** - production company located at 729 Seventh Ave., New York, with Lewis J. Selznick as president.

**National Pictures Co - US - 1915** - production company with studios located at Santa Monica Boulevard, Gower to Lodi Streets, Hollywood, California.

**National-Film Agency - UK - 1913-1914** - distribution company with offices at 64 Victoria St. Manchester.

**Natural Color Kine Co. Ltd. - UK - 1913-1914** - distribution company for Kinemacolor and Nestor Films; offices located at 80 Wardour St., Winchester.

**Natural Color Moving Picture Inc - US - 1915** - production company located at 226 W. 42nd Street, New York.

**Navajo Films - US - 1914-1915** - production company and studio located in Edendale, California; W. H. Bissell was president and Charles K. French was head of production; distribution through Kriterion; in 1915, consolidated with other companies to form Associated Films Service Corp.

**Nazimova Productions - US - 1918-1920 -** production company featuring Nazimova with distribution through Metro Pictures Corp.

**Neal Hart Productions - US - 1921-1922 -** production company located in San Antonio, Texas; produced westerns featuring Neal Hart and released by Capital Film Co.

**Nell Shipman Productions - US - 1920-1924 -** production company located at 643 S. Olive St., Los Angeles, California; formed by Nell Shipman after divorce from Ernest Shipman in Canada; in 1922, formed a filming zoo to make nature films and moved production company to Priest Lake, Idaho; in 1924, shipped animals to the San Diego Zoo and went out of business.

**Nelson Film Co. - US - 1914-1915** - production company formed by J. Arthur Nelson, who had been V.P. of U. S. Films; company closed when Nelson was arrested in 1915 for misappropriation of stockholders' funds.

**Neptune Film Co. - UK - 1914-1920 -** production and distribution company formed by John East, Arthur Moss Lawrence and Percy Nash as general manager; offices located at 13 Gerrard St., Westminster.

**Nero-Film - GERMANY - 1924-1939 -** production company with studios located in Berlin.

**Nestor Film Co. - US - 1911-1919 -** production company formed by David Horsley when he moved his Centaur Films from New Jersey to become the first studio to operate in California and renamed it Nestor; by 1912, had three production units operating in Los Angeles; Thomas Ricketts directed the dramas, Milton Fahrney directed the westerns and Al Christie directed the comedies; distribution was through A. G. Whyte in New York until the formation of the Motion

Pictures Distributing and Sales Co.; when Universal was formed, Nestor moved distribution to them; dispute with Universal in 1913 caused Horsley to go back to New Jersey and reopen Centaur but the Nestor brand was kept active at Universal until it ceased operation in 1919.

**Nevada Motion Picture Co. - US - 1916-1917** - production company formed with F. W. Manson as president and John Ince as head of production; built a studio at 40 W. Mountain St., Pasadena, but it burned down March 24, 1917.

**New Agency Film Co. - UK - 1913-1914** - distribution company with Henry Hayman as general manager; offices located at 81-83 Shaftesbury Ave., Winchester; distributed for Ambrosio, Pasquali, Svea and Nestor Films.

**New Art Film Co. - US - 1918-1921** - production company featuring Dorothy Gish with distribution through Paramount.

**New Bio Exclusives - UK - 1913-1914** - distribution company with offices located at 65 Thornton St., Newcastle.

**New Bioscope Trading Co. - UK - 1904-1922** - distribution company formed by Arthur James Walmsley, Harry Voce Thurgood and Frederick Richard Griffiths as general manager; offices located at 1-5 Cecil Court, Winchester.

**New-Cal Film Corp. - US - 1924-1928** - production company.

**New Century Film Co. - UK - 1913-1914** - distribution company with offices located at 2-4 Quebec St., Leeds.

**New England Film Distributors, Inc. - US - 1916** - distribution company located at 15 State Street, Suite 60, Boston, Massachusetts.

**New England Film Exchange - US - 1908-1910** - distribution company located at 611 Washington Street, Boston, Massachusetts.

**New England Motion Picture Co., Inc. - US - 1917** - production company located in Boston, Massachusetts.

**New Era Films Ltd. - UK - 1924** - distribution company formed by Harry Raymond Nathan, John Thomas Roach Jr. and Charles Warren Lovesy as general manager; offices located at 9 Little St., Holborn.

**New Film Service - UK - 1913-1914** - distribution company formed by Isidore Davison, Horace Dickerson and Francis Hull; offices located at 48 Rupert St., Winchester.

**New Jersey Feature Film Co. - US - 1913** - distribution company located at 800 Broad Street, Newark, New Jersey.

**New Majestic Co. - UK - 1913-1914** - distribution company for Apollo, Nestor, Reliance and Majestic Films; offices located at 5 Gerrard St., Winchester; merged with Western Import Co. in 1914.

**New Orleans Feature Film Co. - US - 1924** - production company formed May 1924 and located in New Orleans, Louisiana, with Leslie Peacock as head of production.

**New Wed Comedies - US - 1921** - trade name for one reel comedy shorts distributed by Dominant Pictures.

**New York Film Co. - US - 1912-1914** - production company located at 145 West 46th Street, New York; predecessors to Equitable Film Producing Co., Inc.

**New York Film Company - 1912 -** distribution company located at 12 Union Square, New York.

**New York Motion Picture Co. - US - 1909-1912 -** production and distribution company formed from merger of Adam Kessel's Empire Film Exchange, Charles O. Baumann of International Film Exchange, and Fred Balshofer; located at 426 Sixth Ave., New York; initially released under the trade name of Bison Life Motion Pictures; distributed films for Ambrosio and Itala; contracted with the Millers 101 Ranch for their winter retreat, renamed Inceville; merged to form the Motion Picture Distributing and Sales Co., but soon left leaving Carl Laemmle as president of what would become Universal Studios. [see New York Motion Picture Corp]

**New York Motion Picture Corp. - US - 1912-1916 -** production company with Adam Kessel as president, Charles Baumann as V. P., and Charles J. Hite as treasurer after leaving the Motion Picture Distributing and Sales Co.; located at 42nd Street & Broadway, New York; used trade names of Broncho and 101-Bison for westerns, Domino for comedies, and Kay-Bee for dramas; distribution through Mutual; in 1916, merged to become part of Triangle Film Corp.

**New Zealand Moving Picture Co. Ltd. - NEW ZEALAND - 1921-1922 -** production company formed in Otaki and released under the trade name Maoriland Films.

**Newcastle Film Supply Co. - UK - 1913-1914 -** distribution company with offices at 177 Westgate Rd., Newcastle.

**Nihon Katsudo Film, Inc. - JAPAN - 1912-current -** production company formed by the merger of Yoshizawa & Co., M-Pathe, Hukuhou-do, and Yokota & Co., which was known as Nikkatsu; Einosuke Yokota was president;

other mergers and changes occurred after the silent era.

**Nijo Castle Studio - JAPAN - 1910-1912** - production studio in Kyoto, Japan. [see Yokota & Co.]

**Nikkatsu - JAPAN - 1912-current** - [see Nihon Katsudo Film, Inc.]

**Nippon Katsudo Shashin - JAPAN - 1912-current** - production company formed September 12, 1912 by the merger of Yoshizawa Shoten, Yokota Shokai, Fukuhodo and M. Pathe; name translates to "Japan Motion Pictures" and shortened to Nikkatsu.

**Nola Film Co. - US - 1915-1916** - production company formed in New Orleans, Louisiana on November 11, 1915 by William Morgan Hannon to acquire Coquille Film Co. at 1347 Moss St. in New Orleans; Hannon was an attorney and a director at Coquille; several films made but they could not get national distribution; late 1916, gave a huge bar-b-que and closed their doors; in August 1917, R. M. Chisholm bought controlling interest and reopened under the name of Diamond Film Co.

**Nolan & Swanson Film Co. - US - 1916-** - distribution company located on Curtis St., Denver, Colorado; distributed through states rights Christie's Comedies, et al, for Colorado, Utah, Wyoming, New Mexico and Montana.

**Norbig Film Manufacturing Co. - US - 1913-1916** - production company and studio owned by Frank E. North in Edendale California and specializing in westerns; did processing and leased the studios to other production companies.

**Norca Pictures - US - 1922-1923** - production company located at 1540 Broadway Street, New York.

**Nordisk Films Kompagni - DEN - 1906-current** - production and distribution company formed by Ole Olsen; in 1908, opened a branch called Great Northern Film Co. to distribute in the U.S.; switched to sound production in 1929; still in existence. [see Great Northern Film Co.]

**Nordisk Film Ltd. - UK - 1911-1921** - distribution company formed by Ole Olsen, Alvieda Paulsen and Axel Severin Paulsen with offices at 25 Cecil Court, Winchester; distributed Nordisk Films; moved to 166-170 Wardour St. in 1915 and to 24 Denmark St. in 1921.

**Norman Film Manufacturing Co. - US - 1920-1928 -** production company formed by Richard F. Norman and specializing in black race films; studios in Arlington, Florida and Boley, Oklahoma.

**Norma Talmadge Film Corp. - US - 1916-1927 -** production company formed in New York by Joseph Schenck to produce films featuring his wife, Norma Talmadge; distributed by Lewis J. Selznick Productions, which became Select Pictures in 1917; distribution was moved to First National in 1920 which became Associated First National.

**North American Film Corp. - US - 1916 -** production company with John R. Freuler as president; located at 71 W. 23rd St., New York with distribution through Mutual Film.

**North-Eastern Film Service - UK - 1913-1914 -** distribution company with offices located at 46 N. Bridge St. Sunderland.

**Northern Feature Film Agency - UK - 1913-1914 -** distribution company with offices located at 68 Victoria St. Manchester.

**Northern Pictures Corp. - CANADA - 1920-1921 -** production company located in Calgary, Canada with Ralph Connor and Ernest Shipman; produced films about the Royal Canadian Mounties. [see Ernest Shipman and Associates]

**Northern Ventures, Ltd - US - 1913 -** distribution company through states rights; located at 145 West 45th Street, Suite 1211, New York.

**Northwestern Film Corp. - US - 1920 -** production and distribution company located in Wyoming.

**Notable Feature Film Company - US - 1914** - distribution company through states rights located at 308 Boston Building, Salt Lake City, Utah; distribution for Jesse L. Lasky Feature Play Co. and Famous Players Film Co. Productions.

**Novagraph Film Co. - US - 1921** - located at 923 Cole Ave., Los Angeles, California.

**Numa Picture Corp. - US - 1920-1922** - production company owned by the Weiss Brothers to produce Tarzan films from Edgar Rice Burroughs; located at 1476 Broadway, New York.

# Ewbank's

Leading UK Entertainment & Memorabilia Auctioneers

Regular Entertainment & Memorabilia auctions throughout 2015.

Including Movie / TV, Music, Sporting Memorabilia and Posters, Photography and Autograph Auctions.

Consignments welcome.
Contact the Auctioneer: 00 (1) 483 223 101          valuations@ewbankauctions.co.uk

**THOUSANDS OF ORIGINAL FRENCH MOVIE POSTERS FROM 1960'S TO NOW DAYS**
contact@FrenchMoviePosters.com
www.FrenchMoviePosters.com

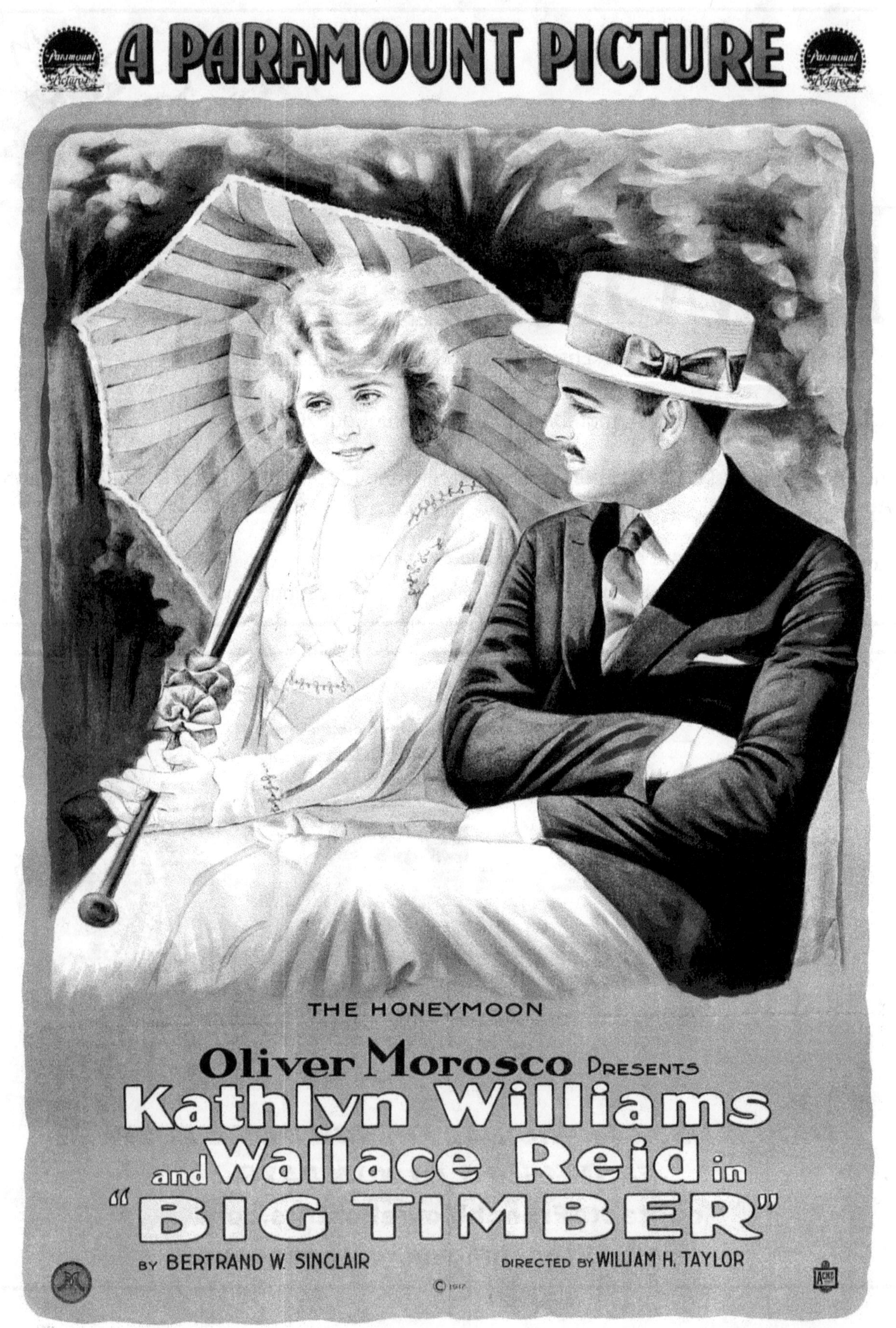
A PARAMOUNT PICTURE
THE HONEYMOON
Oliver Morosco PRESENTS
Kathlyn Williams
and Wallace Reid in
"BIG TIMBER"
BY BERTRAND W. SINCLAIR
DIRECTED BY WILLIAM H. TAYLOR
© 1917

# O

**O'Conor Productions** - US - 1922 - production and distribution company with offices located at 220 W. 42nd Street, New York.

**O. T. Crawford Film Exchange Co.** - 1907-1910 - distribution company located at 1401-05 Locust St., St. Louis, Missouri; 421 4th Avenue, Louisville, Kentucky; and 314 Carondelet Street, New Orleans, Louisiana.

**Oakdale Productions** - US - 1918 - production company.

**Ocean Film Corp.** - US - 1915 - production company with John L. Dudley as president and James D. Goldburg as general manager with offices at 220 W. 42nd St. New York; acquired by the Raver Film Corp.

**Octagon Films, Inc.** - US - 1920 - production company associated with B. A. Rolfe Productions; located in Yonkers, New York; went bankrupt after Houdini film.

**Odessa Film Factory of Ukrainfil'm** - RUS - 1929-1936 - production company formed from Odessa Film Factory of VUFKU. [see next two entries]

**Odessa Film Factory of VUFKU** - RUS - 1922-1929 - production company originally named Odessa Section of the All-Ukraine Kino Factory [see next]; VUFKU meant All-Ukraine Photo-Film Directorate; name was changed again in 1929 to Odessa Film Factory of Ukrainfil'm.

**Odessa Section of the All-Ukraine Kino Factory** - RUS - 1919-1922 - production company originally started in 1919 as part of the Political Department of the 41st Red Army Division; became known as Odessa Section of the All-Ukraine Kino Factory in 1920; name was changed in 1922 to Odessa Film Factory of VUFKU.

**Ogden Pictures Corp.** - US - 1917 - production company formed in Ogden, Utah, with Albert

Scowcroft as president; produced comedy/dramas; office located at 729 Seventh Avenue, New York.

**Oil Field Amusments - US - 1925 -** production company specializing in westerns.

**Oklahoma Natural Mutoscene Co. - US - 1909 -** production company.

**Oliver Films, Inc. - US - 1919-1920 - US - 1919 -** production company located at 308 E. 48th Street, New York, with I. Oliver as president.

**Oliver Morosco Photoplay Co. - US - 1914-1923 -** production company and studio formed by Oliver Morosco; located at 201 N. Occidental Blvd. in Los Angeles, California, with William Desmond Taylor as head of production; distribution through Paramount; on June 28, 1916, company merged with Famous Players-Lasky Corp. but name continued to be used until 1923; moved to 301-2 C. C. Chapman Building, Los Angeles, California.

**Olympian Productions, Inc. - US - 1921 -** located at 110 W. 40th St. New York.

**Olympic Games Film Co. - US - 1912 -** production and distribution company located at Suite 809, Exchange Bldg., 145 W. 45th Street, New York.

**Olympic Motion Picture Company - US - 1915 -** production company located at 220 West 42nd Street, New York.

**Omega Film Co. - UK - 1913-1914 -** distributor with offices at five Blackfriars St., Manchester.

**Onda's Prize Animated Pictures - UK - 1913-1914 -** distribution company with offices located at Picturedrome, Preston.

**101 Bison Co. - US - 1912 -** production company formed by New York Motion Pictures; owners, Adam Kessel and Charles Baumann worked in conjunction with the Miller's 101 Ranch to use their ranch hands; specialized in westerns; winter ranch in California used for the Miller's Wild West Shows and called Inceville.

**Orient Film Syndicate Ltd. - UK - 1913-1915 -** distribution company formed by Sydney Hooton and Arthur B. Heinrich as general manager; offices located at 64 Haymarket Westminster.

**Oriental Film Co. - US - 1913 -** distribution company formed by Benjamin Brodsky of San Francisco to import and distribute films made in China.

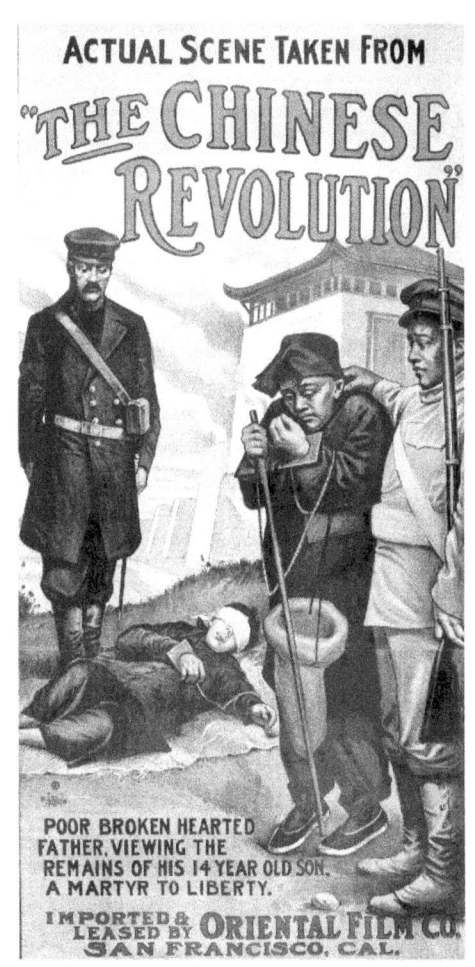

**Oro Pictures Co. Inc. - US - 1917-1921 -** production company formed by H. Grossman with Isadore Bernstein as head of production; offices located at 729 Seventh Ave., New York; acquired Bernstein Productions studio in Los Angeles, California.

**Oscar Rosenberg Co. - UK - 1913 -** distribution company.

**Oswald-Film - GERMANY - 1924 -** production company formed by Richard Oswald.

**Our Gang Comedies - US - 1922-1938 -** trade name for comedy series produced by Hal Roach; distribution was through Pathe Exchange until 1927 when it moved to MGM; changed to sound in 1929 and sold to MGM in 1938 who continued producing until 1944.

**Out of the Inkwell Films, Inc. - US - 1921-1928 -** production company formed by Max Fleischer in New York to produce animated comedy shorts; distribution through M. J. Winkler until 1925 when changed to Red Seal Pictures Corp.; reorganized in 1928 as Inkwell Studios.

**Outing-Chester Pictures - US -** [see C. L. Chester Productions.]

**Outlook Photoplays - US - 1921-1923 -** production company located at 140 W. 42nd St., New York with Myron M. Stearns as general manager.

**Overland Film Company - US - 1917 -** production and distribution company located at 729 Seventh Avenue, New York, with Samuel Krellberg as president.

**Oversea Film Trading Co. Inc. - US - 1921 -** distribution company located at 220 W. 42nd St., New York with Ernest Mattson as general manager; exported films to Scandinavia and Finland.

**Overseas Film Co. - UK - 1914-1916 -** distribution company formed by James Henry Gislingham, William Philip Gislingham and William Baird Laing; offices located at Spenser Road Herne Hill, Lambeth.

**Owen Moore Film Corp. - US - 1922** - production company subsidiary of Selznick Pictures featuring Owen Moore films.

**Owl Features, Inc. - US - 1917** - distribution company located at 5 S. Wabash Avenue, Chicago, Illinois.

**Owl Films - US - 1910** - trade name of films produced by Owl Motion Picture Co.

**Owl Motion Picture Co. - US - 1910** - production company with offices and studio located at 538-540 55th St., New York; released under the trade name of Owl Films; distributed through Motion Picture Distributing and Sales Co.

**Oxford Films - US - 1915** - production company formed by John Barton Oxford.

**Oy Maat ja Kansat - FINLAND** (before independence) **- 1907-1909** - production company formed to produce short documentaries; located in Tampere.

**Oz Film Manufacturing Co. - US - 1914-1915** - production company formed by L. Frank Baum to produce films from his books; offices located at Santa Monica Blvd. from Gower to Lodi Sts, Los Angeles, California; distributed through Paramount; studio closed in November 1914 and reopened in spring 1915 using a different brand name releasing through Alliance.

# Silent Studio Directory

- ORIGINAL VINTAGE MOVIE POSTERS
- RARE FILM POSTERS BOUGHT AND SOLD
- LINENBACKING AND RESTORATION SERVICES
- EXPERT CUSTOM FRAMING

L'IMAGERIE ART GALLERY
In Business Since 1973

www.limageriegallery.com

PHONE: 818-762-8488   FAX: 818-762-8499   EMAIL: limageriegallery@gmail.com

10555 Victory Boulevard - North Hollywood, CA 91606
Tuesday through Saturday from 11:30 to 6:00

---

# kinoart.net

**ORIGINAL MOVIE POSTERS AND LOBBY CARDS**

*12,000 SELECTED VINTAGE INTERNATIONAL POSTERS AVAILABLE*

**WOLFGANG JAHN**
**SULZBURGSTR. 126**
**50937 COLOGNE**
**GERMANY**
**+49 221 1698728**

---

There are 25,000 posters databased and available at www.movieart.com. Inquire to posters@movieart.com. We sell posters to collectors, designers and institutions worldwide. Our staff is friendly. We answer questions.

Selling posters since 1979.

IVPDA
international vintage
P O S T E R
dealers association

KIRBY McDANIEL
MOVIEART

# P

**P. P. Craft - US - 1914 -** distribution company located at 145 West 45th Street, New York.

**Pacific Film Co. - US - 1921-1922** – distribution company for Pacific Productions through states rights; located at 730 S. Olive St., Los Angeles, California, with T. E. Hancock and John J. Hayes.

**Pacific Productions - US - 1921-1922 -** production company located at 730 S. Olive St., Los Angeles, California, with John J. Hayes as president; produced one, two and five reel films with distribution through Pacific Film Co.

**PAGU-Vitascope – GERMANY – 1914-1917 –** production company formed from Projektions Aktiengesellschaft Union headed by Paul Davidson; in 1917, part of merger to form Universum Film AG (Ufa).

**Palatine Film Co. – UK – 1913-1914 –** distribution company with offices at 82 Upper Parliament St,. Nottingham and 60 Victoria St. Manchester.

**Palladium Films – SWEDEN – DENMARK – 1920-1929 –** production company subsidiary of Skandinavisk Filmcentral; produced comedies with Danish director Lau Lauritzen as head of production; sold in 1921 just before Lauriten's comedies became an international success; production continued with distribution by Film Centralen Palladium

**Pallas Pictures - US - 1915-1917 –** production company located at 201 N. Occidental Blvd., Los Angeles, California; shared with Oliver Morosco Photoplay Co. and distribution through Paramount.

**Palo Alto Film Co – US – 1915-1916 –** production company acquired as part of Exactus Photo-film Corp. of Palo Alto.

**Pan-American Film Co. - US - 1914 -** distribution company located at 110 W. 40th Street, New York; distributed for Worcester's Philippine Pictures.

**Pan-American Motion Picture Corp. – US – 1919 –** production company formed by Henry Starr and private investors to produce *Debtor to the Law*, a retelling of the botched bank robbery by Henry Starr after he got out of prison.

**Panama Films – US - 1915-1916 –** trade name used by Balboa Amusement Producing Co.

**Pantheon Pictures Corporation - US - 1921 -** production company with offices at 836 Singer Building, New York and studio located in Port Henry.

**Pantograph - US - 1910s -** production company.

**Paragon Films – US – 1914 –** trade name for two reel dramas produced by Crest Picture Co.

**Paragon Films, Inc. - US - 1915-1917 -** production company located at 924 Longacre Building, New York.

**Paragon Pictures Corp - US - 1920-1934** - production company located in Long Beach, California.

**Paralta Plays, Inc. – US – 1917-1918** – production company formed March 22, 1917 with Carl Anderson as president and Nat L. Brown as general manager; studios located at Melrose Ave. Los Angeles, California; new studio built in 1918 at Melrose Ave and Van Ness; distribution through W. W. Hodkinson; ceased production in fall of 1918 and Robert Brunton took over the studio.

**Paramount Famous Lasky Corp. - US – 1916-1930** – production and distribution company formed by several mergers and headed by Adolph Zukor; name was changed after loss of a federal anti-trust lawsuit.

**Paramount Film Co. - US - 1910** - distribution company with offices located at 61 West 14th Street, New York.

**Paramount Film Co. Ltd – UK – 1914-1915** – distribution company formed by H. B. B. Smith, Ernest Stevens and L. Taylor; offices located at 99a Charing Cross Road, Westminster and then moved to 191 Wardour St.

**Paramount Pictures Corporation - US - 1914-current** – distribution company formed by W. W. Hodkinson May 8, 1914; Adolph Zukor took control in 1916 and changed name to Paramount Famous Lasky Corp. and expanded into production; in 1930, name was changed back; had distribution companies in United Kingdom, France, Germany, Spain, Brazil, Mexico, Japan, Australia and New Zealand. [see Progressive Pictures]

**Park-Whiteside Productions – US – 1920-1921** – production company with distribution through Pioneer Pictures.

**Parufamet - GERMANY – 1925-1931** - distribution company created from the bailout of Ufa by Paramount and MGM; in December 1925, Paramount and MGM loaned Ufa $4 million and in return Ufa had to reserve 75% of its cinema capacity for American productions plus distribute 20 films from each partner per year in Germany.

**Pasquali American - US - 1914 -** distribution arm for Italian film company Pasquali; offices located at 110 W. 40th Street, New York.

**Pasquali and Tempo - ITALY - 1909** - production studio in Turin, Italy.

**Pat Sullivan Comic - US - 1923-1926** – production company owned by Pat Sullivan and distributed through M. J. Winkler; later changed to Bijou Films, Inc. and Educational Film Exchanges in 1926.

**Pathe Cinematographe Co. - US - 1904-1915** – distribution arm of Pathe-Freres of France; distributed about 1/3 of all films in the US between 1905-1908; in 1910, opened production studio in Bound Brook, New Jersey; in 1912, built new studio at 1 Congress Street, Jersey City; the Bound Brook studio changed to handle newsreels; World War I demolished French company and they temporarily moved their international headquarters to the U.S.; in 1914, because of the war, merged the American facilities with Eclectic Films and changed company name to Pathe Exchange, Inc.

**Pathe Exchange, Inc. - US - 1914-1923** – distribution company formed January 1915 by the merger of Eclectic Films and the U.S. offices of Pathe Freres, called Pathe Cinematographe Co.; located at Pathe Bldg. 25 W. 45th St., New York with Paul Brunet as president and J. A.

Berst as V. P. and general manager; distributed for Bray Studios, Hal Roach Studios, Mack Sennett Comedies et al; Pathe Exchange sold to Merrill Lynch in 1923 and changed name to American Pathe.

**Pathe Freres - FRANCE –** [see Societe Pathe Freres]

**Pathe Freres – SWEDEN – 1913 -** production company headed by Siegmund Popert to supply films for the international Pathe distribution; closed later same year due to new film alliances in Sweden with Denmark.

**Pathe Freres Films - UK – 1910-1924 –** distribution company with main office located at 103-109 Wardour St., Winchester and branches in Manchester, Leeds, Liverpool, Glascow, Newcastle and Birmingham; distributed for Pasquali Films, Comika, American, AK, Britannia, Nizza, Thalie, Iberico, Artistic, Film D'Art, Italiana, Literaria, Tanagra, Imperium, Swedish Biograph, Phoenix and Meteo.

**Pathe Russia - RUSSIA - 1907-1915 -** production company opened in 1908 to supply films for the Pathe Empire; sold to Ermolev in 1915, an employee at Pathe Russia, who renamed the studio I. Ermol'ev Co. and gave Pathe exclusive international rights on all films produced.

**Patria Films – SPAIN – 1915-1924 –** production company formed by Benito and Jose Perojo in Madrid.

**Patriot Film Corp. - US - 1916 -** located at 729 Seventh Avenue, New York.

**Paul Gerson Pictures Corp. – US – 1921 –** production company located 353-361 10th St., San Francisco, California, with Paul Gerson as president and general manager; produced films directed by William A. Howell and distributed through National Exchanges and Arrow Film Corp.

**Pax Film – FRANCE – 1927 –** distribution company for Eichberg films et al, with offices located at 34, Rue de la Victoire, in Paris.

**Peerless Feature Film Co. – US – 1914-1916 –** production company formed July 1914 by Jules Brulatour as a subsidiary of Shubert Film Corp.; produced film versions of William A. Brady and Charles A. Blaney plays; owned half of William A. Brady Picture Plays, Inc.; built their own studio in Fort Lee, New Jersey which was used by several other production companies; distribution through World Film Corp.; in 1915, World Film took over Shubert Film, which owned Peerless; Peerless as a production company seems to disappear in 1916 when World Film re-organized.

**Peerless Film Service, Inc. – US – 1915-1917 -** offices located at 100 Golden Gate Ave. San Francisco, California, with branch office at 8th and Broadway, Investment Bldg. Los Angeles; E. H. Emmick was president and general manager; states rights distributor for California, Arizona, and Nevada and distributed Christie Comedies, Mutt & Jeff Cartoons, Katzenjammer Kids, E&R Jungle Comedies and Tweedledum Comedies.

**Peerless Pictures Company - US - 1913-1920 -** production company located at 117 West 46th Street, New York.

**Pelican Films – US – 1915-1916 –** trade name for films released by Eastern Film Co. in Providence, Rhode Island.

**Pena Menichelli Productions – ITALY – 1920-1921 –** production company located in Rome with U. S. and Canadian distribution through Ernest Shipman and Associates.

**Perfection Pictures – US – 1917-1925 –** trade name for productions filmed at the Edison studios and distributed through George Klein exchanges.

**Perret Productions - US - 1918-1920** - production company owned by Leonce Perret and located at 1457 Broadway, New York.

**Perry Pictures - US - 1917 -** trade name for features released by Film d'Art Corporation.

**Peter Pan Film Corp. - US - 1916-1917 -** production and distribution company located at 729 Seventh Avenue, New York.

**Petrova Picture Co. Inc. – US – 1917 –** production company formed to produce films featuring Olga Petrova; Frederick L. Collins was president and Ralph Ince was head of production; filming was at Bacon-Backer studios, 230 W. 38th St., New York; distribution through Super-pictures Distribution Corp.

**Philograph Film Bureau – UK – 1913-1914 –** distributor with offices at 3 Macclesfield St., Winchester.

**Phoebus Films – UK – 1913-1914 -** distributed in the U.K. by Anderson's Film Agency.

**Phoenix Film Agency – UK – 1913-1914 –** distributor for Phoenix Films with offices at 6 Cecil Court, Winchester.

**Phoenix Film Co. - US – 1916 -** distribution company located at Columbus Ave. Boston, Massachusetts; distributed

Christie's Comedies, Carson Films et al, in the New England area through states rights.

**Photo Drama Co. - US - 1912-1914** – production company opened by George Klein with offices at 220 W. 42nd St New York; William Steiner was general manager; studios located in Grugliasco, Italy and Bayonne, New Jersey; later moved to Los Angeles, California; distribution through George Klein with some distribution through Kulee Features.

**Photo Drama - ITALY - 1912-1914** - production studio located at Grugliasco, Italy and founded by George Klein to combat Italian films being supplied to Pathe; World War I shut down the studio and it was moved to the Bayonne, New Jersey.

**Photo Play Productions Co. – US – 1914** – production company formed April 1914; located at 220 W. 42nd St., New York with E. K. Lincoln as president and Frank A. Tichener as general manager.

**Photo Plays Ltd – UK – 1913-1914** – distribution company with offices located at Hartshaed, Sheffield.

**Photo Products Export Co. - US - 1920** - distribution company located at 220 West 42nd Street, New York.

**Photocraft Productions, Inc. – US – 1922** – distribution company formed to rerelease Mack Sennett and Mabel Normand films from Triangle Film; Nathan Hirsh was president; located at 729 Seventh Avenue, New York.

**Photoplay Productions Releasing Co. - US – 1913-1915 –** production company located at 37 South Wabash Avenue, Chicago, Illinois, with A. M. Gollos as president; distributed through Photoplay Releasing Co.

**Photoplay Releasing Co. - US - 1913-1915** - distribution company for Photoplay Productions located at 5 South

Wabash Ave,, Chicago, Illinois, with A. M. Gollos as president.

**Photoplay Serials Co. – US – 1921** – distribution company located at 130 W. 46th St., New York with Joseph Weinstock as president, Benjamin Sherman as V. P., and E. S. Manheimer as treasurer and general manager.

**PhunPhilms – US – 1915-1919 –** trade name used by Rolin Film Co. to release one reel comedies featuring Harold Lloyd and released through Pathe Exchange.

**Physical Culture Photo Play Co., Inc. - US - 1918-1919 -** production company located in the Flatiron Building, New York.

**Picture Playhouse Film Co., Inc. - US - 1914-** distribution company for Interstate Feature Film Co. and Pasquali Co. of Turin; offices located at 71 W. 23rd St., New York.

**Picture Producing Co., Inc. - US - 1917** - distribution company located at 1493 Broadway, Putnam Building, New York, with Jack Goldberg as general manager.

**Picture Supplies Ltd. – UK – 1913-1914 –** distribution company with offices at 74 Victoria St., Manchester.

**Piedmont Pictures Corporation - US - 1917** - distribution company located at 729 Seventh Avenue, New York.

**Pierrot Film Co. Inc. – US – 1914 –** production company formed to produce comedies featuring Louis Simon; used Reliance studios but were stopped by court order from Edison's patent infringement.

**Pike's Peak Photoplay Co. – US – 1914-1916 –** production company in Colorado Springs, Colorado, with Otis B. Thayer as head of production; distribution through United Film Service using the Lariat trade name.

**Pilot Films Corp. - US – 1913-1914 –** production company and studio located at 120 School Street, Yonkers, New York.

**Pina Menichelli Productions, Inc. - ITALY - 1921-1922 -** production company featuring Italian actress Pina Menichelli and located in Italy.

**Pine Tree Pictures, Inc - US - 1921 -** production company located in Augusta, Maine; Frederick W. Hinckley was president, George H. Hinckley was secretary and Carl E. Milliken was treasurer.

**Pinnacle Comedies - US - 1920-1922 –** trade name for two reel comedy shorts featuring Max Roberts and released by Pinnacle Productions.

**Pinnacle Productions, Inc. – US - 1920-1922 –** production company with offices located at 309 Transportation Bldg. Indianapolis, Indiana, 606 Consumers Bldg. Chicago, Illinois and 6575 Fountain Ave. Hollywood, California; Ray M. Southworth was president and Nathan A. Woody was secretary and general manager.

**Pioneer Film Agency – UK – 1912-1915 –** distribution company formed from Williamson Dressler and Co., with offices located at 27 Cecil Court, Winchester.

**Pioneer Feature Film Co. Inc. – US – 1915-1918 –** distribution company formed in New York from the exchanges of Cosmo Feature Film Corp. with Nathan Hirsch as president, Augusta Hirsch and Julian Belman; states rights distributor for New York for Great Northern, Thomas Ince et al; reorganized in 1918 as Pioneer Film Corp.

**Pioneer Film Corp. - US - 1918-1921 –** distribution company formed from Pioneer Feature Film Corp. to distribute through states rights; located at 130 West 46th Street, New York; in 1919, Nathan Hirsch left and M. H. Hoffman merged his releasing company with Pioneer becoming general manager with A. E. Lefcourt as president.

**Pizor Productions - US - 1924-1937** – production company founded by William M. Pizor; specialized in westerns.

**Playgoers Pictures - US - 1921-1923 - US** - located at 35 West 45th Street, New York.

**Plimpton Epic Pictures, Inc. – US – 1915-1918** – production company formed by Horace G. Plimpton, with studio located at 250th St. between Yonkers and Mount Vernon, New York; distribution through Authors' Film Co.; in 1918, merged to form Plimpton-Fischer Photoplays, Inc.

**Plimpton-Fischer Photoplays, Inc. – US – 1918-1920** – production company formed from a merger with Plimpton Epic Pictures; William J. Reed was president, Horace G. Plimpton was V. P. and general manager and David G. Fischer was head of production.

**Plymouth Pictures, Inc. – US – 1921** – distribution company located at 140 W. 42nd St., New York; Nat Levine as president.

**Polar Bear Features – US – 1915** – trade name for a series released by Nordisk Film Co through Great Northern Film Co.

**Poli Films – ITALY – 1918-1928** – production company formed by Gustavo Lombardo in Names released under the trade names Poli Films and Lombardo Films; in 1928, Lombardo moved to Rome and changed the name of company to Titanus Films.

**Pollard Picture Plays Co. - US - 1916-1917** – production company formed by director Harry A. Pollard and his actress wife Margarita Fischer in 1916 in San Diego, California; closed in late 1917.

**Popular Photo Plays Corp. - US - 1914** - production company with offices in the Longacre Building in New York and studio in Fort Lee, New Jersey; Charles O. Baumann was president.

**Popular Pictures Corp - US - 1917** - distribution company located at 218 West 42nd Street, New York.

**Popular Plays and Players, Inc. – US – 1914-1917** – production company formed by Charles O. Baumann with Harry J. Cohen as general manager and treasurer; located at 1600 Broadway in New York; used the studios, roster and crew of Lubin Film Manufacturing Co.; distribution through Alco Film Corp., but moved to Metro Pictures the following year; expanded to release films under 14 different trade names including Canyon, Cee-O-Bee, Continental, Frolic, Gayety, Jester, Longacre, Luna, Niagara, O.K. Palisade, Pastime and Willat; Metro Pictures absorbed the company on May 25, 1917.

**Post Pictures Corp. – US – 1919-1921** – production company located at 527 5th Ave., New York; formed by Albert Redfield and Clyde E. Elliott to produce short travelogues and scenic films that were released under the trade names of Post Nature Pictures, Post Travel Pictures, and Post Scenics.

**Power Feature Film Co. Ltd. – UK – 1913-1918** – distribution company owned by Jane Sarah Coates; Thomas Power was general manager with offices at 100 Shaftesbury Ave. London.

**Powers Co. - US - 1909 -** production company formed by Pat Powers and located in Mount Vernon, New York.

**Powers Photoplays, Inc. – US – 1913-1917** – production company formed from Powers Picture Plays; moved to Hollywood to produce films for Universal; Pat Powers was one of the initial partners.

**Powers Picture Plays - US - 1909-1912** – production company formed by P. A. "Pat" Powers with a studio at 241st St. in Wakefield, New York; reincorporated in May 1913 as Powers Photoplays, Inc.

**Powhantan - US - 1909 -** production company specializing in films with Native American themes.

**Prairie Productions - US - 1922-1923** – production company.

**Prana-Film – GERMANY – 1922** – production company located in Berlin.

**Pre-eminent Films, Ltd. – US – 1915** – production company with W. E. Green as president and general manager.

**Preferred Pictures, Inc. - US - 1920-1926** – production company founded by B. P. Schulberg, J. G. Bachmann and Al Lichtman to produce films featuring Clara Bow; closed in 1926 when Schulberg went back to Famous Players-Lasky.

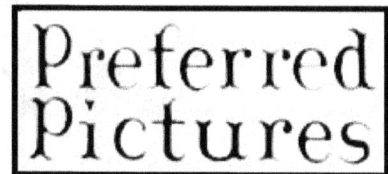

**Premier Film Co. Ltd – UK – 1913-1915** – distribution company formed by Albert Edward Venner and Sidney Walter Venner; offices located at 30 St. Martin's Court, Westminster; distributed for A. R., Cosomograph, Skandinavisk, White Star, Uspafa, Galabert, Cuesta, and Barcelona.

**Premier Films - US - 1914-1915 -** trade name for films produced by St. Louis Motion Picture Co. and distributed through Universal.

**Premier Program Corporation - US - 1915** - production company located at 128 West 46th Street, New York.

**Premium Picture Productions Inc – US – 1923** – production company located in Portland, Oregon.

**Premo Feature Film Co. – US – 1915-1916** – production company with Harry Rapf as president and Harley Knoles as V.P. and general manager and featuring Nat Goodwin; located at 11 E. 14th St. New York; distributed through World Film but moved to Mutual in 1916.

**Preston Film Service – UK – 1913-1914 –** distribution company with offices located at 60 North Rd., Preston.

**Pricefilms, Inc. – US – 1921 –** located at 1540 Broadway, New York, with C. B. Price as president and general manager.

**Primex Pictures Corp. – US – 1921 –** located at 1540 Broadway, New York, with S. H Teabeau as president and C. B. Price as general manager.

**Primagraf Co. – US – 1914 –** production company with studios located at 302 E. 38th St., New York; Irving Billig was head of production.

**Princess Films - US – 1912-1916 –** trade name produced by Thanhouser; released through Mutual in US and Thanhouser Films Ltd. in Europe.

**Principal Distributing Corp. – US – 1922-1925 –** distribution arm of Principal Pictures Corp. with offices located at 5528 Santa Monica Blvd., Hollywood, California.

**Principal Pictures Corp. – US – 1922-1925 –** production company formed by Sol Lesser as president, Mike Rosenberg and Irving M. Lesser; offices located at 1540 Broadway, Suite 1211, New York; distribution through Principal Distributing Corp.

**Primrose Films - US – 1922 –** production company.

**Principal Productions, Inc. – US – 1922-1941** – production subsidiary of Principal Pictures Corp. which produced a wide variety of series including Baby Peggy, Jackie Coogan comedies, Tarzan features, westerns, Bobby Breen musicals, etc.; studio located at 7200 Santa Monica Blvd., Hollywood, California.

**Private Feature and Film Manufacturing Co. – US – 1916-** production company with P. G. Stocky as president and Frank R. Jaffa as general manager; offices located at 712-714 Columbia Bldg., Cleveland, Ohio.

**Pro Patria Films Ltd. – UK – 1928** – distribution company.

**Producers Distributing Corp. - US - 1924-1928** – production and distribution company formed by Jeremiah Milbank; took over the former Ince studios in Culver City; in 1925, D. W. Griffith became head of production with holding company formed called Cinema Corp. of America to control Producers Distributing Corp and Cecil B. DeMille Pictures Corp.; F. C. Munro was president and John C. Flinn was V. P. and general manager; absorbed in re-organization with W. W. Hodkinson as part of an acquisition of Pathe. **NOTE:** PDC didn't seem to use logos on material distributed in the U.S. (they only used a tag line)

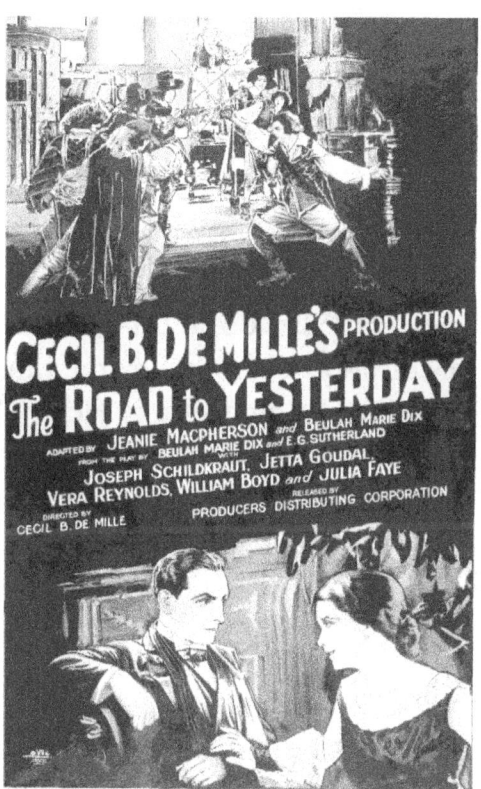

They did use logos in Europe. Here are a couple of samples:

**Producers Distributing Corp. – BELGIUM – 1925-1928 –** distributor of DeMille films in Belgium; managed by Adolphe Max with offices at 68 Boulevard, Bruxelles.

**Producers Distributing Co., Ltd – UK – 1925-1928 –** distributor of DeMille films in the UK with offices at 12 Great Newport St. London.

**Producers Film Co. – US – 1921 -** production company formed in Woodland California by Henry W. Laugenour to produce series called Betty June Travelogues.

**Producers Pictures Corp. – US – 1921 –** production company with offices at 201 N. 7th St. St. Louis, Missouri and studio at 205 S. Broadway Los Angeles, California with H. C. Schaper as president and George H. Kern as general manager.

**Producers' Security Corp. - US - 1919-1924 -** production company located at 516 Fifth Avenue, New York, with Ricord Gradwell as president and general manager.

**Production Reunies – FRANCE – 1916-1918 –** distribution company with offices at 9, des Filles du Calvaire in Paris (which were also the offices for Fernand Weill Films.) [see M. Fernand Weill]

**Progress Film Co. - UK - 1918-1922 –** production company located in Manchester formed by Frank E. Spring with Sidney Morgan as head of production.

**Progress Film Company - US - 1914 -** distribution company located at 110 West 40th Street, New York.

**Progress Picture Producing Assoc. – 1920-1921 –** production and distribution specializing in black race films.

**Progressive Motion Picture Co. - US – 1913-1914 –** distribution company formed by W. W. Hodkinson for independent film distribution as a west coast distributor; located in the Times Building, New York; changed to Paramount Pictures on May 8, 1914. [see Paramount Pictures]

**Progressive Pictures – US – 1925-1926 –** distribution company formed by Arthur C. Bromberg in Atlanta, with branches in Oklahoma City, New Orleans, Dallas and Charlotte.

**Prohibition Film Cororation - US - 1915 -** distribution company located at 220 W. 42nd Street, New York.

**Projektions Aktiengesellschaft Union (PAGU) - GERMANY – 1910-1914 –** production company combined with theaters and distribution formed by Paul Davidson, who owned largest theater chain in Germany; in 1914, divided off the theater chain which he sold to Danish Nordisk Film the following year; PAGU merged to become PAGU-Vitascope.

**Proletkino – RUSSIA – 1923-1926 –** production company formed by the state and headed by Aleksandr Khanzhonkov; studio closed in 1926 from corruption and scandal.

**Public Health Films - US - 1919 -** distribution company located at 1493 Broadway, Suite 211, New York.

**Public Service Film Co. - US - 1915 -** distribution company located at 1482 Broadway, Suite 910, New York.

**Puritan Pictures - US - 1916 –** trade name distributed through Unicorn Distributors.

**Puritan Special Features Co. – US – 1914 –** production company in Boston, Massachusetts with Charles F. Atkinson as president.

**Pygmy Pictures, Inc. – US – 1921** – located at 427 Western Mutual Life Bldg., Los Angeles, California, with Frank A. Woods as general manager.

**Pyramid Comedies, Inc. – US – 1921** – production company located at 220 W. 42nd St., New York.

**Pyramid Film Co. – US – 1913-1914** – production company with distribution by Warner Bros. through Warner's Features.

**Pyramid Films – UK – 1915-1916** – production company formed by the acquisition of Captain Kettle Films at Towers Hall, Bradford; produced comedies featuring Captain Jolly.

**Pyramid Pictures, Inc. – US – 1915** – production company formed by Arthur N. Smallwood as president and general manager with studios at Ridgefield Park, New Jersey.

**Pyramid Pictures, Inc. - US - 1922** - production company located at 150 West 34th Street, New York, and studio located at 361-363 W. 124th Street, with Walter E. Greene as president.

Original Poster .co.uk

Original Vintage Film Posters - For Sale.

British quads, US & UK one sheets, animation art, front of house and lobby cards.

Over 7,000 posters and lobby cards available online!

info@originalposter.co.uk
UK Callers 01905 620 370
Int Callers +44 1905 620370

# Q

**Quality Amusement Co. - US - 1919-1925** - production company; also distributed rereleases.

**Quality Film Productions - US - 1921** - production company formed by George H. Davis and Joseph Brandt with distribution through Metro Pictures.

**Quality Pictures Corp. - US - 1915-1922** - production company formed March 1, 1915 by Fred J. Balshofer (former head of Bison Co.), Joseph Engel and Charles Abrams; studios located at Sunset Blvd. and Gower in Hollywood (old Nestor studio); distributed by Metro Pictures.

**Quality Pictures Corp. - US - 1921** - production company at 526 Holbrook Bldg., San Francisco, California; George Davis was president, Harry Revier was V. P. and Joe Brandt was secretary/treasurer.

**Quo Vadis Film Co. - UK - 1913-1914** - distribution company with offices located at 12 Cecil Court Winchester.

# R

**R. A. Walsh Productions - US - 1921 -** production company located at 5341 Melrose Ave. Los Angeles, California; distribution through First National.

**R. C. Bruce - US - 1922 -** production company formed by R. C. Bruce in Portland, Oregon; distributed through Educational Film Exchanges.

**R. Prieur and Co. - UK - 1913-1914 -** distributor of Blache, Lagium, Parisien, Princess, Sascha, Skandinavia and Lux Films; offices located at 40 Gerrard St., Winchester.

**R. R. Exclusive Film Co. - UK - 1913-1915 -** distribution company with offices located at 49 Greek St., Westminster.

**R. R. Sales Corp. - US - 1921 -** distribution company with offices at 117 W. 46th, New York.

**R - C Pictures Corp. - US - 1921 -** distribution arm of Robertson Cole Co. with offices at 723 7th Ave., New York; R. S. Cole was president.

**R - D Film Corp. - US - 1921 -** production company in Long Beach, California, with William C. Rae as president, Frank L. A. Graham as V. P. and S. B. Drum as secretary/treasurer and general manager.

**Radin Pictures - US - 1920-1921 -** production company located at 729 Seventh Ave., New York, with Matthias Radin as president.

**Radio Film Co. Inc. - US - 1916 -** distribution company with offices located at 1446 Broadway, New York.

**Radiosoul Films, Inc. - US - 1921 -** located at 1400 Broadway, New York with L. E. Miller as president and L. Druskin as V.P.

**Raff and Gammon - US - 1894-1896 -** distribution company for Edison films for all Edison produced equipment.

**Rainbow Comedies - US - 1918-1922 -** trade names used by U.S. Moving Pictures Co.

**Raising-the-Maine Film Co. - US - 1913** - production company located at 145 West 45th Street, New York.

**Ralph Connor Productions - 1920-1921** - production company formed by Ralph Connor to convert his novels into film productions; worked with Dominion Film Co. and Ernest Shipman. [see Ernest Shipman and Associates]

**Ralph Ince Film Attractions - US - 1918-1919** - production company formed to convert novels and stage plays into film productions; distribution through Associated Pictures Inc.

**Ramo Films, Inc. - US - 1913-1916** - production company and studio located in the Columbia Theatre Building, New York; distributed through Exclusive until 1914 when Exclusive went out of business; released under trade name Regent Films.

**Ramona Films - US - 1915 -** production company that specialized in westerns.

**Ranous Motion Picture Co. - US - 1913-1914** - production company formed by W. V. Ranous and distributed by Warner Bros. through Warner's Features.

**Raver Film Corp. - US - 1915-1918** - production company formed by Harry R. Raver in October 1915 and located at 110 W. 40th St. New York; used the W. Lindsey Gordon studio on Staten Island then moved production to Rockville, Long Island; in 1916, took over production by Ocean Film Corp. and in 1918, changed corporate name to Harry Raver, Inc.

**Rayart Pictures Corp. - US - 1924-1931** - production company owned by W. Ray Johnston with offices at 723 7th Ave. New York; distributed through Johnston's Syndicate Film Exchange; international distribution through Richmount Pictures; re-organized in 1931 to form Monogram Pictures.

**Realart Pictures Corp. - US - 1919-1922** - production and distribution company formed by Paramount to handle lesser known titles; offices located at 469 Fifth Ave., New York and studio at 201 N. Occidental Blvd. Los Angeles, California; Morris Kohn was president and J. S. Woody was general manager; forced to divest and close the company in 1922 along with Artcraft as part of Federal settlement.

**Red Feather Photoplays - US - 1916** - trade name used by Universal for their Broadway Features.

**Red Seal Plays - US - 1915** - trade name for series released by Selig.

**Red Seal Pictures Corp. - US - 1924-1926** - formed by Max Fleischer, Lee de Forest, Edwin Miles Fadiman, and Hugo Riesenfeld to distribute short synchronized sound comedies by states rights for animated Out of the Inkwell Films; filed for bankruptcy September 1926.

**Reel Photo Play co., Inc. - US - 1915** - production company located at 1581 Broadway, New York, with Bernard Levey as president; distribution through Gotham Film Co. Inc.

**Reelcraft Pictures - US - 1919-1922** - production company formed from the merger of Bulls Eye Comedies, Emerald Motion Picture Co., Bee Hive Film Exchange, and Interstate Film Co. of New York; offices at 1107 Bronson Ave. Hollywood, California; produced short subjects for the states' rights market featuring Alice Howell, Gale Henry, Billy West, Milburn Moranti, Marcel Perez, and Bud Duncan; filed bankruptcy in 1922.

**Reelplays Corp. - US - 1916 -** production company for westerns with distribution by states rights through Supreme Film Co.

**Regent Film Syndicate - UK - 1913-1914 -** distribution company formed by George Josiah Banfield, Abraham Simons and Frank Milford Smith with offices at 52 Rupert St., Winchester.

**Reggie Morris Productions, Inc. - US - 1921 -** production company located at 5828 Santa Monica Blvd., Los Angeles, California, Reggie Morris was president and Frank H. Marshall was V. P. and general manager; produced two reel comedy shorts.

**Reginald Barker Productions - US - 1920-1921 -** production company with Reginald Barker as president utilizing Goldwyn Studios in Culver City, California.

**Reliance Feature Film Co. - US - 1914 -** production company formed in New York with Benjamin Moss as president; after first production, Moss left to form B. S. Moss Motion Picture Co.

**Reliance Film Co. - UK - 1913-1914 -** distribution company with offices located at 12 Cecil Court, Winchester.

**Reliance Film Company - US - 1910-1916** - production company located at 111 East 14th Street, New York.

**Reliance Motion Picture Corp. - US - 1910-1915** - production company formed by Adam Kessel and Charles Bauman on Coney Island; in 1911, sold to J. C. Graham; distribution through Mutual starting in 1912; in July 1913, moved to new studios and D. W. Griffith came on a few months later as head of production; in March 1914, moved to 4500 Sunset Blvd in Los Angeles with Majestic Motion Picture Co. and became known as Reliance-Majestic Studios with Griffith supervising both until 1915 when they became part of Fine Arts.

**Rellimeo Film Syndicate - US - 1923-1924** - production company formed by Orlando Edgar Miller and located in San Francisco, California.

**Renaissance Films - UK - 1915-1917** - production company formed by Sidney Morgan and John Melvin Payne; Morgan left in 1916 to join Unity Super Films and company closed soon afterward.

**Renco Film Co. - US - 1919** - distribution company located at 29 So. LaSalle Street, Chicago, Illinois.

**Renco Film Co. - US - 1921** - production company located at 724 S. Spring St. Los Angeles, California, with H. J. Reynolds as president.

**Renfax Film Co. - US - 1914-1915** - distribution company formed by Arthur M. Hess and DeWitt Fox as VP with offices located at 110 west 40th Street, New York; distributed phonograph to try to synchronize sound effects with films; exchanges located in New York, Columbus, Ohio, Chicago and Pittsburgh.

**Renown Pictures - US - 1923-1926** - production company.

**Renowned Pictures - US - 1917** - distribution company located at 1600 Broadway, New York, with Akiba Weinberg as president.

**Renters Ltd. - UK - 1914-1921** - distribution company with offices located at 171 Wardour St. in London.

**Reol Motion Picture Co. - US - 1921-1922** - production company formed by Robert J.

Levy to produce black films; production at Tolden Studio in the Bronx.

**Republic Distributing Corp. - US - 1919-1922 -** distribution company formed by Lewis J. Selznick from the 22 exchanges of World Film Corp when they closed; completely separate from Select Films; released under the trade name Republic Pictures; offices located at 130 W. 46th St., New York with Britton N. Busch as president and general manager; released Clark-Cornelius reissues of Charlie Chaplin. (**NOTE:** no affiliation with either the earlier Republic OR the later Republic).

**Republic Film Co. - US - 1911-1912 -** production company located at 145 W. 45th Street, Suite 804-810, New York and part of the merger to form Universal.

**Republic Pictures - US - 1919-1922 -** trade name used by Republic Distributing Corp.

**Reserve Photo Plays Co. - US - 1916-1917 -** production and distribution company located at the Columbia Theatre Building, New York.

**Revier Motion Picture Company - US - 1910-1911 -** production company with offices located at Majestic Theatre Building and studio at Sugar House Station, with H. Revier as president.

**Rex Beach Pictures Co., Inc. - US - 1917-1919 -** production company located at 440 Fourth Avenue, New York.

**Rex Film Co. - US - 1909-1912 -** production company formed by Edwin S. Porter, William

Swanson, and Joe Engel; part of the merger to form Universal in 1912.

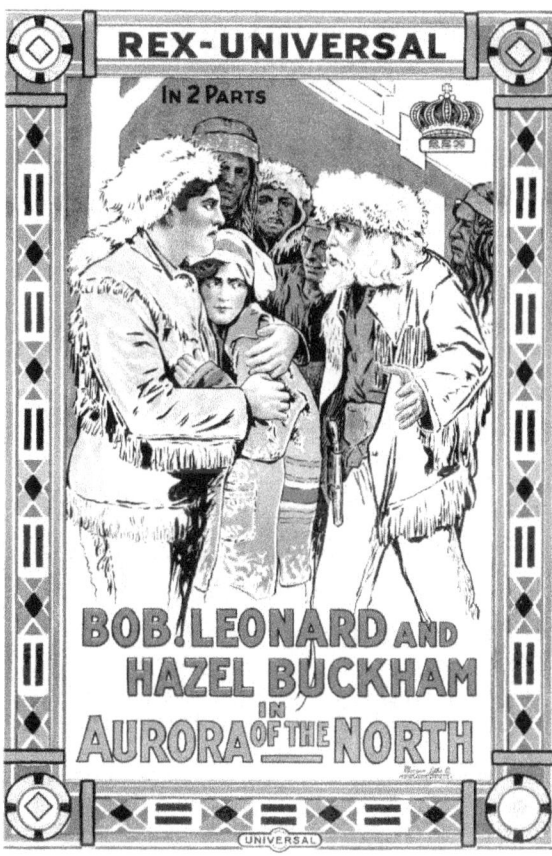

**Rex Motion Picture Masterpiece Co. - US - 1911-1917 -** production company located at 573 Eleventh Avenue, New York.

**Rex Story Comedies - US - 1921 -** production company formed May 1921 by Samuel M. Sargent with Jack S. Nedell as general manager to produce comedies featuring Rex Story; offices located at 4534 Sunset Blvd., Hollywood, California.

**Rialto Productions, Inc. - 1920-1923 -** production company located at 130 West 46th Street, New York, with Lou Rogers as president.

**Rialto De Luxe Productions - US - 1918-1923 -** production company formed in New York by Jesse J. Goldburg; distribution by states rights; went out of business in 1923.

**Rialto Star Features - US - 1915 -** trade name for a series of feature films produced by the Gaumont Company.

**Richard Barthelmess Productions - US - 1923 -** production company formed by Richard Barthelmess with offices at 565 Fifth Ave. New York.

**Richard Kipling Enterprises - US - 1921 -** production company formed by Richard Kipling, R. A.

Sullivan and S. J. Sullivan to make five reel westerns; offices located at 516 5th Ave., New York; used the Balshofer studio with distribution through Kipling Film Exchange, Inc.

**Richard Talmadge Productions - US -** [see Carlos Productions]

**Richard Walton Tully Productions - US - 1922-1923 -** production company with Richard Walton Tully as head of production and Philip Krova as general manager.

**Richmount Pictures, Inc. - US - 1923-1925 -** distribution company formed to export U.S. films; distributed for Rayart.

**Robert C. Bruce Scenics - US - 1916-1934 -** production company creating travelogue style short documentaries and distributed by Educational Film Corp. of America.

**Robert Brunton Productions - US - 1918-1921 -** production company and studios located at 5341-5601 Melrose Ave., Los Angeles, California, with Robert Brunton as president and general manager.

**Robert L. Fargo Productions - US - 1921 -** production company located at 1116 Lodi St., Hollywood, California; produced one reel comedies featuring Hank Mann and distributed by Arrow Film Corp.

**Robertson-Cole Co. - US - 1918-1922 -** formed as import/export business for automobiles by Harry F. Robertson and Rufus Sidman Cole with films as a sideline; soon changed strictly to film distribution; offices located at 780 Gower St. Los Angeles, California; distributed for Haworth Pictures, B. B. Features, National Film Corp. of America, Jess D. Hampton Feature Corp. and Brentwood Film Corp.; in 1922, restructured with Film Booking Offices of America for distribution; opened Robertson-Cole Pictures Corp. to expand into production; later became RKO.

**Robertson-Cole Pictures Corp. - US - 1922-1928 -** production company formed by division of Robertson-Cole Co. with distribution through their sister company Film Booking Offices of America.

**Robert W. Paul - UK - 1895-1910 -** created first production studio in the UK called Muswell Studios; closed and destroyed everything in 1910.

**Robin's Photoplays, Inc - US - 1914-1915** - production company with distribution through Kriterion; merged to form Associated Film Service Corp. in 1915.

**Rockett Film Corp. - US - 1921** - production company located at 3800 Mission Road Hollywood, California, with Ray R. Rockett as president and general manager.

**Rogell-Brown Production Co. - US - 1921-1922** - production company formed by Harry Joe Brown, producer of western films, and director Albert S. Rogell; located in Los Angeles, California; released under trade name of Cactus Features.

**Rogers Film Corporation - US - 1919** - production company located at the Capitol Theater Building, Broadway & 51st Street, New York.

**Roland West Film Productions - US - 1921** - production company located at 260 W. 42nd St., New York with Roland West as president and Charles H. Smith as general manager; produced films featuring Jewel Carmen.

**Rolands Feature Film Co. - US - 1914** - production company formed by George K. Rolands and Samuel Q. Edelstein as general manager with offices located at 145 W. 45th St., New York.

**Rolfe Photoplays, Inc. - US - 1914-1917** - production company owned by B. A. Rolfe and formerly called B. A. Rolfe Photoplays; distributed through Alco Film Corp. but soon changed to Metro Pictures Corp.; in 1915, bought Dyreda Art Film Corp. and used their studios located at 3 West 61st St, New York; in May 1917, absorbed by Metro with Rolfe becoming the general manager; in April 1918, Rolfe left to form Rolfe Productions, Inc.

**Rolfe Productions, Inc. - US - 1918-1920 -** production company formed by B. A. Rolfe after Rolfe Photoplays were acquired by Metro Pictures; ad material during this time shows B. A. Rolfe Productions; in 1920, Rolfe moved to head of production for A. H. Fischer Feature Films at the old Thanhouser studio.

**Rolin Film Co. - US - 1915-1922 -** production company formed by Hal Roach and Dan Linthicum to produce one reel comedies featuring Harold Lloyd using the trade name Phun Philms and Rolin Comedies; distribution was by Pathe.

**Rollo Sales Co. - US - 1922 -** distribution company.

**Roma - ITALY - 1913 -** distributed in the U.K. by Anderson's Film Agency.

**Romance Productions, Inc. - US - 1926 -** production company with distribution by Educational Film Exchanges.

**Romayne Super-Film Co. - US - 1918-1921 -** production company formed in July 1918 with H. Y. Romayne as president and E. D. Ulrich as V. P. and general manager; offices were located at Marsh Strong Bldg., Los Angeles and filming at David Horsley Studios; distribution through states rights.

**Rosenberg and Co. - UK - 1913-1914 -** distributor for S. R. H. Films with offices at Lime St., Liverpool.

**Rosfil'm - RUSSIA - late 1920s-1934 -** production company and studio in Leningrad; formerly named Kinosev; name changed several times and finally in 1934, name was changed to Lenfilm as it remains today.

**Rossi & Co. - ITALY - 1907-1908 -** production company renamed Itala Film [also Carlo Rossi & Co.]

**Rothacker Film Manufacturing Co. - US - 1910-1925 -** production and distribution company located 1339-1351 Diversey Parkway, Chicago, Illinois.

**Rothapfel Pictures Corp. - US - 1919 -** production company formed by Samuel L. Rothapfel with Frank G. Hall as V. P.; distribution through Independent Sales Corp.

**Royal Comedies - US - 1921 -** trade name for two reel comedies released by Reelcraft Pictures Corp.

**Royal Film Agency - UK - 1913-1914 -** distribution company with offices located at 270 Corporation St., Birmingham.

**Royal Gardens Motion Picture Co. - US - 1920 -** production company located at 459 E. 31$^{st}$ St., Chicago, with Sam T. Jacks as head of production; specialized in black films.

**Ruby Feature Film Co. - US - 1914 -** production company formed by Leon J. Rubenstein with studios located at 217 E. 24$^{th}$ St., New York.

**Ruffell's Imperial Bioscope Syndicate - UK - 1910-1914 -** distribution company formed by Charles Warren Lovesy, Harry Raymond Nathan and John Thomas Roach Jr.; offices located at 8-9 Long Acre, Winchester; specialized in rereleases.

**Russell Clark Syndicate, Inc. - US -1922 -** distribution company located at 1540 Broadway, New York.

**Russell Productions - US - 1921-1925** - production and distribution company located at 8 S. Dearborn St., Chicago, Illinois with B. D. Russell as manager of production and W. D. Russell as manager of distribution; produced two reel and five reel westerns and six reel dramas.

**Russell-Greiver-Russell - US - 1920-1921** - distribution company with offices in Chicago, Illinois; distributed for Doubleday Productions, Tusun Productions and Capital Films.

**Russian Art Film Corporation - US - 1917** - distribution company for Russian films; located at 729 Seventh Avenue, New York.

**Ruth Roland Serials - US - 1921** - trade name for production featuring Ruth Roland and produced by Hal E. Roach Studios.

**Ryno Film Co., Inc. - US - 1913** - production company with offices located at 220 W. 42nd Street and studio in City Island, New York with John Noble as head of production.

**583 Pacific Street - Stanford CT 06902**
**203.324.9750**
**www.posterconservation.com**

*Before*

*After*

**LINEN BACKING AND RESTORATION SERVICES**

---

Posters ~ Comics
Comic Art ~ Books
Magazines ~ Memorabilia

Four Color Comics LLC
Robert Rogovin

P.O. Box 1399
Scarsdale, NY 10583
TEL: (914) 722-4696
FAX: (914) 722-7656

WEB: www.fourcolorcomics.com

EMAIL: rob@fourcolorcomics.com

*Femmes Fatales & Fantasies*

**Visit our Museum/Gallery**
**Femmes Fatales &**
**Fantasies**
**7013 E. Main Street**
**Scottsdale, AZ 85251**
**480.429.6800**

# S

**S - L Enterprises - US - 1918-1921** - production and distribution company formed by Arthur H. Sawyer and Herbert Lubin, (both from General Enterprises, Inc.) to produce and distribute their films and films by Ralph Ince Film Attractions; offices located at 1476 Broadway, New York.

**S - L Productions - US - 1921 -** production company with distribution through Metro Pictures Corp.

**S & E Enterprises - US - 1920 -** distribution and production company formed by J. Shenfield and Bert Ennis; located at 1476 Broadway, Suite 907, New York.

**S. A. Lynch Enterprises, Inc. - US - 1917-1920 -** distribution company formed by S. A. Lynch, owner of a theater chain and part owner of Triangle Distributing Corp.; when Triangle Film Co. closed, Lynch bought out the other two partners of Triangle Distributing (Hodkinson and Pawley) and began rereleasing some Triangle films through S. A. Lynch Enterprises; Hallmark Pictures acquired Triangle Distributing from Lynch in 1920. [see Triangle Distributing Corp. and Hallmark Pictures Corp.]

**S. A. Feature Film Co. - UK - 1914-1915 -** distribution company formed from South American Feature Film Co. Ltd. by Nathan Arthur Reichlin and Joseph Worssan; offices located at 38 Bedford St., Westminster.

**S. L. K. Serial Corp. - US - 1919 -** production company located at 112 West 42nd Street, New York, with S. S. Krellberg as president.

**S. L. Warner - US - 1918 -** production company formed by S. L. Warner and located at 220 W. 42nd Street, New York.

**S. P. C. Films - UK - 1913-1914 -** distribution company with offices at 95 Norfolk St. Sheffield.

**Sable Productions - US - 1924-1925 -** production company with William D. Russell as president.

**Sack Amusement Enterprises - US - 1920-1972 -** distribution company formed by Alfred N. Sack in San Antonio, Texas and moved to Dallas; became known for production and distribution of black films from 1930 to 1947; continued in distribution until 1972.

**Sacred Films, Inc. - US - 1921 -** production company in Burbank, California with Harwood Huntington as president, J. D. Taylor as V. P. and Frank Jenal as secretary/treasurer; produced two reel religious films.

**Safety Bioscope Co. Ltd. - UK - 1909-1914 -** production and distribution company formed by William Bailey Ransom, Alice Thompson and Mary Wernyes with William Dewhurst Walker as general manager; offices located at 84 Southhampton Road, Haverstock Hill, Hampstead.

**SAFFI-Comerio - ITALY - 1907-1909 -** production company and studio formed in Milan by merger of Comerio Production Co. and Adolfo Croce's Societa Anonima Fabbricazione Films Italiane; in 1909, changed company name to Milano Films.

**Saint (St.) Louis Motion Picture Co. - US - 1912-1915 -** production company and studio located at 25th and Montgomery Streets, St. Louis, Missouri; produced for Universal under the brand name Shamrock Film in 1912, Frontier Films in 1913-1914, and then in 1914-1915 as Premier Films.

**Salient Films, Inc. - US - 1920-1921** - production company located at 522 Fifth Avenue and 220 West 42nd Street, New York, with Max F. C. Goosmann as president.

**Salvation Army Limelight Department - AUSTRALIA - 1896-1901** - production of magic lantern shows and moved to film production in 1897; built first Australian production studio in 1898 at 69 Bourke St., Melbourne; in 1901, production company separated from Salvation Army department and became officially Australian Kinematographic Company.

**Sammy Burns Comedies Inc - US - 1921-1926** - production company located at 311 5th Ave., New York, with Sammy Burns as president.

**Samson Film Co. - UK - 1914-1915** - distribution company with offices located at 20 Frith St., Westminster.

**Samuel Bischoff Productions - US - 1922-1928** - production and distribution company for Bischoff Comedies; in 1924, purchased studio at 1424-1426 Beachwood Dr., Los Angeles, California.

**Samuel Goldwyn, Inc. - US - 1922-1960?** - production company formed by Samuel Goldwyn upon his leaving Goldwyn Pictures; battle over use of the Goldwyn name ensued; early productions were released as Howard Productions after his wife Frances Howard; distribution through United Artists during the silent era.

**Samuelson Film Manufacturing Co., Ltd - UK - 1914-1920** - production company formed by George Berthold Samuelson with offices and studio at Worton Hall, Isleworth.

**Samuel Zierler Photoplay Corp. - US - 1922-1923** - production distributed through Metro Pictures Corp.

**Sanford Productions - US - 1925-1926** - production company.

**Santa Barbara Motion Picture Co. - US - 1914-1915** - production company formed by Dr. Elmer J. Boeske and other Santa Barbara businessmen with Lorimer Johnston as head of production; distribution through Sawyer Film Mart and then moved to Kriterion; merged to form Associated Film Service Corp. in 1915.

**Sascha Studios - AUSTRIA - 1912-1938** - production and distribution company founded by Count Sascha Kolowrat-Krakowsky, a nobleman from Bohemia which became one of the largest studios in Austria;

confiscated by Nazis in 1938 and integrated into one state studio, Wien-Film.

**Satex Film Co. - US - 1910-1913 -** production company formed in San Antonio Texas by Paul W. Tilley and Wesley Hope Tilley; in 1911, moved production to Austin, Texas, producing features and shorts; distribution through Warner's Features; ceased operation July 1913.

**Sawyer, Inc. - US - 1914-1915 -** [see A. H. Sawyer Film Features, Inc. and Sawyer Film Corp.]

**Sawyer Film Corp. - US - 1914-1915 -** distribution company formed December 1914 from Sawyer, Inc. and A. H. Sawyer Film Features, Inc. with the idea to purchase the films from all the production companies; quickly ran out of money and closed March 1915.

**Sawyer-Lubin Productions - US - 1922 -** production company with distribution through Metro Pictures Corp.

**Schiller Film Company - US - 1914 -** production company located in the Schiller Building, Chicago, Illinois.

**Screen Art Pictures - US - 1920 -** distribution company located at 1331 Vine Street, Philadelphia, Pennsylvania with Michael Lessy.

**Screen Classics, Inc. - US - 1918 -** trade name used by Metro Pictures Corp.

**Screen Snapshots, Inc. - US - 1920** - production company specializing in presenting news about the celebrities.

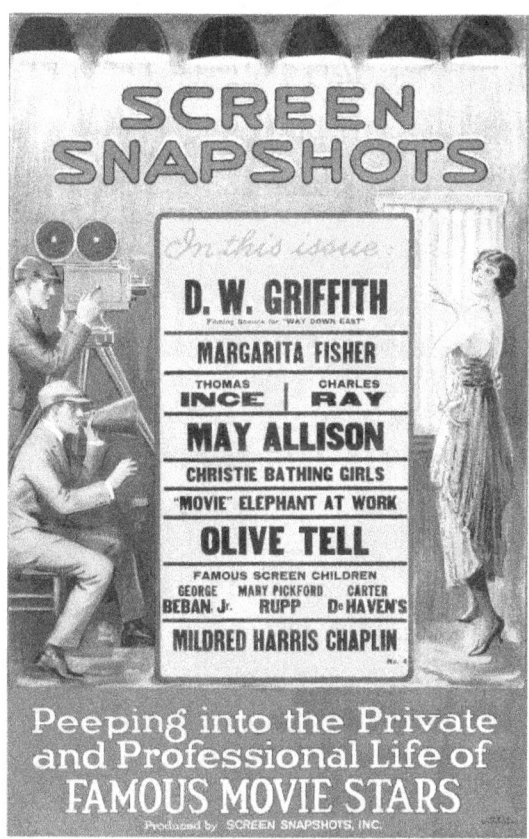

**Screencraft Pictures - US - 1918** - production company located at Longacre Building, 1476 Broadway, New York, with studios located at 46 Main Street, New Rochelle, New York.

**Seattle Film Co. - US - 1914** - production company formed by Edward S. Curtis in Seattle, Washington.

**Second National Film Corp. - US - 1922-1923** - distribution company formed to distribute independent films similar to First National Pictures; offices located at 140 W. 42nd St., New York.

**Select Film Booking Agency, Inc. - US - 1915-1916** - distribution company formed by Famous Players Film Co. to distribute longer and more expensive films.

**Select Photo-Play Producing Company - US - 1914** - production company located at 71 West 23rd Street, Suite 812-812 Masonic Building, New York.

**Select Pictures Corp. - US - 1917-1923** - distribution company formerly called Lewis J. Selznick Productions; offices at 729 7th Ave., New York; Aldolph Zukor bought controlling interest of Selznick Productions to eliminate Selznick's name from the company; went bankrupt in 1923.

# Silent Studio Directory

**Selecto Film Co. Inc. - US - 1916 -** production company formed by Richard Wallace in Los Angeles California, to produce comedy shorts; closed April 1916.

**Selexart Pictures - US - 1918 -** production and distribution company specializing in westerns.

**Selig Polyscope Co. - UK - 1912-1916 -** distribution arm of Selig Polyscope Co. formed by E. H. Montagu; offices located at 12 Gerrard, St. Winchester.

**Selig and Rork - US - 1921 -** production company located at 3800 Mission Road, Los Angeles, California, with William Selig and Samuel E. Rork; produced one and two reel animal comedies for Educational Film Corp.

**Selig Polyscope Co. Inc. - US - 1896-1918 -** production company formed from W. N. Selig Co. by William N. Selig in Chicago; formed to produce travelogues; established temporary studio in New Orleans in 1909 through Francis Boggs; Boggs moved operations to California and set up the first studio in California at Edendale in 1909; in 1913, bought 32 acres near Los Angeles and turned it into a zoo; in 1915, moved the Chicago and Edendale studios into the zoo and formed V-L-S-E for distribution; in 1916, when V-L-S-E closed, distributed by states rights; in 1918, stopped production and focused on supplying animals for other film studios.

**Selsior Film Co. - UK - 1913-1914** - distributor for Searchlight Films; offices located at 3 Denman St. Winchester.

**Selznick Co. - US - 1923 -** production company formed by David O. Selznick (Lewis' son).

**Selznick Distributing Corp. - US - 1923-1924 -** distribution company formed by Lewis J. Selznick after the bankruptcy of Select Pictures.

**Selznick Pictures Corp. - US - 1919-1923 -** production company formed by Myron Selznick (Lewis' son), with brother Howard Selznick as assistant and brother David as treasurer; financed by their mother with offices at 729 7th Ave., New York and using studios at Fort Lee, New Jersey.

**Selznick Productions - US - 1916-1917 -** [see Lewis J. Selznick Productions, Inc.]

**Serial Film Corp. - US - 1916-1917 -** production company with William Steiner as president and head of production; formed to make serials and comedy shorts; studio located at Cliffside, New Jersey, with some filming done in Jacksonville, Florida; distribution through Unity Sales Corp. and then Metro Pictures Corp. in 1917.

**Serial Publication Corp. - US - 1915 -** distribution company located at 29 Union Square, New York.

**Sessua Hayakawa Productions - US - 1918-1920** - [see Haworth Pictures Corp.]

**Sevzapkino - RUSSIA - 1920s-current** - production company and studio in Leningrad formerly named Kinosev; after several changes, in 1934, name was changed to Lenfilm and it remains today.

**Sfinks Studio - POLAND - 1909-1936** - production company formed in Warsaw by Aleksander Hertz; in 1914, absorbed Kosmofilm owned by Henryk Finkelstein and expanded into distribution, becoming the dominant studio in Poland; created the Polish star system (primarily with Pola Negri and Mia Mara); Hertz died in 1928 and Finkelstein took control until 1936 when the studio closed due to the Nazis.

**Shaftesbury Feature Film Co. Ltd. - UK - 1912-1914** - distribution company formed by David Walter Beck and George Soole with offices at 55-59 Shaftesbury Ave., Westminster; distributed for Continental Kunstfilm.

**Shamrock Film - US - 1912-1913** - trade name for films produced by St. Louis Motion Picture Co. and distributed through Universal.

**Shamrock Photoplay Corp. - US - 1917-1923** - production company formed from reorganization of the Lone Star Co. in San Antonio, Texas; specialized in westerns.

**Sheffield Photo Co. - UK - 1913-1914** - distribution company for Shamrock Films with offices located at 95 Norfolk St., Sheffield.

**Sheriott Pictures Corp. - US - 1917** - production company located at 218 West 42nd Street, New York and 203 Schiller Building, Chicago, Illinois.

**Sherlock Holmes Series Inc. - US - 1922** - production company with offices in New York; distribution through Educational Film.

**Sherman Pictures Corp. - US - 1917** - production company formed by Harry A. Sherman; located at Sherman Pictures Building, 218 West 42nd Street, New York.

**Sherman Productions Corp. - US - 1920** - production company formed by Harry A. Sherman; located at 1476 Broadway, New York.

**Sherman-Elliott, Inc. - US - 1916 -** distribution company located at 220 West 42nd Street, Suite 1702, New York.

**Sherman Krellberg Productions - US - 1919 -** [See S. L. K. Serial Corporation]

**Sherry Service - US - 1918 -** distribution company located at 729 7th Avenue, New York; formed by William L. Sherry, former VP of Paramount, to distribute "Broncho Billy" Anderson films.

**Shochiku Cinema Co. - JAPAN - 1920-current -** well established Kabuki production company owned by Matsujiro Shirai and Takejiro Otani since 1895; moved into film production in 1920; acquired Taikatsu in 1922 and began to modernize the Japanese film industry with new equipment and creation of the star system; produced Japan's first "talkie" in 1931, (*The Neighbor's Wife and Mine* aka *The Lady Next Door and My Wife*); silent films continued to be produced until the late 1930s.

**Short Films Syndicate, Inc. - US - 1925-1927 -** distribution company of short films by states rights with Joseph Pincus as general manager; offices at 729 7th Ave., New York.

**Shubert Film Corp. - US - 1914-1916 -** production company formed to handle material of William A. Brady, Charles A. Blancy and Owen Davis; offices were located at 223 West 44th St., New York, with Joseph L. Rhinock as president and Jules Murry as general manager; distribution through World Film Corp.

**Sid Films - US - 1914 -** trade name used by Sid Olcott International Features.

**Sid Olcott International Features - US - 1914 -** production company formed by Sid Olcott after leaving Gene Gautier Feature Players to produce films for Warner's Features; used trade name Sid Films and produced in Jacksonville, Florida until June 1914 when they moved to Ireland.

**Sierra Pictures - US - 1923-1928 -** production company.

**Sigla Film Co. - ITALY - 1909-1928 -** distribution company formed in Naples by Gustavo Lombardo; in 1928, moved to Rome and changed name to Titanus.

**Signal Film Corp. - US - 1915-1921 -** production company formed by John P. McGowan and Helen Holmes with S. S. Hutchinson as president and general manager (Hutchinson was also head of American Film Corp.); distribution through Mutual as Signal-Mutual Films; offices located at 4560 Pasadena Avenue, Los Angeles, California, and 222 S. State St., Chicago, Illinois; later moved to 6227-6235 Broadway, Chicago.

**Signet Film Co. - US - 1916 -** distribution company located at 220 West 42nd Street, New York.

**Signet Picture Supplies, Ltd. - UK - 1913-1914 -** distribution company located at 116 Dale St., Liverpool.

**Sila Film - POLAND - 1911-1913 -** production company formed in Warsaw by Mordka Towbin to produce Yiddish films of the Kaminski Troupe.

**Skandias Filmbyra - SWEDEN - 1923-1924 -** distribution company located in Stockholm for U.S. films.

**Skandinavisk Film-Central - SWEDEN - 1915-1921 -** distribution company formed by Lars Bjorck in Stockholm and expanded into production in 1919 and created subsidiary company Palladium Films to produce comedies with Danish director Lau Lauritzen as head of production but had financial trouble and filed for bankruptcy in 1921. [see Palladium Films]

**Smallwood Film Corp. - US - 1913-1915 -** production company formed from U. S. Film Corp. in Cincinnati with Arthur Smallwood as president; distribution was through Warner's Features and then United Film Service when they took over Warner's.

**Snakeville Comedies - US - 1911-1917 -** trade name for a series of comedy shorts produced by Essanay Films.

**Snowy Baker Productions - US - 1921 -** production and distribution company featuring Snowy Baker; located at 3800 Mission Rd. Hollywood, California; organizers were W. N. Selig, Sam E. Rork, Snowy and Ethel Baker.

**Snub Pollard Comedies - US - 1921 -** trade name for comedy shorts featuring Snub Pollard produced by Hal E. Roach Studios.

**Societa Anonima Ambrosio - ITALY -** [see Ambrosio]

**Societa Anonima Stefano Pittaluga (SASP) - ITALY - 1920-1934 -** production and distribution company formed by Stefano Pittaluga and he began purchasing studios; acquired the F.E.R.T. studio in 1924; by 1929, SASP had acquired all the distributors in the Italian Cinematographic Union (UCI) including Cines, Itala and Palatina; in 1929, began equipping them for sound production; Pittaluga died in 1932.

**Societe des Films Artistiques - FRANCE - 1924-1928 -** production and distribution company that specialized in financing and distributing independent films all over Europe; used the trade name SOFAR Film

**Societe Francaise des Films Artistiques - FRANCE - 1921-1922 -** production and distribution company located at 71, Rue de Choiseul, Paris, France.

**Societe Francaise des Filmes et Cinematographes Eclair - FRANCE - 1907-1986 -** production and distribution company formed by Charles Jourjon with studio at Epinay sur Seine outside of Paris; started producing their own camera in 1912; slowly moved out of film production and into producing cameras.

**Societe Pathe Freres - FRANCE - 1902-current -** translates as Pathe Brothers Co.; acquired Lumiere patents and set up multiple production companies and distribution in most industrialized countries; started first newsreels in 1908, and dominated world film production until World War I; in 1921, sold off U.S. production arm which was renamed Pathe Exchange; later merged to become RKO.

**Societe Universelle de Distribution - FRANCE - 1927-1928 -** distribution company located in Paris.

**Society Italian Cines - US - 1904-1908 -** distribution company located at 143 E. 23rd Street, New York; formed to import and distribute Cines films.

**Sofar Film - FRANCE - 1924-1928**
[see Societe des Films Artistiques]

**Sokal-Film GmbH - GERMANY - 1926-1933** - production company.

**Sol Lesser Productions - US - 1920-1958** - production and distribution company located at 634 H. W. Hellman Building, Los Angeles, California; produced films under the names Progressive Film Co. and Principal Pictures Corp.

**Solax Film Corp. - US - 1910-1916** - production company formed September 7, 1910 by Alice Guy Blache, Herbert Blache and George A. Magie; Alice Guy was the world's first woman director with Gaumont; production for Solax was at the Gaumont studio on Congress Ave., Flushing, New York until their studio was built in 1912 in Fort Lee, New Jersey; in 1912, Guy directed what is considered one of the first all black films titled *A Fool and His Money;* continued releasing films under the Solax trade name; in 1914, company was re-organized as Blache Features and United States Amusement Co. to make more feature length films; originally distributed through Motion Picture Distributing and Sales and moved to Metro Pictures in 1916; studios used by numerous other production companies.

**Solitary Sin Corporation - US - 1919 -** distribution company located at 1482 Broadway, New York.

**Sono Art-World Wide - US - 1927-1933 -** production company; merged with Rayart to form Monogram.

**South Coast Feature Film Co. - US - 1912 -** distribution company through states rights; located at First National Bank Bldg., Suite 746, Chicago, Illinois.

**South Wales Film Agency - UK - 1913-1914 -** distribution company with offices at Glebeland St., Merthyr, Tydfil.

**Southern Cross Feature Film Co. - AUSTRALIA - 1918-1925 -** production company formed in Adelaide by Sir David Gordon et al.

**Southern Feature Film Corp. - US - 1918 -** production and distribution company located at 1476 Broadway, Suite 801-806, New York.

**Sovkino - RUSSIA - 1925-1931 -** production company and studio located in Leningrad; reformed and absorbed Goskino, Proletkino and Sevzapkino.

**Special Film Co. Ltd. - US - 1912 -** distribution company located at 5 West 14th Street, New York.

**Special Pictures Corp. - US - 1920-1921 -** production and distribution company located at 7100 Santa Monica Blvd. Hollywood, California, with Frank G. Collier as president and general manager; distributed Comedyart Comedies, Comiclassics, Clayplay Comedies, Moranti Comedies and Chester Conklin Comedies.

**Spencer Productions, Inc - US - 1921 -** production company located at 2435 Wilshire Blvd. Santa Monica, California, with A. Spencer Livingston as president and Samuel Howie as V. P.; produced six reel westerns and dramas; distributed through Associated Photoplays.

**Spencer's Pictures - AUSTRALIA - 1905-1914 -** distribution company formed by Canadian businessman Charles C. Spencer who, in 1908, moved to production and established a studio to produce documentary shorts and newsreels; expanded to feature films in 1910; in 1911, incorporated as Spencer's Pictures Ltd. and built a new studio at Rushcutter's Bay in Sydney; by 1912, largest film importer in Australia but, while he was out of the country, his board elected to merge with West's Pictures and Amalgamated Pictures to become General Film Co. of Australasia; Spencer retired in 1918 and went back to Canada.

**Sport Film Co. - UK - 1913-1914 -** distribution company for Splendor Films with offices located at 3-7 Southampton St., Winchester.

**Spotlight Comedies - US - 1921 -** trade name for one reel comedies released by Arrow Film Corp.

**Standard Cinema Corp. - US - 1923-1924 -** distribution company for shorts; located at 831 S. Wabash Avenue, Chicago, Illinois; formed by L. D. Darmour as president; some distribution through Selznick Distribution Corp.

**Standard Feature Film Co. - UK - 1913-1916 -** distribution company formed by merger of Standard Feature Film and Art Cinema Plays with Rhonda Gay, Emily O'Hara, William Robert Paterson, Beatrice Alice Coomber Renton, and Percy Renton; offices located at 79 Shaftesbury Ave., Winchester; in September 1914, moved to 55 High St., New Oxford and then in October 1916 to Film House, Gerrard St.

**Standard Film Attractions - US - 1924 -** distribution company located at 1322 Vine Street, Philadelphia, Pennyslvania.

**Standard Photo-Play Distributors - US - 1915 -** [see Standard Pictures, Inc.]

**Standard Pictures, Inc. - US - 1915 -** distribution company located at the Times Building, New York, and formed by Al Lichtman, A. Warner and H. M. Warner to replace United Film Service, which went bankrupt; Standard picked up distribution for Albuquerque, Crystal, Erbograph, Grandin, Ideal, Mittenthal, Pike's Peak, Smallwood, and St. Louis film companies et al.

**Standard Pictures, Inc. - US - 1921** - located at 205 International Bldg. Los Angeles, California; formed by Emmett Dalton, M. J. Graves and Arthur C. Webb.

**Stanley Film Agency - UK - 1915** - distribution company located at Sherwood St., Stanley House, Westminster.

**Star Comedies - US - 1920** - trade name of comedy series released by Universal.

**Star Film Agency - UK - 1915** - distribution company with offices at 59-61 New Oxford St., Holborn.

**Star Film Co. - DENMARK - 1917-1920** - production company formed by William Gluckstadt and Alex Christian; closed due to scandal and Christian committing suicide.

**Star Film Co. - FRANCE - 1896-1914** - production company located at Theatre Robert Houdin, 8. Boulevard des Italiens, Paris and founded by magician Georges Melies; Melies is credited for creating many of the special effects that are still in use today; Melies produced and directed 531 films between 1896 and 1913; in 1902, released a *Trip to the Moon*, which is considered to be the most pirated movie EVER; Melies sent his brother, Gaston to the U. S. in an attempt to stop some of the piracy; in 1914, studio was confiscated by the French government in World War I.

**Star Film Co. - US - 1903-1908** - Georges Melies used Biograph Co. for U.S. distribution but film piracy was so rampant that he sent his brother Gaston to open a U.S. office in 1902 located at 204 E. 38th St. New York; Melies films were released under the first trade name known Star Films; Gaston opened a production facility as Fort Lee; in 1910, moved production company to San Antonio to the Star Film Ranch and released approximately 70 films under G. Melies with the trade names Wild West Films and American Wild West Films. [see Star Films American Wild West Productions]

**Star Film Company - US - 1917 -** production company with offices and studio located at Ridgely Avenue and Factory Street, Springfield, Illinois.(**NOTE:** NOT associated with Melies)

**Star Film Service - UK - 1902-1914 -** distribution company with offices located at 4 St. Anne St., Liverpool.

**Star Film Trading Co. - UK - 1908** - distribution arm of Melies films with offices at 7 Rupert Court, Westminster.

**Star Films American Wild West Productions - US - 1911-1913 -** trade name used for Gaston Melies western productions; in 1910, production company was moved to San Antonio, Texas and the studio called the Star Films Ranch where they began producing westerns; in 1911, name was changed to Star Films American Wild West Productions and moved to Santa Paula, California; in 1912, Gaston travelled the south seas with a crew making exotic films using the G. Melies tag and the American Wild West logo, but the quality was not marketable, basically bankrupting the company; company closed in 1913 and sold to Vitagraph. [see Star Films; Melies Manufacturing Co.]

**Star Productions - US - 1920-1922** - trade name used by Realart.

**Star Serial Corp. - US - 1922 -** production company formed by Joseph Brandt.

**Starfilms Limited - US - 1916 -** distribution company located in the Starfilms Building, Montreal, Canada; distributors for Metro Pictures, et al.

**State Film Agency - UK - 1914-1915 -** distribution company with offices located at 191 Wardour St., Westminster.

**State Pictures Corp. - US - 1922-1923** - production company.

**State Rights Independent Exchanges - US - 1912-1962** - distribution company.

**States Rights Distributors, Inc. - US - 1917** - distribution company formed August 22, 1917 by a conglomerate to distribute films patterned after First National Pictures with Sol Lesser as president, Louis Haas as V. P. and Louis B. Mayer as treasurer.

**Steiner Productions - US - 1921-1925** - production company formed by William Steiner [see William Steiner Productions]

**Stellar Photoplay Co. - 1913-1914** - production company located at the Longacre Bldg., New York with Frank J. Carrol as president, C. A. "Doc" Willat as V. P. and William A McManus as secretary/treasurer; production was done at the Ruby Twinplex studio.

**Stereoscopic Film Co. - US - 1925** - production company headed by Max O. Miller in Hollywood, California.

**Sterling Camera and Film Co. - US - 1913-1915** - production company located at 145 West 45th Street, New York, and formed by Fred J. Balshofer to showcase films featuring comics Fred Sterling and George Nash; distribution through Universal as Sterling Pictures.

**Sterling Comedies - US** - comedy shorts featuring Al St. John and distributed through Famous Players-Lasky Corp.

**Sterling Pictures - US - 1913-1915** - trade name used by Sterling Camera and Film Co.

**Sterling Pictures - US - mid 1920s-1931** - production company owned by Trem Carr; specialized in westerns; in 1931, merged with W. Ray Johnston to form Monogram Pictures.

**Stoll Film Co., Ltd - UK - 1918-1922** - production company formed by Sir Oswald Stoll with offices in Surbiton; in 1919, moved into their new studio, Cricklewood.

**Stoll Film Corp. of America - US - 1920-1921** - distribution company formed by Sir Oswald Stoll; located at 130 West 46th Street, New York, with George King as president; imported five and six reel dramas produced by Stoll English Studios; distributed through Pathe Exchange.

**Storey Pictures - US - 1921 -** distribution company located at 17 W. 42nd St., New York with A. D. V. Storey as president and general manager; distributed short subjects by states rights.

**Storyart Pictures Corp. - US - 1921 -** located at 90 West St., New York, with Charles F. Ames as president and Arling Alcine as V. P. and general manager.

**Strand Comedies - US - 1917-1918** - trade name for one reel comedies produced by Caulfield Photoplay Co. and distributed by Mutual Film Corp.

**Strand Film Company - US - 1914** - distribution company located at 145 West 45th Street, New York.

**Studio Alvise - EGYPT - 1927-1928** - production company formed by Alvise Orfanelli; Orfanelli had two studios in Alexandria: one located at 18 Qaid Gohar St. and the other at 2 Maumoud Pasha el Falaki St.; Oranelli later moved to Cairo and became a major producer.

**Studio Lama - EGYPT - 1928-1929** - production company and studio formed by Ibrahim Lama in Victoria; released under the trade name of Condor Films; later moved to Cairo at 18, Naguib Shakour Pasha St., el Quobbeh Gardens.

**Studio Togo Mizrahi - EGYPT - 1929-1946** - production company formed by Togo Mizrahi and located in Bacos, Alexandria; produced numerous films and in 1939 moved to Cairo and used the Studio Wahbi until his exile in 1946.

**Submarine Film Co. - US - 1914-1918** - production company formed by Capt. Charles Williamson to shoot underwater footage; offices located at 1482 Broadway, New York with T. S. Southgate as president and J. Ernest Williamson as general manager; initial distribution was through Thanhouser Films; moved to Universal who produced *20,000 Leagues Under the Sea* and other underwater films.

**Sudfilm - GERMANY - 1929** - distribution company.

**Suitu Exclusive Picture Co. - UK - 1913-1914** - distribution company with offices located at Peel Square, Barnsley.

**Sullivan Films - US - 1923-1926** - production company owned by Pat Sullivan and distributed through M. J. Winkler; in 1926, changed name to Bijou Films, Inc. and distributed through Educational Film Exchanges [see Pat Sullivan Comics]

**Sun Photoplay Co. - US - 1914-1915** - production and distribution company located at 218 West 42nd Street, New York with A. C. Langan as president and general manager.

**Sun Motion Pictures Corp. - US - 1921-1926** - production and distribution company located at 220 W. 42nd St. New York with Sam Efrus as general manager.

**Sun-Lite Comedy - US** - trade name for comedies produced by Schiller Productions and distributed by Reelcraft.

**Sunbeam Comedies - US - 1918-1919** - trade name for two reel comedies released by Florida Film Corporation.

**Sunbeam Motion Picture Corp. - US - 1917** - production company located at 220 West 42nd Street, New York, with John J. Lordan as president.

**Sunny South and Sealight Film Co. - UK - 1914-1915** - production company formed by F. L. Lyndhurst and Will Evans to make one reel comedies.

**Sunnywest Film Co. - US - 1921** - distribution company located at

126 W. 46th St., New York to distribute westerns.

**Sunrise Film Mfg. Co - US - 1919 -** production and distribution company located in San Francisco and owned by Benjamin Brodsky; formed to make and export films to China.

**Sunrise Pictures Corp. - US - 1921** - distribution company located at 729 7th Ave., New York, with Max Carnot as president, Nat N. Dorfman as V. P. and Sylvester Rubenstein as general manager.

**Sunset Comedies - US - 1921 -** trade name for one reel comedies featuring Fatty Bellstein produced and distributed by Sunset Comedy Co.

**Sunset Comedy Co. - US - 1921 -** production and distribution company located at South Heights and Irma Ave. Youngstown, Ohio with H. C. Kunkleman as president and general manager and A. M. Schaeflein as V. P.; produced one reel comedies featuring Fatty Bellstein under the trade name of Sunset Comedies; distributed through states rights.

**Sunset Motion Picture Co. - US - 1914** - production company located at Suite 401, World's Tower Building, 110 W. 40th Street, New York and 1015-1016 Hearst Building, San Francisco, California.

**Sunset Motion Picture Corp. - US - 1914-1915** - production company formed with M. E. Cory as general manager in association with Sunset Magazine and some Senators and judges; formed to produce documentaries of expeditions.

**Sunset Pictures - US - 1916 -** production company specializing in western dramas; distributed through Unicorn Film Services.

**Sunset Productions - US - 1918-1927** - production company located in San Antonio, Texas with Frank Powell as head of production; formed to produce western dramas; offices in New York and distribution through W. W. Hodkinson Corp and then later through Awyon Film.

**Sunshine Comedies - US - 1917-1921** - trade name for comedy shorts produced by Sunshine Comedy Co. and distributed by Fox Film.

**Sunshine Comedy Co. - US - 1917-1922** - production company formed March 1917 with William Fox as president and Harry Lehrman as V. P. and head of production; Films were released as Sunshine Comedies and distribution through Fox Film.

**Sunshine Film Corp. - US - 1914-1915** - production company specializing in comedy shorts and released under the trade names of Juno Comedies, Magnet Comedies and Mars Comedies; distribution was through Warner's Features until they were forced by court order to change to United Film Service.

**Suomen Filmkuvaamo - FINLAND - 1919-1921** - production company formed by Erkki Karu but changed their name to Suomi Filmi in 1921.

**Suomi-Filmi - FINLAND - 1921- still in existence** - production company formed from Suomen Filmkuvaamo with Erkki Karu as president; by the end of silent era, Suomi-Filmi was largest production studio in Finland.

**Super Film - FRANCE - 1920 -** distribution company located in Paris.

**Superba Comedies, Inc. - US - 1921** - production company of comedy shorts located at 6040 Sunset Blvd., Hollywood, California.

**Superior Feature Film Co. - US - 1912** - distribution company located at 32 Union Square, New York.

**Superior Features - 1916- -** distribution company located in Detroit for Christie's Comedies et al for Michigan; distributed by states rights.

**Superior Film Mfg. Co. - US - 1914-** production company located in Des Moines, Iowa.

**Superior Foto-Play Co. - US - 1921** - production company and studio located at Englewood, Denver, Colorado, with Otis B. Thayer as president and general manager and F. A. Stone as secretary/treasurer.

**Superior Pictures - US - 1919-1920** - trade name used by Robertson-Cole Distributing Corp.

**Superpictures Distributing Corp. - US - 1917** - distribution company reformed from Superpictures with Hodkinson, Collins and Pawley after the buyout of Triangle Distributing Corp. by S. A. Lynch; began distributing for Petrova Pictures with Collins also president of Petrova.

**Superpictures, Inc. - US - 1916** - distribution company formed with W. W. Hodkinson as president, Frederick L. Collins as V. P., and Raymond Pawley as treasurer; almost immediately merged to form Triangle Distributing Corp., a separate distributing arm of Triangle Pictures.

**Superlative Pictures - US - 1927-1928** - production company.

**Superlative Pictures Corp. - US - 1917** - production company formed June 1, 1917 in the merger of Lois Meredith Pictures, Inc. and Irving Cummings Pictures, Inc., with Morris F. Tobias as president.

**Supreme Comedies - US - 1915-1921** - trade name for comedy series released by Vim Comedy Co. and rereleased by Robertson Cole in the early 1920s.

**Supreme Feature Film Co. - US - 1912-1913** - distribution company through states rights; located at 4 East 14th Street, New York, with Jacob Berg as general manager.

**Supreme Feature Films, Inc. of California - US - 1917** - production and distribution company located at 1600 Broadway, New York, with D. S. Markowitz as general manager.

**Supreme Film Co. - US - 1916** - distribution company for Reelplays Corp. with offices located at 207 S. Wabash St., 6th Floor, Chicago, Illinois.

**Supreme Film Co. Ltd. - UK - 1914-1915 -** distribution company formed by William Chapman, Nathaniel Lyons and Eugene Solmersitz; offices located at 11 Charing Cross Road, Westminster.

**Supreme Pictures Corp. - US - 1916 -** production company with distribution through Unicorn Film Service.

**Supreme Pictures, Inc. - US - 1919-1921 -** production company headed by Louis Grossman, Arthur B. Reeve and John W. Grey as president; formed to make the Harry Houdini films; in 1921, J. A. Forney became president and distribution was through Pioneer Film; offices were located at 101-103 W. 42nd St., New York and studio in Flushing, Long Island New York.

**Svenska Biografteatern AB - SWEDEN - 1911-1919 -** production company called Svenska Bio and formed by investment group headed by Charles Magnusson, Frans Wiberg and Nils Nylander; offices located at Kristianstad; later that year they built Sweden's first production studio with offices located at Kungsgatan 24, Stockholm; distribution was through Pathe Freres. World War I drastically expanded company production;. in 1919, merged with Filmindustri Inc Skandia to form Svensk Filmindustri.

**Svensk Bios Filmbyra - SWEDEN - 1922** - distribution company for Fox Films.

**Svensk Filmindustri - SWEDEN - 1919-current** - production company formed by the merger of Filmindustri Inc Skandia and Svenska Bio with Charles Magnusson as president; Svensk Filmindustri is still in existence today.

**Sydney Polytechnic - AUSTRALIA - 1897-1899** - production company formed by Mark Blow in Sydney Australia to produce local short films.

**Sylvanite Productions - US - 1921** - production company located at 802 S. Olive St., Los Angeles, California, with Robert Sullivan as general manager; specialized in westerns by states rights distribution; production was done at Santa Ynez Canyon, Santa Monica, California.

**Synchofilms - UK - 1927** - production company.

**Syndicate Pictures - US - 1928-1930** - production company specializing in westerns and formed by Lillian Cunningham, Peter Lewis and Henry R. Danziger in New York

**Syndicate Superfeatures - US - 1921** - trade name for higher budget feature films distributed by George Kleine.

# T

**Taikatsu - JAPAN - 1920-1922** – short name for Taisho Katsuei.

**Taisho Katsuei - JAPAN – 1920-1922** - production company formed by Ryozo Asano; acquired by Shochiku Cinema in 1922.

**Tatra Film Corp. – CZECHOSLOVAKIA – 1920-1921** – production and distribution company formed by Jaroslav Saikel.

**Tattenham Productions, Inc. – US – 1921** – production company located at 4534 Sunset Blvd., Los Angeles, California; distributed by Pinnacle Productions.

**Tec-Art Studio - US - 1913-1931** – production company founded by William H. Clune and known as Clune Studio.

**Teikoku Kinema Geijutsu - JAPAN – 1920-1921** – (translates as Imperial Cinema Art Co.) production company a/k/a Teikine for short.

**Tennenshoku Katsudo Shashin - JAPAN – 1914-1919** – production company formed from remnants of Fukuhodo; introduced first animated films; was acquired in 1919 by Kokkatsu.

**Tenkatsu - JAPAN – 1914-1919** – short name for Tennenshoku Katsudo Shashin.

**Terra Filmkunst - GERMANY – 1926-1949** – production and distribution company.

**Terriss Film Corp. – US – 1916** – production company formed by Tom Terriss; distribution through Unity Sales Corp.

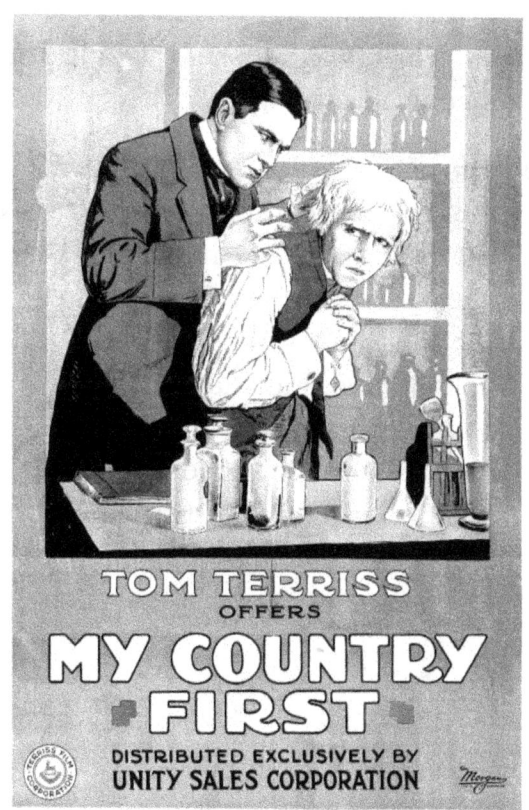

**Texas Film Corp. - US - 1914 -** distribution company located at 1917 Main Street, Dallas, Texas, with E. T. Peter as president and Albert Russell as general manager.

**Texas Films Co. - US – 1920 –** production company in Austin, Texas, that specialized in native American films.

**Texas Guinan Productions - US - 1921 -** production company specializing in westerns; located at Suite 712, 1819 Broadway, New York, with Jesse J. Goldburg as general manager.

**Thanhouser Co. - US - 1909-1912** – production company formed by Edwin Thanhouser in an old skating rink in New Rochelle, N. Y.; opened a winter studio in Jacksonville, Florida in 1912; sold the studio to a group from Mutual later the same year. [see Thanhouser Film Corp.]

**Thanhouser Film Corp. - US - 1912-1918** – production company formed by the purchase of Thanhouser Company by Charles Hite, Crawford Livingston and Wilbert Schallenberger with Hite as president; Hite took control in January 1913 but the studio burned down; rebuilt in 1914 and shortly afterward Hite died in car accident; Mutual asked Edwin Thanhouser to come back and manage, which he did until he retired February 1918 and the studio was closed; studio was loaned to Clara Kimball Young; in 1919 acquired by A. H. Fischer Features Inc.

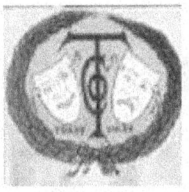  

**Thanhouser Films Ltd. – UK – 1914-1917** – distribution company formed by John Frank Brockliss and William Percy Guillet with Paul Kimberley as general manager and offices located at 100 Charing Cross Rd. London; distributed Thanhouser films under their trade names of Princess Films and Falstaff Films; moved to 166-168 Shaftsbury Ave in July 1915 and then to 167-169 Wardour St in February 1917.

**Theatre Film and Supply Co. - US - 1912 -** distribution company located at 64 E. 14th Street, New York.

**Thistle Films – US – 1914 –** trade name for two reel comedies produced by Crest Film Co.

**Thomas A. Edison, Ltd. – UK – 1910-1914 –** distribution arm of Edison Films with offices at 25 Clerkenwell Rd. E. C.

**Thomas A. Edison, Inc. - US - 1911-1918 –** formed as reorganization of Edison Manufacturing Co. April 1911 for film production; offices located at 239 Lakeside Ave., Orange, New Jersey, with distribution through General Film Corp; after numerous legal losses, sold to Lincoln & Parker Film Company in 1918.

**Thomas H. Ince Productions, Inc. - US - 1914-1925 –** production company and studio with Thomas Ince as president and Clark W. Thomas as head of production; studio located in Culver City California; distribution through Metro Pictures Corp. and Associated Producers.

**Tianyi Film Co. – SHANGHAI – 1925-1937 –** production and distribution company formed by Runje Shaw, Runde Shaw, Runme Shaw and Run Run

Shaw; **NOTE:** In 1925, they released Swordswoman Li Feifei which was the first Chinese martial arts film; Tianyi closed in 1937 in the Japanese invasion.

**Tiffany Films Corp. - US – 1914-1923 -** production company formed by Robert Z. Leonard and his wife Mae Murray; located at 1465 Broadway, New York, with Herbert Brenon as head of production; distribution through Metro Pictures Corp; Brenon soon left to join the newly formed Fox Film Corp.

**Tiffany Productions - US - 1921-1932 -** production company formed in 1921 with studio on Sunset Blvd. Los Angeles, and offices at 1540 Broadway New York; M. H. Hoffman was general manager; formed to produce westerns and dramas; from 1927-1929, produced films by director John Stahl and released as Tiffany-Stahl Productions; in 1929, moved to 729 7th Ave. New York; ceased operations in 1932.

**Tiffany-Stahl Productions - US - 1927-1929 -** films released through Tiffany Productions that were directed by John Stahl and released as Tiffany-Stahl Productions.

**Tilford Cinema Corp. – US – 1922-1924 –** production company formed by W. F. Tilford with offices in New York and production in Florida.

**Timely Films Inc. – US – 1920-1922 –** production company with Amadee J. Van Beuren as president and general manager; offices located at 1562 Broadway,

New York, with distribution through Pathe. [see Adventure Films, Inc.; AyVeeBee Film Corp; V. B. K Film Corp; Timely Topics Inc.; Fables Pictures Inc.; ]

**Timely Topics Inc. – US – 1920-1922** – production company with Amadee J. Van Beuren as president and general manager; offices located at 1562 Broadway, New York with distribution through Pathe. [see Adventure Films, Inc.; V. B. K Film Corp; AyVeeBee Film Corp; Fables Pictures Inc.; Timely Films Inc.]

**Tip Top Films - US – 1916** – production and distribution company formed from the Frank Merriwell series of books released by Tip Top Weekly, a weekly publication of Street & Smith Publishers; books were released from 1896-1916.

**Titan Pictures Corporation - US - 1917** - production company located in the Century Building in Chicago, Illinois, with Frederick Russell Clark as president; produced one reel comedies distributed through American Military Relief Association.

**Titanus – ITALY – 1928-current** – distribution company formed by name change of Sigla Film Co. when it moved from Naples. [see Sigla Film Co.]

**To-Day Feature Film Corporation - US - 1917-** production company located at 1564 Broadway, New York, with Harry Rapf as general manager.

**Topical Film Agency – UK – 1913-1914** – distributor for Thanhouser Films with offices located at 76 Victoria St., Manchester.

**Topicals Syndicate – UK – 1913-1914** – distributor for Thanhouser Films with offices at Kingsgate House, High Holborn.

**Topnotch Motion Pictures - US - 1915** - production company with distribution through Authors Film Co., Inc.

**Torchy Comedies – US – 1922** – trade name for two reel comedy shorts featuring Johnny Hines; produced by C. C. Burr Pictures and distributed by Mastodon Films, Inc.

**Tournament Film Company - US - 1910** - production company located in Toledo, Ohio.

**Towarzystwo Udzialowe Pleograf – POLAND -** [see Sfinks Studio]

**Towarzystwo Udziałowe Sfinks – POLAND – 1909-1936 –** [see Sfinks Studio]

**Tower Film Corp. – US – 1918-1921** – distribution company located at 71 W. 34rd St., New York.

**Toyland Films, Inc. - US - 1917** - production and distribution company located at 6242 Broadway, Chicago, Illinois, for Motoy Comedies.

**Trans-Atlantic Film Co. – UK – 1913-1930** – distribution company formed by James Dalton and John Dewey Tippett as general manager; offices located at 37-39 Oxford St. Winchester, London; distributed for Bison, Crystal, Frontier, Gem, Gold Seal, Joker, IMP Films, L-Ko, Nestor, Powers, Rex, Sterling. Thanhouser, Universal, and Victor; Carl Laemmele bought out John Tippett in 1914; moved in 1921 to 91 Shaftsbury Ave.; Laemmele sold out in 1924 but the company continued until 1930.

**Trans-Oceanic Films - US - 1913** - distribution company located at 145 West 45th Street, New York.

**Transatlantic Film Company of America, Inc. - US - 1919-1920** - production and distribution company located at 729 Seventh Avenue, New York, with H. C. Hoagland as V. P. and general manager.

**Trem Carr Productions - US - 1926-1931** – production company owned by Trem Carr; merged with W. Ray Johnston to form Monogram Pictures. [see Sterling Pictures]

**Tri-Stone Pictures Inc. – US – 1923** – distribution company located at Straus Building, 565 Fifth Avenue, New York; handled some Triangle rereleases.

**Triangle Distributing Corp. – US – 1915-1919** – owned by W. W. Hodkinson, Raymond Pawley and S. A. Lynch; distributed films for Triangle Film Corp.; when Triangle Film Corp. folded, Lynch bought out Hodkinson and Pawley to become sole owner of Triangle Distributing and began rereleasing some of their films under a separate distribution company he formed called, S. A. Lynch Enterprises. [see S. A. Lynch Enterprises and Superpictures Distribution Corp.]

**Triangle Film Corp. - US - 1915-1919** - production company formed by Harry Aitkens, Adam Kessel, Robert Bauman, D. W. Griffith, Thomas Ince and Mack Sennett to collectively market their independent production; offices located at the Brokaw Bldg., Broadway and 42$^{nd}$ St. New York, sales office at 71 W. 23rd and studio in Culver City California; in 1916, Triangle Distributing Corp. was formed separately to market their films; in late 1916, owners started leaving because of over spending; went bankrupt in 1918; in 1919, Triangle Studios was acquired by Goldwyn.

**Triangle-Fine Arts Pictures Co. - 1915-1919 -** trade name for films released through Triangle produced by Fines Arts Pictures Co. [see Fine Arts Pictures Co.]

**Triangle-Ince - 1915-1918 -** trade name for films released through Triangle produced by Thomas Ince.

**Triangle-Keystone Films - US - 1915-1919 –** trade name for films released through Triangle produced by Mack Sennett.

**Triart Picture Co. - US - 1921-1922** - production company located in New York.

**Triumph Film Co. Ltd – UK – 1913-1918** – distribution company formed by Max Baer, Sidney Brinney, Paul Hill, Charles P. Whittle, and Nathaniel Emmanuel Woolfe; offices at 66 Old Compton St. Westminster; in October 1914, Max Baer left due to World War I and Paul Hill died in 1916; closed January 1918.

**Triumph Film Corp. - US - 1915-1917** - production company formed September 1915 as a subsidiary to Equitable Film Corp. to boost production; Julius Steger was president and Joseph Golden was head of production; took over the old Horsley studio in Bayonne, New Jersey; distribution through World Film Corp.; absorbed by World Film as part of the stock buyout of Equitable.

**Truart Film Corp. - US – 1922-1926** - production and distribution company founded by L. A. Young at 1540 Broadway, New York, and associated with M. H. Hoffman; distribution was by states rights.

**True Feature Co. - US - 1912-1914** - distribution company located in the World's Tower Building, 110-112 West 40th Street, New York.

**Tumlingfilm – DENMARK – 1923-1924** – production company with distribution through Fotorama.

**Tusun Comedies – US – 1921** – trade name for one reel comedy shorts released by Capitol Film Co.

**Turner Films, Ltd – UK – 1913-1914** – production company for films featuring Florence Turner; distributed in the UK by Hepworth Film Manufacturing and in the US by Vivaphone Film & Sales Corp.

**20th Century Feature Film Company - US - 1914 -** production company located at 216 West 42nd Street, New York.

**Tyler Film Co. – UK – 1910-1916 –** production and distribution company formed by Edgar Holman Bishop, Harold Roswell Bishop, Lawrence Collier Bishop and Richard Collier by acquiring Walter Tyler Ltd.; offices located at 13 Gerrard St. Westminister; distributed for Broadwest, Broncho, Continental, Éclair, Eiko, Gloria, Herkomer, Itala, Keystone, Kunst, T. F. C., Victoria, and Southern Star of Australia.

**Tyrad Pictures, Inc. - US - 1918-1920** - production and distribution company located at 729 7th Avenue, New York.

# THE CINEMATRADE.COM

*Your source for original posters and memorabilia*

*Classics to current... and everything in between*

**BUY - SELL - TRADE**

**SEARCH & SPECIAL ORDER**

*thewildbunch@yahoo.com*

---

**Intemporel Gallery opened in 1982. We specialize in vintage movie posters.**

22 rue Saint-Martin
Paris, 75004 France
Phone: 1.42.72.55.41

email: choko@intemporel.com
website: www.intemporel.com

---

**JOHN REID**
**VINTAGE MOVIE MEMORABILIA**

**ORIGINAL MOVIE POSTERS, LOBBY CARDS, MOVIE STILLS AND MEMORABILIA**

JOHN REID VINTAGE MOVIE MEMORABILIA
PO Box 92 ~ Elanora ~ Qld 4221 ~ Australia

info@moviemem.com
http://www.moviemem.com
ebay userid: johnwr

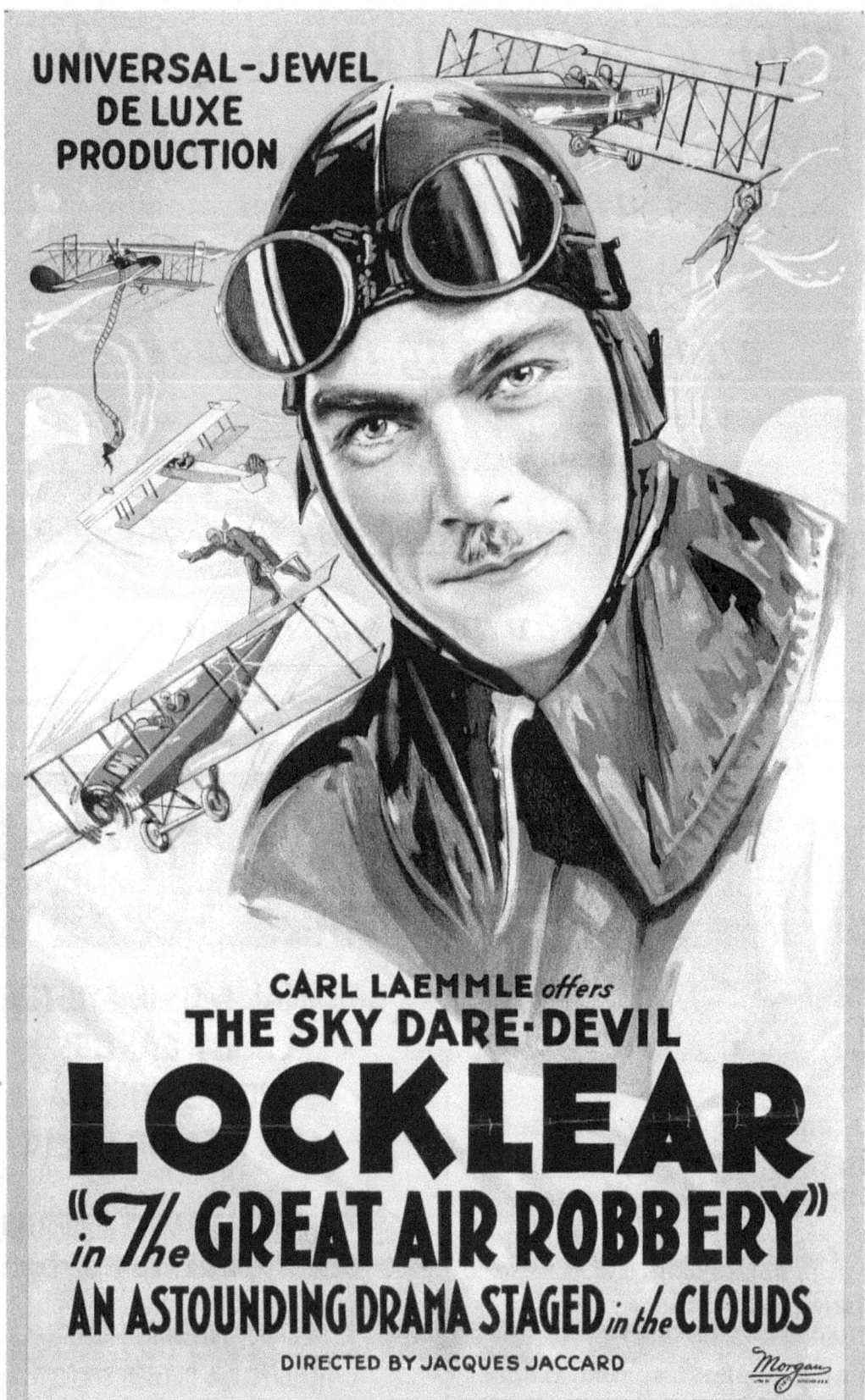

# U

**UCI - ITALY -** [see Unione Cinematografica Italiana]

**Ufa - GERMANY - 1917-1945** [see Universum Film Aktiengesellschaft]

**U. S. Amusement Corp. - US - 1916- -** production company owned by Alice Guy Blache and Herbert Blache; produced films for Solax Film Co.; located in Fort Lee, New Jersey.

**U. S. Exhibitors' Booking Corp. - US - 1917 -** distribution company located at the Top O' The Times Building, New York, with Frank G. Hall and William Oldknow.

**U. S. Feature Film Co. - US - 1914-1915 -** production company located in Oroville, California.

**U. S. Film Corp - 1908-1913 -** production company formed in Cincinnati, Ohio and specializing in westerns; absorbed by Smallwood Film Corp. in 1913.

**Ultra Film Co. - ITALY - 1920 -** production company located in Rome with Dr. Francisco Stame as president; distribution in the U.S. and Canada was through Ernest Shipman and Associates.

**Ultra Pictures Corp - US - 1917 -** distribution company located at 729 Seventh Avenue, New York.

**Uncle Sam Films - US - 1910 -** trade name for films produced by Yankee Film Company.

**Unicorn Film Service Corp. - US - 1912-1916 -** distributor releasing under trade names Hippo, Lily, Supreme, Hiawatha, Puritan, et al; roster was taken over by Belmont Film.

**Union Artistic Films - FRANCE - 1924 -** distribution company for F.P.S. Films.

**Union Features - US - 1912-1914 -** distribution company located at 225 W. 42nd Street, New York.

**Union Film Co. - US - 1921 -** production company located Sherman, California, with Alexander Alt as president, J. T. Whitlaw as V. P. and general manager, and Helen Howell as secretary/treasurer; produced Alt and Howell Comedies.

**Union Film Publishing Co. Ltd - UK - 1912-1916 -** production and distribution company formed by Sidney Harrison Callow, Archibald Leslie Gibson, John Edward Hookway, and George William Pearson in association with Pathe; located at 167-169 Wardour St., Westminster, and studio at Great Portland St.; produced comedy series under trade name of Big Ben Films.

**Union-Film - GERMANY - 1912- -** distribution company for imported films.

**Union Photoplay Co. - US - 1914-1915 -** production company formed by Charles R. Macauley to produce cartoon shorts.

**Unique Film Co. - SHANGHAI - 1925-1937 -** [see Tianyi Film Co.]

**Unique Film Co. Inc. - US - 1913 -** production and distribution company located at 110-112 West 40th Street, New York.

**United Artists Corp. - US - 1919-1983 -** production and distribution company formed April 17, 1919 with offices located at 729 7$^{th}$ Ave. New York; Oscar Price was president, but was soon replaced by Hiram Abrams and Dennis O'Brien as V. P.; initially set up for the production of Mary Pickford, Charles Chaplin, Douglas Fairbanks and D. W. Griffith but expanded to major distribution companies all over the world; distribution in France as Les Artistes Associes S. A.

**United Booking Office Feature Co. - US - 1915 -** located at Palace Theatre Building, 1564 Broadway, New York.

**United Feature Film Co. - US - 1912 -** distribution company located at 559 Spitzer Building, Toledo, Ohio.

**United Film Corp. of Los Angeles - US - 1918 -** production company.

**United Film Service - US - 1914-1915 -** distribution company formed by court order to replace Warner's Features; P. A. "Pat" Powers was president; later changed to J. C. Graham as president and general manager; offices located at 130 West 46th Street, New York, and distributed for American Gaumont, Colonial Motion Picture, Lariat Co., Luna Films, Premier, Pyramid Pictures, Regent Film Co, Sunshine Film Co, Starlight and Superba. including the trade names of Empress, Juno, Magnet and Mars comedies; in June, 1915 went bankrupt and distribution moved to Standard Pictures, Inc.

**United Keanograph Film Manufacturing Co. - US - 1915-1916 -** production company founded in Fairfax, California by James Keane; reorganized as James Keane Feature Photoplay Productions.

**United Kine Exclusive Film Co. Ltd. - UK - 1913-1916 -** distribution company formed by Alexander Anderson, John Frank Brockliss, Howard Hopkins, John Hopkins, George Edward King and Arnold Fred Taylor with offices at 87 Shaftesbury Ave. Winchester.

**United Kingdom Films - UK - 1913-1915 -** distribution company formed by Augustine Charles Joseph Brean, Joseph Herbert Brean, Nicholson Ormsby-Scott and Henry Thomas Roberts with offices at 11 Cecil Court Westminster; distribution in the U.S. was by states rights through James McEnnery Heidelberg Bldg. New York.

**United Kingdom Photoplays - 1913-1915 -** production company with distribution through United Kingdom Films.

**United Photo Plays Co. - US - 1917 -** production company located at 2332-38 N. California Ave., Chicago, Illinois.

**United Picture Productions Corp. - US - 1919 -** production company formed by principals of United Picture Theatres of America, Inc.; formed to supply films.

**United Picture Theatres of America, Inc. - US - 1918-1919 -** distribution company formed as a co-operative to release films financed by exhibitors; offices located at 1600 Broadway, New York, with J. A. Berst as president; in 1919, merged with World Film Corp.

**United States Amusement Corp. - US - 1914-1918 -** production company formed by Herbert Blache and Alice Guy Blache; a reformation and division of Solax Studio; production was done at Solax and distribution first through World Pictures, then Art Dramas, Inc., and finally through Metro.

**United States Exhibitors Booking Corp. - US - 1917-1919 -** distribution company formed by Frank G. Hall and William Oldknow; purchased productions and rented them direct to exhibitors in an attempt to eliminate the states rights distributors; went out of business in 1919.

**United States Film Co. - US - 1912** - distribution company located at 145 West 45th Street, New York.

**United States Motion Picture Corp. - US - 1916-1917** - distribution company located in Wilkes Barre, Pennsylvania with J. O. Walsh as president; distributed Black Diamond comedies.

**United States Moving Picture Corp. - US - 1915-1922** - production studio built in August 1915 in Wilkes-Barre, Pennsylvania with James O. Walsh as president and Fred W. Hermann as V. P.; produced comedy shorts released through Paramount under the trade names of Rainbow Comedies and Black Diamond Comedies.

**United Photoplays Co. - US - 1917-1920** - production and distribution company located at 207 South Wabash Avenue, Chicago, Illinois, with Frank Zambreno as president.

**United Picture Corporation - US - 1916** - production company with distribution through United Sales Corporation.

**Unity Sales Corp. - US - 1916-1917** - distribution company formed May 1916 with Andrew J. Cobe as president and general manager; offices located at 729 7th Ave. New York; distributed for Eagle Film, Serial Film, Tom Terriss Film, Unity Pictures, et al.

**Unity Super Films - UK - 1917 -** production company with Sidney Morgan as head of production; Morgan left at the end of the year to join Progress Film Co. and the company closed.

**Universal Film Co. Ltd. - UK - 1911-1922 -** distribution company formed by Arthur Bliss, Harold Bliss, Montague Browne and James Dalton; offices located at 5 Denman St Westminster; reorganized in 1915 and distributed for Sun, Windmill, Unitas, Champion, Heron, Scientific, Dansk Filmfabrik, Edko, Solograph, Veritas, Lama, Motograph, Big 5, Favourite, Pennent, Crusade and SB Films; declared nonexistent in 1922.

**Universal Film Manufacturing Co., Inc. - US - 1912-1922+ -** distribution company formed April 30, 1912 by Carl Laemmle, Mark Dintenfass, Charles O. Baumann, Adam Kessel, Pat Powers, William Swanson, David Horsley, and Jules Brulatour in the merger to release under the trade name of Bison, Champion, Republic, Rex, Bluebird, Jewel, Joker, et al.

**University Film, Inc. - US - 1914 -** production company located at 110 West 40th Street, New York, with Joseph Sullivan as president.

UNIVERSITY FILM INC.

**Universum Film Aktiengesellschaft (Ufa) - GERMANY - 1917-1945-** production company owned by the German government; formed in a merger with the largest production companies in Germany including Messter, PAGU, and German Nordisk; Paul Davidson was head of production; in 1921, Ufa was privatized causing instability so in 1923, Erich Pommer merged his company Decla-Bioskop into Ufa and took control; to break the moratorium against German films, Pommer created Exportverband der Deutschen Filmindustrie to send unmarked films to Scandinavian countries and reship them to Allied countries, therefore breaking the moratorium; unfortunately, overspending abounded; when they made Metropolis, they went bankrupt; in 1925, Paramount and MGM bailed them out and created an import company to supply the U.S. with German films called Parufamet; Nazis took control of Ufa in 1937; after World War II, the Soviets renamed Ufa as DEFA (Deutsche Film AG). [see Parufamet]

**Uranus Films - UK - 1913 -** distribution company located in the U.K. by Anderson's Film Agency.

**Urban Trading Co. Ltd. - UK - 1914 -** distribution company [see Charles Urban Trading Company; Urban Eclipse; Urbanora Films; Warwick Trading Co.]

**Urbanora Films - UK - -1914 -** trade name used for films produced by Charles Urban Trading Co.

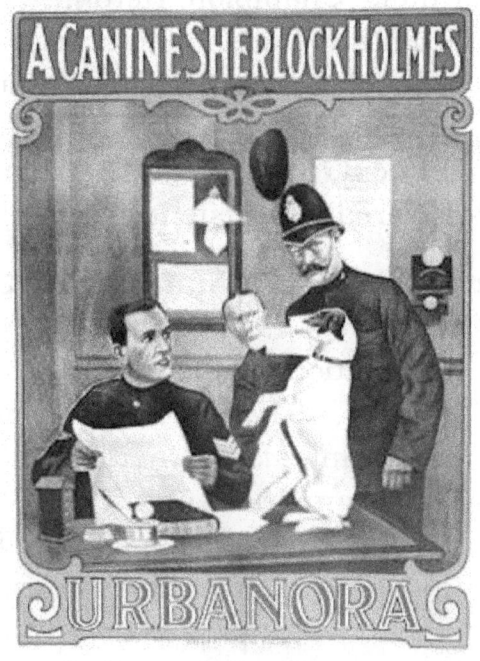

**Usla - US - 1924-1925 -** production company specializing in westerns.

### MovieArt GmbH

one of Europe's largest
selection of movie posters
- silent to present -
over 6000 titles online

Walchestrasse 17
8006 Zurich Switzerland
phone ++41 44 363 50 26
fax ++ 41 44 363 50 27

www.movieart.ch

# V

**V. B. K. Film Corp. - US - 1920-1922** - production company with Amadee J. Van Beuren as president and general manager; offices located at 1562 Broadway, New York; distribution through Pathe. [see Adventure Films, Inc.; AyVeeBee Films; Timely Topics Inc.; Fables Pictures Inc.; Timely Films Inc.]

**V-Films Ltd - UK - 1914-1915** - distribution company located at 15 Cecil Court Westminster.

**V-L-S-E, Inc. - US - 1915-1916** - distribution company formed April 13, 1915 by Vitagraph, Lubin, Selig and Essanay for distribution of their films; Albert Smith was president, William Selig was treasurer, George Spoor was secretary and Walter W. Irwin was general manager; dissolved September 1916 by Vitagraph buying out partners; Selig and Essanay joined George Kleine and Edison to form K-E-S-E Service.

**Van Dyke Films - US - 1916-1917** - production company located at 251 W. 19th St. New York with distribution through Art Dramas.

**Vanity Comedies - US - 1919-1921** - trade name used for two reel comedies produced by Christie Film Co. and distributed by Educational Film.

**Vanity Fair Maids Comedies - US - 1921** - trade name for comedy shorts featuring Eddie Boland; produced by Hal E. Roach Studios and distributed by Pathe.

**Variety Feature Film Co. - US - 1914** - distribution company located at 1482 Broadway, New York, with Charles Penser as general manager.

**Venus Features Co. - US - 1913-1914** - production company formed in Hollywood with Thomas W. Evans as head of production.

**Verafilm Co. - ITALY - 1914** - distribution export subsidiary of Cines Co. of Rome with an American office called Inter-Continent Film Co.

**Vesuvio Films - ITALY - 1908-1914** - production company distributed in the UK by A. E. Hubsch & Co.

**Vesuvio Films - UK - 1908-1912 -** distribution arm in the UK for the Italian Vesuvio Films; located at 18 Charing Cross Road, Westminster; in 1913-1914, Vesuvio production was handled in the UK by A. E. Hubsch & Co.

**Vickers and Edwards Ltd - UK - 1913 -** distribution company located at 155 Wardour St., Westminster.

**Victor Adamson Productions US - 1927-1928 -** production company formed by Victor Adamson (a/k/a Denver Dixon, Art Mix, Al Mix, Al James); studio located in Monrovia, California, called Studio Santa Fe. [see Art Mix Productions]

**Victor Film Co. - US - 1912-1917 -** production company formed by Florence Lawrence and her husband Harry Salter; located in Fort Lee, New Jersey with distribution through Universal; Universal took over the studio in 1914 and the name changed in 1917.

**Victor Kremer Film Features, Inc. - US - 1915-1921 -** production and distribution company located at 126-130 West 46th Street, New York with Victor Kremer as president and Curt Kremer as V. P.; used Francis Ford Studios to produce Texas Guinan westerns.

**Victoria Film Agency - UK - 1913-1914** - distribution company with offices located at 58-60 High St., Bedford.

**Victory Feature Films Ltd. - UK - 1913-1915** - distribution company located at 29a Charing Cross Road, Westminster.

**Victory Film Mfg. Co. - US - 1918** - production company located at 218 W. 42nd St., New York and distributed through General Film.

**Victory Pictures - US - 1918** - trade name distributed as Fox-Victory Films.

**Victus Exclusive Photoplay Co. - UK - 1914-1915** - distribution company located at 99a Charing Cross Road, Westminster.

**Vim Comedy Co. - US - 1915-1917** - production company founded by Mark Dintenfass and Louis Berstein; offices at 326 Lexington Ave., New York, with studio in New Jersey; acquired Lubin Manufacturing Co. Jacksonville studio located at 750 Riverside Ave. when it closed; primarily produced two reel comedies which included the Pokes and Jabbs series starring Bobby Burns and Walter Stull and the Plump and Runt series starring Billy Ruge and Oliver Hardy; released under the trade name of Supreme Comedies; internal legal battles between Dintenfass and Berstein caused their closure in 1917 with Amber Star Film Corp. taking over the Jacksonville studio; Berstein retained the New Jersey studio and continued producing Billy West Comedies under the trade name of King Bee Films.

**Vitagraph Co. Ltd. - UK - 1913-1922** - distributor formed from a name change of the British company of Vitagraph Company of America with offices at 31-33 Charing Cross Rd. Winchester.

**Vitagraph Company of America - UK - 1907-1913 -** British distribution arm of Vitagraph Company of America located at 23 Cecil Court Westminster; changed name to Vitagraph Co. Ltd. in 1913 and moved.

**Vitagraph Company of America - US - 1897-1925** - production company formed by J. Stuart Blackton, Albert A. Smith, Ronald A. Reader and William T. "Pop" Rock; in 1898, set up the first studio on rooftop of Morse Bldg. Nassau St. New York; opened studio in 1905 in Brooklyn; opened studio in California in 1911 at 1438 2nd St. in Santa Monica; in 1915, formed V-L-S-E with Lubin, Selig and Essanay for distribution; in 1921, offices at 469 5th Ave. New York with Albert E. Smith as president and John M Quinn as general manager; acquired by Warner Bros April 20, 1925 but the Vitagraph name continued to be used into the 1950s.

**Vital Exchanges, Inc. - US - 1925 -** production company.

**Vitascope GmbH - GERMANY -** [see Deutsche Vitaskop]

**Vivaphone Film & Sales Co. Inc. - US - 1913-1914 -** distribution company formed from Vivaphone Sales Company of America with Albert Blinkhorn as president; offices located at the Longacre Bldg., 1480 Broadway St., New York; imported and distributed films for Turner Film Co. and Hepworth Manufacturing Co.

**Vivaphone Sales Company of America - US - 1913 -** formed by Albert Blinkhorn in April 1913 to distribute films by states rights; in May 1913, incorporated under the name Vivaphone Film & Sales Co. Inc.

**Vivian Martin Productions Inc. - US - 1921 -** production company located at Capitol Theatre Bldg. Broadway and 51st St. New York, with Messmore Kendall as president.

**Vogue Films, Inc. - US - 1915-1917 -** production company formed October, 1915 by Samuel Hutchinson, (also president of American Film) with Joseph H. Finn as general manager; produced comedy shorts using the Signal Film Co. studios (old Lubin studio) located at 4560 Pasadena Ave., Los Angeles, California and sales offices at 222 S. State St. Chicago, Illinois.

**Vogue Comedies - US - 1915-1917 -** trade name for comedy shorts produced by Vogue Films, Inc. which featured Owen Evans and Ben Turpin.

# SIMON DWYER!

GENUINE VINTAGE MOVIE POSTERS
DATING FROM THE 1920's
TO THE 1970'S BROUGHT
FROM CINEMA HOARDINGS
AROUND THE WORLD TO
YOUR FRONT DOOR

Simon Dwyer
7 Epirus Mews
London SW6 7UP
United Kingdom

www.SimonDwyer.com
SIMON.DWYER@LAKESVILLE.COM

## DO YOU HAVE POSTERS YOU WANT TO SELL?

THERE IS **NO** AUCTIONEER OF VINTAGE MOVIE PAPER WHO HAS LOWER FEES OR WHO DELIVERS CONSISTENTLY HIGHER PRICES THAN EMOVIEPOSTER.COM, AND WE ARE THE ONLY AUCTIONEERS WHO CAN TAKE **ALL** OF YOUR MOVIE PAPER!

EMOVIEPOSTER.COM
P.O. BOX 874
306 WASHINGTON AVE.
WEST PLAINS, MO 65775
WWW.EMOVIEPOSTER.COM
417-256-9616 · MAIL@EMOVIEPOSTER.COM

---

## channingposters

ORIGINAL
MOVIE POSTERS,
LOBBY CARDS, AND
AUTOGRAPHED ITEMS

CHANNING THOMSON
P. O. BOX 330232
SAN FRANCISCO, CA 94133-0232

Email: channinglylethomson@att.net
ebay: http://stores.ebay.com/CHANNINGPOSTERS

## kinoart.net

ORIGINAL
MOVIE POSTERS
AND LOBBY CARDS

12,000 SELECTED VINTAGE
INTERNATIONAL POSTERS
AVAILABLE

WOLFGANG JAHN
SULZBURGSTR. 126
50937 COLOGNE
GERMANY
+49 221 1698728

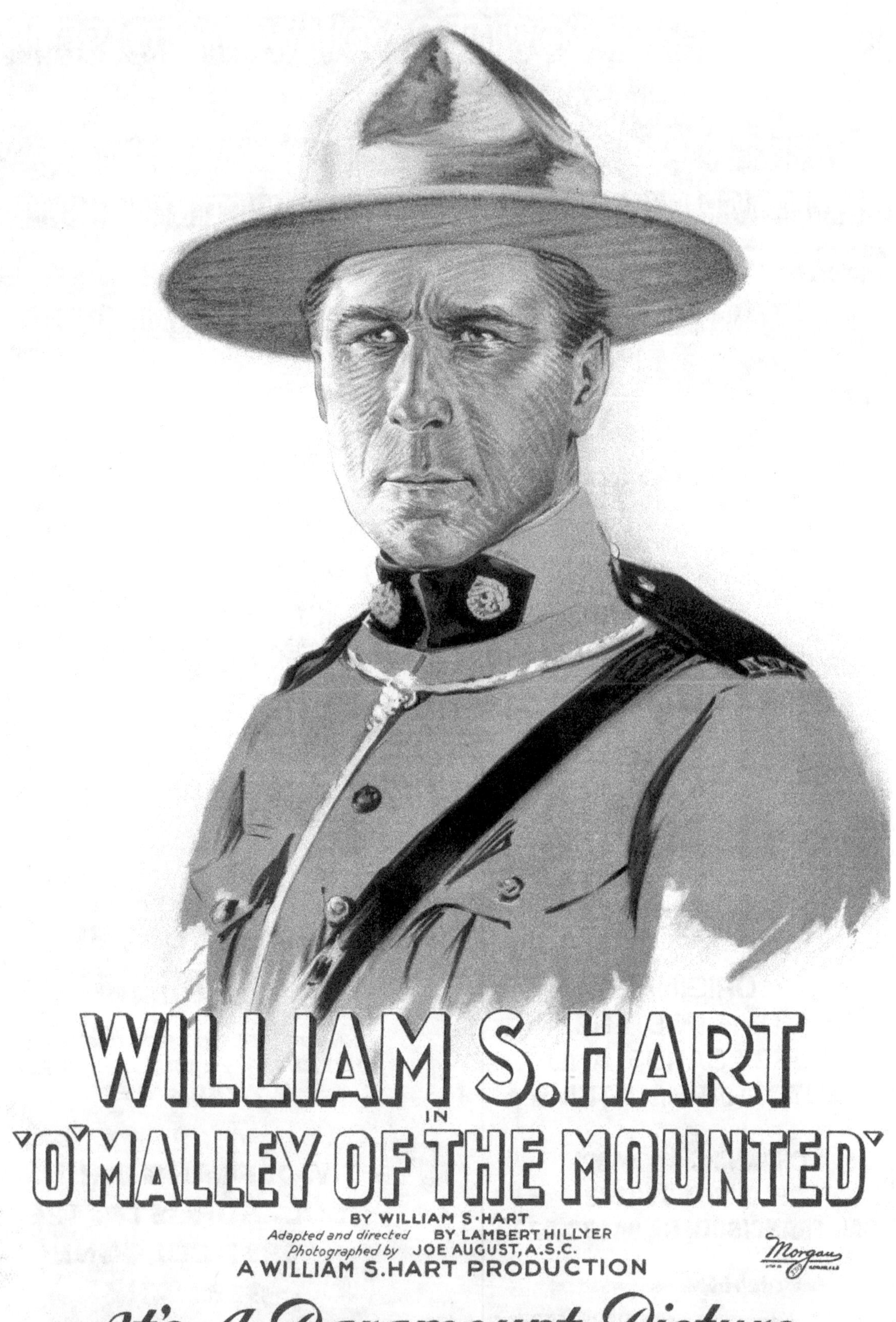
WILLIAM S. HART
IN
"O'MALLEY OF THE MOUNTED"
BY WILLIAM S·HART
Adapted and directed BY LAMBERT HILLYER
Photographed by JOE AUGUST, A.S.C.
A WILLIAM S.HART PRODUCTION
Morgan
It's A Paramount Picture
© FAMOUS PLAYERS-LASKY CORP. 1921

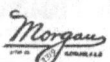

# W

**W. & F. Film Service Ltd. - UK - 1928-1929 -** distribution company with offices located at 74-76 Old Compton St., London.

**W. & Y. Film Services Ltd. - UK - 1921 -** distribution company.

**W. Butcher and Sons - UK - 1913-1914 -** distribution company with offices located at Farringdon Ave. E. C.

**W. E. Greene Film Exchange - US - 1909-1910 -** distribution company located at 228 Tremont Street, Boston, Massachusetts.

**W. H. Clifford Photo Film Co. - US - 1917-1918 -** production company located at 17 W. 44th Street, New York, with Victor Kremer as general manager; produced Shorty Hamilton Series.

**W. H. Productions Co. - US - 1916-1921 -** distribution company located at 71 W. 23rd St., New York.

**W. M. Smith Productions - US - 1921-1922 -** production company specializing in westerns.

**W. N. Selig Co. - US - 1896 -** [see Selig Polyscope Co. Inc.]

**W. W. Hodkinson Corp. - US - 1917-1924 -** distribution company located at 527 5th Ave. New York; formed by Hodkinson after he was unseated as head of Paramount; distributed for numerous companies, such as Artco Production, Bessie Barriscale (before becoming B. B. Features), Deitrich-Beck, Great Authors, Paralta and Zane Grey Pictures; in late 1918, released films through Pathe.

**Wah Ming Motion Picture Co. - US - 1921 -** production company located at 753 S. Boyle Ave. Los Angeles, California, with James B. Leong as general manager; produced feature films with Chinese casts.

**Walgreene Film Corp. - US - 1921 -** located at 220 W. 42nd St., New York with Walter Greene as general manager.

**Walker's Exclusives - UK - 1913-1914 -** distribution company with offices located at 112 Shaftesbury Ave., Winchester; in 1914, name was changed to Walker's World Films Ltd.

**Walker's World Films Ltd. - UK - 1914-1921 -** distribution company located at 166-170 Wardour St., Westminister; formed from Walker's Exclusives by James Herbert, Herbert Page, Alfred Tildsley and James D. Walker with John J. Fraser as general manager.

**Walt Disney Productions - US - 1929-current -** production company incorporated from Walt Disney Studio.

**Walt Disney Studio - US - 1926-1929 -** production company reformation of the Disney Bros. Studio in their new studio on Hyperion Ave. Los Angeles; in 1929, incorporated as Walt Disney Productions.

**Walturdaw Co. - UK - 1913-1923 -** distribution company located at 40 Gerrard St., Winchester, Cardiff and Birmingham; distributor of Solax Films, Bavaria Film, Behr Bros. Duskes and Deutsche Bioscop.

**Ward's Films Ltd. - UK - 1914-1915 -** distribution company located at 121 Wardour St., Westminster; formed by Harry Bawn, Henry Lundy, John George Lundy, Wright Lundy and Harry Ward.

**Wardour Films, Ltd - UK - 1925-1927 -** distribution company with offices located at 173 Wardour St. London.

**Warner Brothers Pictures, Inc. - US - 1923-1969 -** production company formed April 4, 1923 by Harry, Albert, Samuel and Jack Warner.

**Warner's Features, Inc. - UK - 1913-1914 -** distribution company located at 126 West 46th Street, New York; distributor for independent productions from Gene Gauntier Feature Players, Lederer's Celebrities Film Co., Ranous Motion Picture Co., Imperial Film Mfg Co., Whitman-Warren Co., Tampa Films Inc., Marion Leonard Features, Mittenthal Film Co., Albuquerque Film Mfg. Co., Pyramid Film Co., Satex Film Co., Great West Motion Picture Co., and Helen Gardner Picture Players; offices were located at 99 Charing Cross Rd., London.

**Warner's Features, Inc. - US - 1913-1914 -** distribution company formed to distribute independent productions from Gene Gauntier Feature Players, Lederer's Celebrities Film Co., Ranous Motion Picture Co., Imperial Film Mfg Co., Whitman-Warren Co., Tampa Films Inc., Marion Leonard Features, Mittenthal Film Co., Albuquerque Film Mfg. Co., Pyramid Film Co., Satex Film Co., Great West Motion Picture Co., Éclair Film Co., Ambrosio Film Co., Milano Film Co., and Helen Gardner Picture Players; offices were located at 126 W. 46th St. New York with branches in Chicago, Cleveland, Minneapolis, Buffalo, Pittsburg, Boston, Philadelphia, Washington, San Francisco, Seattle, Denver, Dallas, Kansas City, Atlanta, St. Louis, New Orleans, Indianapolis, Cincinnati, Spokane and Los Angeles. [see United Film Service]

**Warren and Clark - US - 1917 -** distribution company located at 305-306 Garrick Theater Building, Chicago, Illinois; distributed through states rights for Illinois, Indiana and Wisconsin.

**Warrenton Photoplays Film Distributing Co. - US - 1917 -** production and distribution company for Lule Warrenton Photoplays.

**Warwick Trading Co. - UK -** production and distribution company located at 172 Charing Cross Road, Westminster; owned by Charles Urban; distributors for Lumiere, Melies, Hepworth, Ambrosio, and Continental.

**Waterloo Film Co. - US - 1913 -** states rights distribution company located at 145 West 45th Street, New York with P. P. Craft as general manager.

**Watson's Pictures - UK - 1913-1914 -** distribution company with offices located at 21 Gt. Ducie St. Manchester.

**Wedepict Motion Picture Corp. - US - 1913 -** production and distribution company located at 115 Broadway, New York.

**Weisker Bros. Ltd. - UK - 1913-1914 -** distribution company with offices located at London Rd., Liverpool and 13 Pottinger's Entry, Belfast.

**Weiss Brothers-Artclass Pictures Corp. - US -** located at Loew Bldg., New York with Bert Ennis as general manager.

**Werbe Luescher, Inc. - US - 1915 -** distribution company located at 1520 Broadway, New York.

**West End Exclusives, Ltd - UK - 1914-1916 -** distribution company located at 18 Cecil Court, Westminster, with Harold Frederick Phillips as general manager.

**Westart Pictures - US - 1921 -** production company.

**Western Feature Productions, Inc. - US - 1921-1922 -** production company located at 5545 Hollywood Blvd. Hollywood, California, with F. M. Sanford as president; produced five and six reel westerns.

**Western Film Exchange - US - 1906-1910 -** distribution company formed by John R. Freuler, Harry E. Aitken and Roy Aitken in Milwaukee, Wisconsin.

**Western Import Co. - US - 1914-1915 -** distribution company located at 71 West 23rd Street, New York.

**Western Import Co. - US - 1918 -** distribution company located at 1010 Brokaw Building, New York.

**Western Import Company of London - UK - 1912-1914 -** distribution company for Ammex, Apollo, Broncho, Brooklyn, Domino, Excelsior, Flying A, K.B., Keystone, Komic, Majestic, Punch, Reliance, Welt and Thanhouser films; offices located at 4 Gerrard St., Winchester, and 7 Rupert Ct., Westminster.

**Western Pictures Exploitation Co. - US - 1921-1923 -** distribution company located at 576 5th Ave., New York with Irving M. Lesser as president and general manager, and 5528 Santa Monica Blvd, Los Angeles, California, with Mike Rosenberg as general manager.

**Western Photoplays, Inc. - US - 1918 -** production company headed by Joseph A. Golden and A. Alperstein to produce westerns for Pathe; acquired in 1918 by Astra Film Corp., who continued their production.

**Western Star Productions - US - 1921 -** production company located at 620 Sunset Blvd. Los Angeles, with Phillip Goldstone as general manager; produced five reel westerns.

**West's Pictures - AUSTRALIA - 1910-1914 -** production and distribution company formed by Thomas James West to produce newsreels and shorts and distribute short comedies such as Keystone Comedies; in 1912, merged with Amalgamated Pictures and Spencer's Pictures to form General Film Co. of Australasia, but continued use of West's Pictures trade name. [see General Film Co. of Australasia; Spencer's Pictures; Amalgamated Pictures]

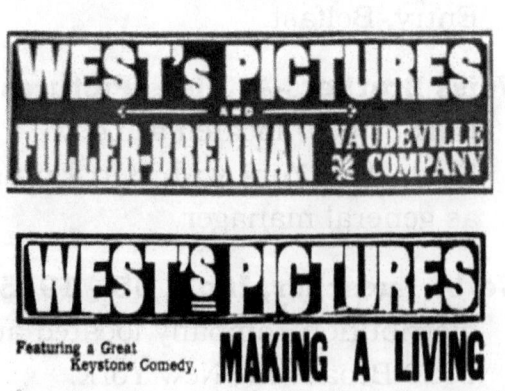

**Wharton, Inc. - US - 1914-1919 -** production company located in Ithaca, New York; founded by brothers Theodore W. Wharton and Leopold Wharton; started production May 1, 1914; produced serials for Pathe; in 1916, started producing for other companies; went out of business in 1919.

**Wheeler-Loper Film Co. - US - 1908-1917 -** distribution company located in Dallas, Texas, with a branch in San Antonio; formed by J. D. Wheeler; referred to as J. D. Wheeler Film Co.; distributors in Texas for Edison films, General Film Corp. and Mutual Film Corp. of Texas.

**Whitman Bennett Productions - US - 1919-1925 -** production company located at 537 Riverdale Ave., Yonkers (old Fine Arts studio); W. O. Hurst was general manager; distribution through First National and United Artists; leased studio to other production companies.

**Whitman Features Co. - US - 1914 -** production company located at 110 W. 40th Street, New York with Martin J. Faust as head of production; distribution by states rights through Blinkhorn Photoplays Corp.

**Whitman Warren Co. - US - 1913-1914 -** production company headed by Giles R. Warren; distribution by Warner Bros. through Warner's Features.

**Wholesome Films Corp. - US - 1917 -** production company located at Consumers Building, 222 So. State St., Chicago, Illinois, with Milton Daily as president, A. M. Allen as V. P., P. W. Stanhope as secretary/treasurer and M. J. Weisfeldt as general manager.

**Wiener Kunstfilm - AUSTRIA - 1912-1938 -** production company formed as Erste Osterreichische Kinofilms-Industrie until 1938 when the

Nazis confiscated all studios and merged them into one, Wein-Film.

**Wild West Films - UK - 1911 -** trade name for western films produced by Gaston Melies' Star Films and distributed through J. F. Brockliss, Ltd.

**Wild West Productions - US - 1923-1927 -** production company specializing in westerns; later expanded to distribution.

**Wilkar Films - US - 1914 -** distribution company located at 1482 Broadway, New York.

**Wilkins & Bros. Ltd. - UK - 1913-1914 -** distribution company with offices located at 27-35 Duke St., Liverpool.

**Willat Productions - US - 1921 -** production company located in Culver City, California, with C. A. Willat as president and general manager.

**William A. Brady Picture Plays, Inc. - US - 1914-1916 -** production company formed to convert the plays of William A. Brady into films; half owned by Peerless Feature Film Co. which had a studio in Fort Lee, New Jersey.

**William Christy Cabanne Producing Co. - US - 1919-1921** - production company located at 780 Gower St., Hollywood, California; worked with Robertson Cole.

**William D. Foster Film Co. - US -** production and distribution company specializing in black race films.

**William Desmond Productions - US - 1921 -** production company located at 5341 Melrose Ave., Los Angeles, California; owned by William Desmond and William La Plante; formed to produce westerns featuring William Desmond.

**William H. Swanson & Co. - US - 1910** - distribution company located at 304-5-6 Railroad Building, Denver, Colorado.

**William L. Sherrill Feature Corp. - US - 1916-1917 -** production company formed by William L. Sherrill; distributed by Art Dramas, of which Sherrill was also president.

**William L. Sherrill Feature Film Co. of New York - US - 1913-1916 -** distribution company opened March 15, 1913 for states rights distribution.

**William L. Sherrill Service - US - 1916-1919 -** distribution company formed by William L. Sherrill on September 26, 1916 to distribute nationwide when Sherrill left as president of Art Dramas; distributed for De Luxe Pictures, Edgar Lewis Productions, and Frank A. Keeney Productions; in 1918, moved distribution through General Film until May 1919, when they changed to the Film Clearing House exchanges.

**William L. Sherry Feature Film Co. - US - 1914 -** states rights distribution company located at 126 West 46th Street, New York; controlled New York City and state rights for The Famous Players Film Co. and The Jesse L. Lasky Feature Play Co.

**William M. Kraft - US - 1921 -** distribution company for states rights located at 1664 Broadway in New York.

**William M. Pizor Productions - US - 1920-1936 -** production and distribution company with offices in New York.

**William Mix Productions - US - 1924-1927 -** production company formed by William (Bill) Mix; specialized in westerns.

**William S. Hart Productions, Inc. - US - 1918-1925 -** production company located at the Apollo Theatre Bldg., Hollywood, California. with distribution through United Artists.

**William Steiner Productions - US - 1919-1937** - production company located at Suite 605-611, 220 West 42nd Street, New York.

**William Sievers Co. - US - 1916 -** distribution company owned by William Sievers with offices at Grand Central Theater Bldg., St. Louis, Missouri; distributor of Christie's Comedies, et al for Missouri by states rights.

**William Stoermer Enterprises - US - 1919** - production company located at Suite 707, 729 Seventh Avenue, New York.

**Williamson & Co. - US - 1908-1910** - distribution company located at 145 E. 23rd Street, New York for Williamson Kinematograph Co. Ltd.

**Williamson Brothers Submarine Film Corporation - 1914-1917 -** production company formed by the Williamson Brothers; located on the Eighth Floor, Longacre Building, New York; studios located in Nassau, Bahamas with Ernest Shipman as general manager.

**Williamson Kinematograph Co. Ltd. - UK - 1898-1910 -** production and distribution company formed by chemist and photographer James A.

Williamson; acquired by Charles Urban's Natural Colour Kinematograph Company in 1910 to make Kinemacolor films.

**Williamson Kine. Co. Ltd. - UK - 1913-1914** - distributor for Welt Films, with offices at 28 Denmark St. Winchester.

**Wiltwyck Feature Film Co., Inc. - 1914-present** - distribution company with headquarters in Kingston, New York.

**Winnipeg Productions Inc. - CANADA - 1920-1921** - production company formed by Ernest Shipman and Ralph Connor. [see Ernest Shipman and Associates]

**Wistaria Productions - US - 1919-1921** - production company located at 1520 Broadway, New York, with Frank F. Gallagher as president and R. E. Shanahan as general manager.

**Wizard Motion Picture Co. - US - 1915** - production company formed July 1915 by Louis Burnstein, Walter Stull and Bobby Burns; produced comedy shorts with distribution through World Comedy Stars Film Corp; created the Pokes and Jabs series starring Burns and Stull which was absorbed by VIM Comedy Co. with the same owners.

**Wolf & Wilson's Life Motion Pictures - US - 1902-1905** - production company.

**Wolff Philip - UK - 1900-1901** - distribution company located at 9 Southampton St., Holborn, Winchester, with Mr. Hessberg as general manager.

**Wondergraf Production Corp. - US - 1920-1921** - production company located at 6050 Sunset Blvd., Hollywood, California, with C. H. Gowman as president and Charles J. Wilson as V. P. and general manager; produced one and two reel novelties.

**Woolf and Freedman Film Service - UK - 1926-1930** - distribution company.

**Worcester's Philippine Pictures - US - 1914 -** production company formed by Dean Conant Worcester and distributed by Pan American Pictures.

**World Comedy Stars Film Corp. - US - 1915 -** production and distribution company formed by Phil Gleichman to make comedy shorts from vaudeville acts; Edmund Lawrence was head of production; distributed for Wizard Motion Picture Co.; went out of business in August 1915.

**World Film Corp. - US - 1913-1919** - production and distribution company formed February 1914 by E. Mandelbaum, Phil Gleichman and a group of Wall Street investors headed by W. A. Pratt; offices located at 130 West 46th Street, New York; G. L. P. Vernon was president and Mandelbaum and Gleichman each V.P.'s; after a few months, Mandelbaum sold his interest and Lewis J. Selznick became V. P. and general manager; acquired Charles E. Blaney Feature Film Co.; signed Clara Kimball Young, set up 24 distribution exchanges; set up distribution for California Motion Picture, Colonial Motion Picture, Dyreda Art Film, and Peerless; in 1915, took over Shubert Film and Paragon Studios while adding distribution of Equitable Motion Picture, William A. Brady Picture Plays, and Wizard Motion Picture; in February 1916, re-organized with Arthur Spiegel as president; Selznick left World and took Clara Kimball Young and others with him to form Lewis J. Selznick Productions; in January 1919, merged with United Picture Theaters; Republic Distributing Corp. took over all of World's exchanges.

**World Film Corporation - US - 1920-1921 -** distribution company located at 130 West 46 Street, New York with Milton C. Work as president.

**World Film Manufacturing Co., Inc. - US - 1908-1909 -** production company located at 27th and Upshur Streets, Portland, Oregon; released under the trade name World Films.

**World Films - US - 1908-1909 -** trade name for films released by World Film Manufacturing Co., Inc.

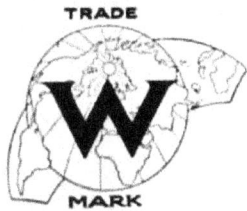

**World Pictures - US - 1914-1919 -** trade name used by World Film Corp.

**World Special Films Corp. - US - 1913-1914 -** distribution company located at 110 West 40th Street, New York.

**World-Wide Films, Inc. - US - 1928** - distribution company located in New York; formed by J. D. Williams and John Maxwell to import films by British International Pictures.

**World-wide Pictures - US - 1922 -** distribution company located at 15 West 44th Street, New York with Holmes Walton as manager of export services.

**World's Best Film Co. - US - 1911-1913 -** production and distribution company located at 145 W. 45th St., New York; imported films and produced animal pictures for Universal.

**World's Exclusives - UK - 1913-1914 -** distribution company with offices located at 112 Shaftesbury Ave., Winchester.

**Worlds Leader Features - US - 1913-1914 -** distribution company located at Suite 619 Candler Building, 220 West 42nd Street, New York.

**Wörner-Filmgesellschaft - GERMANY - 1919-1923 -** production and distribution company.

**Wray Film Agency Ltd. - UK - 1913-1914 -** distributor with offices at Wellington Chambers, Leeds.

**Wright & Sons Ltd. - UK - 1913-1914 -** distributor for Welt Films with offices at 40 Gerrard St. Winchester.

**Wynn Taylor and Co. - UK - 1915 -** distribution company located at 35 Leicester Sq. Westminster.

# X - Y - Z

**XL Exclusive and Feature Film Co. - UK - 1915** - distribution company located at 58 Dean St., Westminster.

**Yale Feature Film - US - 1913** - production company located at 1547 Broadway, Suite 619, Gaiety Theatre Building, New York, with Charles A. Pryor as president and general manager.

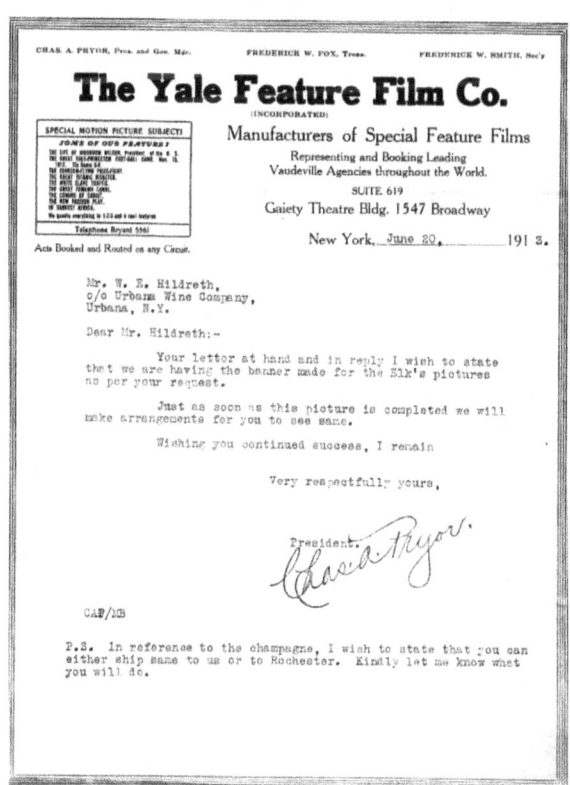

**Yankee Film Co. - US - 1909-1911** - production company with William Steiner as head of production and Isadore Bernstein as general manager; located at 344 East 32nd St., New York; released under Uncle Sam Films trade name and distributed by Motion Picture Distributing and Sales Company.

**Yankee Photo Corporation - US - 1920** - distribution company located at 1476 Broadway, New York.

**Yokota & Co. - JAPAN - 1902-1912** - distribution company in Kyoto; formed by name change from Yokota Bros. & Co.; in 1904, expanded into production of documentaries during the Russo-Japanese War and into feature production in 1907; first dominant film studio in Japan; shot films on location until opened Nijo Castle Studio in 1910; after two years, built larger studio in Kyoto called Hokke-do Studio; in 1912, merged with Yoshizawa & Co., M-Pathe, and Hukuhou-do to form Nihon Katsudo Film, Inc., which was known as Nikkatsu. [see Yoshizawa & Co. - Hukuhou-do - M. Pathe Co.]

**Yokota Bros. & Co. - JAPAN - 1901-1902** - distribution company founded by Masunosuke and Einosuke Yokota in Kyoto, Japan; imported Lumiere films; in 1902, Masunosuke left the business and the name changed to Yokota & Co.

**Yorke Film Corp. - US - 1916-1918** - production company distributed through Metro Pictures Corp.

**Yorkshire Cine Co. - UK - 1915** - distribution company formed from Yorkshire Film Co.; located at 30 Gerrard St., Westminster; distributed for Bamforth.

**Yorkshire Film Co. - UK - 1912-1915** - distribution company with offices at Greek St., Leeds; distributed for Bamforth and Co. and Pyramid Films; became Yorkshire Cine Co.

**Yoshizawa & Co. - JAPAN - 1905-1912** - production company formed in Toyko to produce documentaries from the Russo-Japanese War; in 1909, built first major studio in Toyko called Meguro Studio; in 1912, merged with Yokota & Co., M-Pathe, and Hukuhou-do to form Nihon Katsudo Film, Inc., which was known as Nikkatsu. [see Yokota & Co. - M. Pathe Co. - Hukuhou-do]

**Zane Grey Pictures, Inc. - US - 1918-1919** - production company located at 5341 Melrose Ave. Los Angeles, California and formed to produce films from Zane Grey books; distributed by W. W. Hodkinson Corp. until sale to Paramount Pictures.

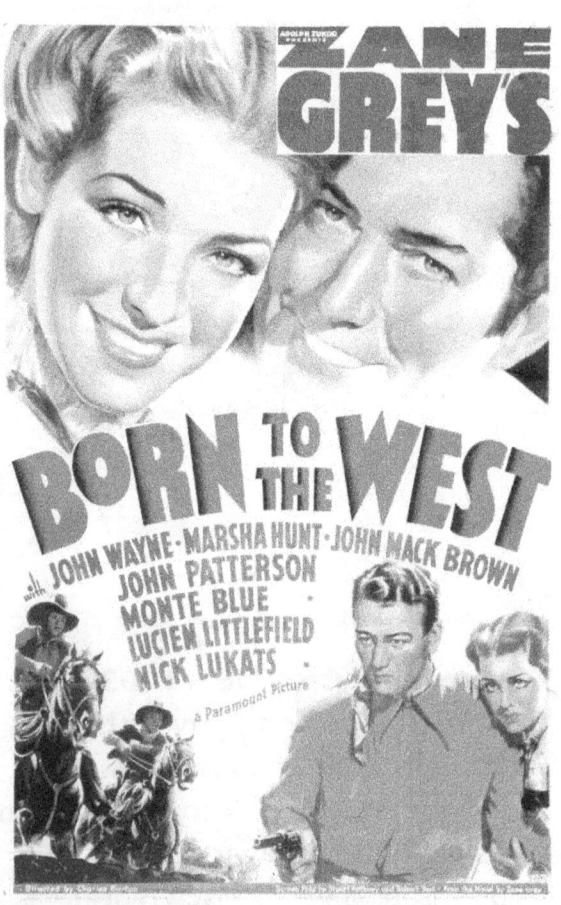

**Zenith Feature Film Co. - US - 1916** - distribution company with offices located at Produce Exchange Bldg. Minneapolis, Minnesota with branch in Milwaukee; States rights distributor of Christie's Comedies et al for Wisconsin, North Dakota, South Dakota and Minnesota.

**Zenith Features, Inc. - US - 1921** - offices located at 3800 Mission Road, Los Angeles, California.

**Zenith Film Co. - UK - 1913-1915** - production company located at Whetstone and taken over in 1915 by British Empire Films.

**Ziegfeld Cinema Corp. - US - 1921** - located at Delmonico's 5th Ave and 44th St. New York with W. K. Ziegfeld as president.

**Zion Films, Inc. - US - 1918-1919** - production company located at 1400 Broadway, New York and formed with S. Adler as president to produce Jewish oriented films

**Zodiac Film Manufacturing Co. - US - 1915** - production company and studio with Thomas S. Nash as president and Albert S. Ruddell as general manager; purchased J. A. C. Film Manufacturing Co. in Los Angeles and renamed it Zodiac.

# Movie Poster Frames
*Direct from Studio Supplier*

*Specializing in framing your collectibles since 1984*

*Made to order custom frames*
*At Wholesale Prices*
*~ Delivered to your door ~*

www.hollywoodposterframes.com
*(800) 463-2994*

9260 Deering Ave
Chatsworth, CA 91311

Open to public:
Thur-Fri: 10-5 p.m.
Sat: 9-2 p.m.

## L'Imagerie gallery

- ORIGINAL VINTAGE MOVIE POSTERS
- RARE FILM POSTERS BOUGHT AND SOLD
- LINENBACKING AND RESTORATION SERVICES
- EXPERT CUSTOM FRAMING

L'IMAGERIE ART GALLERY
In Business Since 1973

www.limageriegallery.com

PHONE: 818-762-8488   FAX: 818-762-8499   EMAIL: limageriegallery@gmail.com

10555 Victory Boulevard - North Hollywood, CA 91606
Tuesday through Saturday from 11:30 to 6:00

---

## PROTECT YOUR POSTERS

with
MAILING TUBES
from

Erdie Industries, Inc.
1205 Colorado Avenue
Lorain, Ohio 44052
1-800-848-0166
www.erdie.com

**FILM/ART**

Original Film Posters

Hollywood, CA

323.363.2969

filmartgallery.com

**GOT POSTERS?**

**SPOTLIGHTDISPLAYS.COM**

Movie Posters ~ Music Posters
TV Posters ~ Celebrity Posters
Star Wars & James Bond
Harry Potter

Collectormania
17892 Cottonwood Dr
Parker, CO 80134

1-866-630-1648

questions@posterplanet.net
posterplanetfile@aol.com

There are 25,000 posters databased and available at www.movieart.com. Inquire to posters@movieart.com. We sell posters to collectors, designers and institutions worldwide. Our staff is friendly. We answer questions.

Selling posters since 1979.

**IVPDA**
international vintage
P O S T E R
dealers association

KIRBY MCDANIEL
MOVIEART

---

**Louisiana film research – where it all began**

77 different Louisiana film prints
Only at our store at HollywoodOnTheBayou.com and Amazon.com

# Chapter Dividers

**A –** Artcraft Pictures - stock

**B –** Blache Features, Inc. – Fighting Death

**C –** Consolidated Film Corp. – Crimson Stained Mystery

**D –** D. W. Griffith – Birth of a Nation

**E –** Éclair–Universal – Link in the Chain

**F –** Filmbyran S. B. D. – Burlesque on Carmen

**G –** Goldwyn Pictures – Peck's Bad Girl

**H –** Hepworth Film – stock

**I –** Imperial Comedy – Heartbreaker

**J –** Joker Comedies – Heroes

**K –** Kalem – Fighting Heiress

**L –** Lubin – Snare of Society

**M –** Mack Sennett – Love Comet

**N –** Norman Film Mfg. Co. – Bull-Dogger

**O –** Oliver Morosco – Big Timber

**P-Q –** Pathe – Matrimonial Martyr

**R –** Rolin Film Co. – Marathon

**S –** Sunshine Comedy – Cupid's Elephant

**T –** Thanhouser Co. – Star of Bethlehem

**U –** Universal-Jewel – Great Air Robbery

**V –** Vitagraph – Vamps and Variety

**W –** William S. Hart Productions – O'Malley of the Mounties

**X-Y-Z –** Zane Grey – Code of the West

## Archival tools for cataloguing and processing

Only at your LearnAboutMoviePosters.com Bookstore and Amazon.com

---

### Where can you go to get instant access to:

- 50,000 production codes
- 25,000 NSS codes
- 18,000 trailer codes
- 1000s lithography plate #s
- 100s artist signatures
- studio logos and info
- int'l censorship and markings
- advance research and **more**

**ONLY when you become a LAMP Member**
LearnAboutMoviePosters.com

---

### AVAILABLE SOON!

**Webinars on Film Accessories**

- U.S. movie poster basics
- Int'l movie poster basics
- Latest dating techniques
- Legality and copyright
- how to use production codes
- how to use lithography numbers
- how to use NSS numbers
- how to use censorship markings

**Contact us for more info and scheduling**
edp@LearnAboutMoviePosters.com

---

### Louisiana film research – where it all began

**77 different Louisiana film prints**
Only at our store at HollywoodOnTheBayou.com and Amazon.com

## Chapter Dividers

**A –** Artcraft Pictures - stock

**B –** Blache Features, Inc. – Fighting Death

**C –** Consolidated Film Corp. – Crimson Stained Mystery

**D –** D. W. Griffith – Birth of a Nation

**E –** Éclair–Universal – Link in the Chain

**F –** Filmbyran S. B. D. – Burlesque on Carmen

**G –** Goldwyn Pictures – Peck's Bad Girl

**H –** Hepworth Film – stock

**I –** Imperial Comedy – Heartbreaker

**J –** Joker Comedies – Heroes

**K –** Kalem – Fighting Heiress

**L –** Lubin – Snare of Society

**M –** Mack Sennett – Love Comet

**N –** Norman Film Mfg. Co. – Bull-Dogger

**O –** Oliver Morosco – Big Timber

**P-Q –** Pathe – Matrimonial Martyr

**R –** Rolin Film Co. – Marathon

**S –** Sunshine Comedy – Cupid's Elephant

**T –** Thanhouser Co. – Star of Bethlehem

**U –** Universal-Jewel – Great Air Robbery

**V –** Vitagraph – Vamps and Variety

**W –** William S. Hart Productions – O'Malley of the Mounties

**X-Y-Z –** Zane Grey – Code of the West

## Archival tools for cataloguing and processing

Only at your LearnAboutMoviePosters.com Bookstore and Amazon.com

---

### Where can you go to get instant access to:

- 50,000 production codes
- 25,000 NSS codes
- 18,000 trailer codes
- 1000s lithography plate #s
- 100s artist signatures
- studio logos and info
- int'l censorship and markings
- advance research and **more**

**ONLY when you become a LAMP Member**
LearnAboutMoviePosters.com

---

### AVAILABLE SOON!

**Webinars on Film Accessories**

- U.S. movie poster basics
- Int'l movie poster basics
- Latest dating techniques
- Legality and copyright
- how to use production codes
- how to use lithography numbers
- how to use NSS numbers
- how to use censorship markings

**Contact us for more info and scheduling**
edp@LearnAboutMoviePosters.com

---

### Louisiana film research – where it all began

77 different Louisiana film prints
Only at our store at HollywoodOnTheBayou.com and Amazon.com

# LAMP SPONSORS

Amazing 3rd Planet – 333

Bags Unlimited – 88, 312

Bonhams Auctions – 105

Channing Posters – 121, 313

Christie's Auction – intro

Cinema Retro - 214

Conway's Vintage Treasures – 214

Dominique Besson – 77

eMoviePoster.com – intro, 313

Erdie Ind. – 155, 332

Ewbank's Auction - 215

Femme, Fatales and Fantasies – 257

Film Art Gallery – 121, 333

Four Color Comics – 257

French Movie Poster – 215

Heritage Auctions – intro, back cover

Hollywood Poster Frames – int, 331

Illustration Gallery – 223

Intemporel – 295

John Reed Vintage Movie Memorabilia - 295

KinoArt – 222, 313

L'Imagerie Gallery – 222, 332

Last Moving Picture Show – 305

Limited Runs – 305

Movie Art GmbH – 305

Movie Art of Austin – 222, 334

Movie Poster Exchange - 223

Original Poster – 242

Past Posters – 305

Poster Conservation – 257

Poster Planet – 76, 334

Posteropolis – 312

Robert Edwards Auctions – 89

Simon Dwyer – 312

Spotlight Displays – 76, 333

The Cinema Trade – 295

Unshredded Nostalgia – 163

Yazoo Mills – 294

Please take time to notice the ads throughout this book and support these wonderful people as they have invested financially in YOUR education by sponsoring this book.

www.ingramcontent.com/pod-product-compliance
Lightning Source LLC
Chambersburg PA
CBHW080529170426
43195CB00016B/2515